ENTERING THE BEHAVIORAL HEALTH FIELD

This text provides new clinicians with an overview of the tasks involved in behavioral health treatment as it is practiced in community-based training organizations. The text's specific focus is on the application of theoretical and academic knowledge to clinical work as a psychotherapist or case manager, with a case example that follows treatment from the first session through termination. It contains an overview of all aspects of treatment that are required in these organizations, which are the primary settings for practicum, internship, and post-graduate training.

Diane A. Suffridge, PhD, is Assistant Professor at Dominican University of California (tenure track) and has provided training and supervision to many students, post-graduates, and licensed clinicians for over 25 years. She has served as Clinical Director at several behavioral health centers in the San Francisco Bay Area, and has over 25 years of experience as a psychologist.

ENTERING THE BEHAVIORAL HEALTH FIELD

A Guide for New Clinicians

Diane A. Suffridge

Routledge
Taylor & Francis Group

NEW YORK AND LONDON

First published 2016
by Routledge
711 Third Avenue, New York, NY 10017

and by Routledge
2 Park Square, Milton Park, Abingdon, Oxon, OX14 4RN

Routledge is an imprint of the Taylor & Francis Group, an informa business

Library of Congress Cataloging-in-Publication Data
Names: Suffridge, Diane A., author.
Title: Entering the behavioral health field: a handbook for new clinicians / Diane A. Suffridge.
Description: New York, NY: Routledge, 2016. Includes bibliographical references and index.
Identifiers: LCCN 2015045016 | ISBN 9781138186491 (hbk: alk. paper) | ISBN 9781138186507 (pbk: alk. paper) | ISBN 9781315643809 (ebk)
Subjects: | MESH: Psychology, Clinical—methods | Counseling—methods | Mental Health Services | Handbooks | Case Reports
Classification: LCC RC454 NLM WM 34 | DDC 616.89—dc23
LC record available at http://lccn.loc.gov/2015045016

ISBN: 978-1-138-18649-1 (hbk)
ISBN: 978-1-138-18650-7 (pbk)
ISBN: 978-1-315-64380-9 (ebk)

Typeset in Bembo
by codeMantra

To the students and post-graduates who I have supervised and trained during the last 27 years. You taught me as much as I taught you.

CONTENTS

ACKNOWLEDGMENTS

When the idea for this book came to me on a morning walk in December 2011, I was completely uninformed about the journey on which I was embarking. Since then I have been privileged to have many friends and colleagues who have accompanied and supported me while I have proceeded with this project from the original idea to final publication. I first want to thank Nancy McWilliams for her encouragement and mentoring of me for many years. Her statement, "Yes, I think this book is needed and you're a great person to write it," gave me the confidence to begin writing. Lynn Greenberg and Michael Rothschild were also enthusiastic when I mentioned, "I'm thinking of writing a book," while visiting them for New Year's a few weeks after the original idea came to me.

I am blessed to have wonderful friends, and they have been a huge source of support during the long and sometimes lonely writing process. My gratitude goes to Nancy Cavender, Karla Clark, Jen Cross, Janice Cumming, Lorrie Goldin, Carol Kerr, Anita Moran, Jolyn O'Hare, Marian Price, Curran Reichert, Louie Sheridan, Katherine Shine, and Karen Willcox. Each of them asked me about the writing periodically, and they cheered my progress no matter how slow it sometimes seemed. Lois Lane was a consistent supporter and reflected her understanding of the commitment it took to bring this project to fruition. My spiritual community at Community Congregational Church in Tiburon, California, is an ongoing source of support and inspiration for me, especially the women who attended the annual women's retreat in 2012 through 2015. They have been a source of unconditional acceptance and encouragement.

Many colleagues also encouraged me personally and professionally: Rachelle Averbach, Sarah Chapman, and other therapists and supervisors at Family Service Agency of Marin; Carin Grove and supervisors at Bay Area Community Resources in San Rafael; and Robin Gayle, Vince Nevins, and Rande Webster at Dominican University of California. I am indebted to all of the clinicians I have supervised and trained at Community Institute for Psychotherapy in San Rafael, San Francisco Child Abuse Prevention Center, and Family Service Agency of Marin. My work with them is the inspiration for this book. Feedback from my students at Dominican University of California also helped me clarify concepts as I made final editing changes.

I thank Rachelle Averbach, Cristin Brew, Janice Cumming, Cynthia Duxbury, the late Elisabeth Hathaway, Annette Holloway, Dan Kalb, Marian Price, Robert Reiser, Joan Roane, Kathy Truax, and Karen Willcox for their review of portions of the book while it was in development. Greg Bodin, Molly Dahlman, Caitlin Severin, and Daniela Sylvers Weise provided feedback from the perspective of clinicians in training. I had editing support from Barbara Brauer of Wordsworth of Marin and from Sandra Eastburn Weil. The book benefitted from all of their comments and input, and any remaining mistakes are mine alone. Maureen Ladley and Clair Tannenbaum have provided technical support for my website and biweekly blog.

Finally, I thank my parents, Ted and Gladys Suffridge, who have been examples of teaching, mentoring, and giving to the next generations. My father's long career in teaching was a model of meaningful, rewarding work and instilled in me the value of accompanying others on the path of learning and growth. My daughters, Christina Greenberg and Teresa Bilinski, are exceptional women, and they and their husbands, Brian and Greg, have dedicated their talents to education. My grandchildren Jonah, Daniella, and Lander are a continual source of joy, and they often provided needed respite from the keyboard and screen.

INTRODUCTION

This book is based on my 30 years of experience as a psychotherapist and over 25 years as a supervisor, consultant, and trainer with other counselors and psycho-therapists. My experience has taught me that to become skilled in clinical work, integrating conceptual knowledge with emotional responsiveness is of primary importance. As clinicians, we need to develop the capacity to become aware of our own thoughts and feelings as we sit with individuals and families in distress. This self-awareness then guides our understanding and our decisions as we inter-act with them to foster their healing and growth. My book contains information, advice, guidance, examples, and tools for you to use in the early months and years of your clinical training and practice. While there is no formula that can guarantee success, I can assure you that the information contained in this book has been well-tested and has proven to be of great value in my own work and that of the clinicians I have supervised and trained.

I wrote this book for students and post-graduates in the fields of clinical psy-chology, marriage and family therapy, counseling psychology, and social work. The case example that runs throughout the book and the short illustrations contained in the body of each chapter focus on individual adult psychotherapy. However, many of the concepts and suggestions are also relevant to case management and crisis intervention. I have included variations in approach or technique for work-ing with children, couples, and families, although that is not my primary focus.

My intention in writing this book is to provide a bridge between academic learning and clinical training. Academic study gives you the conceptual knowledge for clinical work, and clinical training gives you the applied experience of working with individuals and families as a case manager, psychotherapist, crisis intervention specialist, or behavioral health practitioner. This introduction describes important features of clinical training, the terminology and scope of the book, and three areas of clinical practice that are addressed in each chapter.

Features of Clinical Training in the Early Twenty-First Century

Most of my work as a supervisor, consultant, and trainer has taken place in out-patient community-based organizations in California, which have a large clinical training component in their model of service provision. I have seen the following four significant changes in these organizations and in the field of psychotherapy in the United States since the late 1980s that have significantly affected the nature of clinical training:

- Increase in distress and complexity in the client population,
- Pressure to achieve measurable results in a short period of time,
- Use of evidence-based treatment approaches and principles, and
- Emphasis on a strength-based, recovery model of treatment.

The *increase in the level of distress and complexity in the client population* served by clinicians in training can be traced to a number of social, economic, and political factors in American society. During your years of clinical training, you are likely to work with individuals and families who have multiple diagnoses, are living with serious psychosocial stressors, are part of cultural communities that have been disenfranchised and oppressed, and present significant interpersonal challenges in treatment.

As a new clinician, you are likely to feel overwhelmed and to find it difficult to apply your academic knowledge to the reality of your clients' lives. Supervision will help you orient and ground yourself, and you will gain skill and confidence as you move through your clinical placements. However, recognize that you may face the most complex and challenging clinical situations at the earliest stage of your career when you are least prepared. This is the context for the intense emotional demands of clinical training. Throughout the book, I have included reminders and tools to help you understand and manage these emotional demands as well as examples that illustrate a variety of ways to engage the individuals and families under your care. You will need to be flexible in trying different approaches and interventions with clients whose life situations are more complex and diverse than those of participants in research studies of effective treatment.

The *pressure to achieve measurable results in a short period of time* is influenced by third-party funding requirements and by client expectations. This pressure can lead to a decreased emphasis and value placed on the time required to develop a therapeutic relationship. Most of us are motivated to do clinical work by feelings of compassion and a desire to help others, and it can be difficult to balance these motivations with the pragmatic requirements of doing a thorough early assessment that leads to focused and behaviorally measurable goals.

One resolution of this dilemma is to view assessment and treatment planning as paperwork that is separate from the therapeutic relationship and rapport building. Another approach is to focus on the task of assessment and treatment planning without considering the establishment of a therapeutic relationship. These solutions are not ideal. In fact, I believe it is a mistake to compartmentalize in this way, and my book illustrates ways to integrate all aspects of treatment into the therapeutic relationship. The treatment you provide will be more effective when you approach all of your interactions with your clients in a therapeutic manner.

The *use of evidence-based treatment approaches and principles* has improved the treatment effectiveness for a number of conditions and has expanded the population that can benefit from treatment. However, these advances have been accompanied by a general bias toward behavioral and cognitive-behavioral theoretical perspectives and away from the principles developed by psychodynamic and humanistic theorists.

Your graduate education may have led you to believe that you should use only behavioral or cognitive-behavioral theory in order to provide effective treatment. I have taken a different approach as a supervisor and trainer, and that approach is reflected in this book. I integrate the knowledge from multiple theoretical perspectives, including psychodynamic and humanistic, to emphasize the quality of the therapeutic relationship as the basis for treatment. The principles and illustrations in this book provide strategies to develop a comprehensive understanding of the client, and emphasize the quality of the therapeutic relationship when using evidence-based techniques and interventions.

Psychodynamic psychotherapy in particular has a long and rich history of explaining complex and puzzling psychological phenomena and is a source of insights for case formulation and for adaptation of evidence-based interventions with many clients who are treated in clinical training settings.

In recent years, the field of psychotherapy and behavioral health treatment has seen *an emphasis on a strength-based, recovery model of treatment*. There has been particularly strong advocacy for this approach for individuals with serious mental illness and members of non-dominant cultural communities. One implication of this model is that all assessments should include a description of the client's strengths and strategies for coping with difficult life circumstances. The client's symptoms and difficulties should also be interpreted in a cultural context that provides meaning to the client's behavior. My book contains examples and tools that place value on the client's strengths and cultural identities and that consider the function of symptoms in managing stressful and traumatic life circumstances.

Terminology

I use the term *behavioral health* to refer to settings that offer treatment for one or more mental health and substance use conditions through psychotherapy, social work, counseling, and case management. My use of the term behavioral health does not connote a behavioral or cognitive-behavioral treatment approach but is an umbrella term for various treatment settings. Behavioral health care is sometimes provided in a medical setting as an adjunct to physical health care, and the term is also used to refer to freestanding outpatient clinics and treatment centers.

I use the term *treatment* in my discussions of interactions between clinicians and clients. I chose this term to facilitate the application of the principles I discuss to different types of clinical work, i.e., psychotherapy, case management, crisis intervention, or a combination.

I use the term *clinician* to refer to someone who is working with individuals or families in any behavioral health setting using one or more treatment modalities. Common job titles are intern, trainee, psychotherapist, social worker, case manager, or counselor. I am writing primarily for clinicians who are in the training phase of their career, working under the supervision of a licensed clinician and meeting the requirements for independent licensure in one of the behavioral health fields.

I use the term *client* to refer to the individual or family unit requesting services in a behavioral health setting. I am aware that other terms are used by some treatment providers (e.g., patient, consumer), but client is a term that seems to have the widest usage at this time. When I use the word client, I refer to an individual or to multiple individuals who are seen as a couple or family.

The shorter vignettes and illustrations I use throughout the book can apply equally to male or female clients. It is cumbersome to use the construction *he or she* in each example, and it is artificially exclusive to use only one pronoun throughout the book. I have resolved this dilemma by using *male and female pronouns in alternate chapters*. The composite case example in the book describes a female supervisor, female clinician, and female client, since most behavioral health treatment settings have a predominance of female staff and clients. Please keep in mind that the situations discussed in each chapter and in the case example apply to both genders.

Scope of the Book

My professional practice for over 25 years has been in the state of California, and the information in this book is *directly applicable to behavioral health settings in California*. When discussing areas of practice that are affected by state law and may vary from state to state, I have noted this fact. My book does not contain legal advice, so you should consult with a supervisor, senior clinician, and/or attorney who specializes in behavioral health law regarding any legal issue you encounter in your practice, whether in California or another state.

Areas of Clinical Practice

The *task of integrating what we know in our heads with what we feel in our hearts* is ongoing throughout our careers as psychotherapists. Most of us have a natural inclination to either escape into our minds or become awash with feelings when we are engaged in an intensely emotional interaction. Identifying your default response is a first step toward developing greater awareness of your less developed side and beginning to balance intellectual knowledge with emotional responsiveness. I have found that this integration of head and heart takes place gradually over the years, and I encourage you to be patient and compassionate with yourself as you work to become more conscious of your automatic reactions and to achieve greater balance in your response to your clients.

Assisting you in this task of integrating head and heart is the primary goal of my book, and I have identified three areas of clinical practice in which this integration is achieved.

1. Using yourself as an instrument of hope, change, and healing.
2. Becoming confident in your authority and professionalism.
3. Developing interpersonal skills that strengthen the therapeutic relationship.

Each chapter contains guidance and examples relevant to these areas of clinical practice, and each chapter summary reviews the principles contained in the chapter in light of these three areas. A case example illustration follows this summary.

I recommend reading the book as a continuous narrative. However, individual chapters can also be used as a reference for specific topics when they are relevant to a specific client, a new training setting, or a new phase in your professional development. You have chosen a career path that will bring many rewards and challenges. I hope this book will serve you as you develop your skills and grow in your self-knowledge.

1

PERSONAL PREPARATION

(Note: This chapter will use the male pronoun for supervisor, clinician, and client.)

In the behavioral health field, the clinician is an instrument of hope, change, and healing. Therefore, it is essential that we develop self-awareness and self-reflection in order to increase our capacity to be effective instruments. Personal growth and development are an integral part of clinical training and often require that we make changes in familiar parts of ourselves and some of our automatic reactions. This growth is often uncomfortable and even painful, but rewards come from increased emotional strength and flexibility. I describe some of the relationships between individual identity and professional identity as a clinician. I recommend returning to this chapter as you progress in your training, so you can recognize the growth you have made.

Personal Vulnerability and Growth

Motivations for Becoming a Clinician

You probably decided to train as a behavioral health clinician for many reasons: some you are aware of and some you may only discover in the course of clinical training and practice. One commonality for most of us, including myself, is that we enter the field with a *desire, often primarily unconscious, to resolve issues that originated in our relationships early in life.* We may have adopted a caretaking style toward others because it was rewarded or because we felt comfortable in that role. Perhaps we weren't cared for in important ways and we now identify deeply with others who are asking for help. For some of us, relationships carry such a danger of rejection and disappointment that engaging with others in a role that is structured and limited allows us to meet our own needs for intimacy without feeling exposed and vulnerable. We also may have had a role model—parent, therapist, mentor, teacher—who we wish to emulate.

In addition to these deeply personal, partially hidden motivations, we generally make the decision to become a psychotherapist, counselor, or social worker based on *experiences that give us a taste of what it would be like* to be a behavioral health clinician. We may have done rewarding volunteer work or counseled friends successfully or become fascinated with the workings of the human psyche, and we long to learn more. As expected, we find rewards and gratification in working as a professional clinician (McWilliams, 2004).

Unexpected emotions. What most of us do not expect is that this work will lead us to feel emotions, both familiar and alien, that test our inner strength and lead us to doubt our ability to withstand the flood of suffering to which we open ourselves in our clinical work. These emotions are often discordant with our general view of ourselves as well as our view of what a clinician does or should feel. We expect to feel patient, understanding, caring, and valued. We don't expect to feel angry, disgusted, helpless, disoriented, impatient, or worthless but, like most clinicians, I have experienced all of these emotional reactions at different times. These often disturbing reactions to our clients can help us understand ourselves and those who come to us for help, but at the same time they challenge our emotional equilibrium.

Support for Personal Growth

As a beginning clinician, you are about to embark on a journey of personal and professional growth. Your emotional reactions on this journey may surprise you with their intensity and unpredictability. I recommend using a variety of methods to develop and strengthen your capacity for self-awareness and self-reflection early in your professional training. The following methods have been especially helpful to me and colleagues:

- Personal psychotherapy,
- Mindfulness practices, and
- Supportive relationships with peers.

Personal psychotherapy is required by many training programs, but it is often difficult to find both the time and money for psychotherapy during your training. You may be paying for graduate school, working in clinical training positions for little or no pay, and juggling all of this with family life and other paid work. However, investing in your personal and professional well-being by seeking personal psychotherapy will generate benefits throughout the training process and beyond. It can help you

- Understand the conscious and unconscious motivations that led you to enter clinical training,
- Increase your self-awareness, and
- Manage the intense and distressing feelings that arise in your work.

Many experienced professional psychotherapists set aside a few hours in their schedule for working with clients at a reduced fee, and they are usually particularly interested in working with new clinicians. Help in finding a therapist is often available from professors or the office of training in academic programs and from supervisors in clinical training programs.

Mindfulness practices increase our ability to be open to inner experience without making judgments or rushing into action. Building a repertoire of rituals and skills to help you find calm in the midst of emotional upheaval, both yours and the client's, is a critical part of becoming a professional clinician. Although a formal practice of meditation is one way to cultivate this calm, there are many other ways to incorporate mindfulness practices in your daily or weekly routine (Hanh, 2009; Siegel, 2011).

Supportive relationships with peers who are at a similar stage of training also support the growth that occurs during clinical training. Friends and life partners can offer understanding and caring, but there is a unique empathic bond between clinicians who face the overwhelming emotions and feelings of responsibility inherent in this work. I suggest you seek out peers who are willing to share openly and to listen while not attempting to advise you or solve your problems. It may take time to find people whose personality and interpersonal or therapeutic style are a good match for yours, so be persistent. I recommend attending a support or process group for clinicians in training if one is available at your training site. This could be a peer group or a group led by someone who does not have an administrative or evaluative role in the training program. Talk with your peers about coming together for mutual support if your agency doesn't offer a formal group, and let a supervisor or administrator know you are doing so, in order to eliminate the appearance of secrecy and to raise their awareness about your needs.

Transference and Countertransference

Emotions Present in Clinicians and Clients

I have introduced you to some of the emotions that clinicians feel when they sit with clients who are in distress. These emotions can be comfortable, like patience and understanding, or uncomfortable, like anger, fear, hopelessness, and self-doubt. On the clients' side, they may enter treatment with emotions related to depression and anxiety, have difficulty managing the strong emotions that are related to their life circumstances, and come to treatment feeling discouraged about getting the help they need. The degree of healing that takes place in the therapeutic relationship is directly related to the strength and nature of these emotions.

Definition of Terms

Freud used the terms *transference* and *countertransference* to describe the intensely powerful emotions that arise between analyst or therapist and patient or client

(McWilliams, 2004). *Transference,* or the set of patient reactions to the analyst as though the analyst were a past attachment object, was initially viewed as an obstacle to analysis but came to be viewed as necessary for the resolution of past conflicts in attachment relationships. Similarly, *countertransference*, or the set of analyst reactions to the patient that go beyond the professional desire to be helpful, was viewed as potentially problematic. Contemporary psychoanalytic theory has moved toward a relational perspective in which the interpersonal experiences of both analyst and patient are considered active in the therapeutic relationship. Transference and countertransference are seen as inevitable and necessary in the healing process (McWilliams, 2004).

Currently, the term countertransference is used by practitioners of psychodynamic and other theoretical perspectives to describe the clinician's emotional response and reactions to the client. Some practitioners limit the term countertransference to the clinician's unresolved conflicts while others include all responses that arise in relation to the client (Hayes, Gelso, & Hummel, 2011).

Using Countertransference Responses

I recommend identifying and reflecting on your countertransference responses to clients because your responses provide information about the client and yourself. Specifically, countertransference is

- A source of information about the client's inner world of internalized relationships, and
- A way to deepen your understanding of your interpersonal patterns and responses.

If you work in a training setting that uses psychodynamic theory as its foundation, your supervisors will probably encourage you to identify and discuss your countertransference. This will help you to use your emotional responses to inform the treatment and develop greater skill in working with difficult interpersonal patterns. Supervisors from other theoretical perspectives may also inquire about countertransference as a way to help you identify your emotional response and your contribution to the quality of your therapeutic relationships with clients.

Cultural Identities

The *cultural influences that have shaped your sense of self* are part of your therapeutic presence. You may have greater awareness of some aspects of your cultural background than of others, and this may be especially true if there are ways in which your background places you outside the dominant cultural group. Also, your feelings about different aspects of your cultural background probably vary. For example, you may feel confident about being a Jewish man and embarrassed that you speak with an accent due to immigrating to the United States as a teenager. Your experiences with others who are similar to and different from you have shaped your understanding of and comfort in interpersonal interactions, and you bring all of this self-awareness and prior experience into your relationship with your clients.

There are many *aspects of cultural identity*, which are more or less salient in different social contexts. One helpful framework for examining these multiple influences (Hays, 2008) uses the acronym ADDRESSING.

- Age and generational influences
- Developmental disabilities
- Disabilities acquired later in life
- Religion and spiritual orientation
- Ethnic and racial identity
- Socioeconomic status
- Sexual orientation
- Indigenous heritage
- National origin
- Gender including gender identity

In *examining your cultural identities*, one or more of these identities may feel central to your sense of self and others unimportant. Often, the features of your cultural identity that match those of the dominant cultural group seem less significant because their impact on your development is less obvious. Being part of the dominant group is associated with privilege: a set of unearned benefits and advantages (Dressel, Kerr & Stevens, 2010). If you were born and raised in the United States and are Caucasian, middle class, male, and/or heterosexual, you may not have spent much time reflecting on how those factors influenced your personality, beliefs, values, and interpersonal style. I encourage you to do so as part of your clinical preparation in order to become aware of assumptions and cultural blind spots that may be present for you.

Most graduate school programs include academic courses to increase awareness of the influence of culture. You will find these courses to be a beginning step in developing cultural sensitivity and knowledge. You may also need to seek out other experiential opportunities to gain self-understanding of the impact of cultural experiences on your personal and professional identity (Cornish, Schreier, Nadkarni, Metzger, & Rodolfa, 2010).

Professional Boundaries

Definition

The concept of professional boundaries may be unfamiliar to you, unless you have prior experience in a behavioral health setting, a social service agency, or another service profession. The term *professional boundaries* refers to *the structure and limits that are placed on the contact between clinician and client* in order to ensure that the focus of their time together is on the client's needs and welfare and that the intense feelings that can arise in clinical work are managed differently than they are in other relationships.

Reasons for Professional Boundaries

Maintaining professional boundaries is crucial, in order for treatment to be helpful to the client in managing his difficulties. Professional ethics codes require that the client's welfare remain the clinician's primary concern, and this is only possible when the safety and security of both client and clinician are ensured by the presence of professional boundaries in their relationship (American Association for Marriage and Family Therapy [AAMFT], 2001; American Psychological Association [APA] 2002; Barnett, 2011; National Association of Social Workers [NASW], 2008).

In addition to this ethical requirement, maintaining professional boundaries is *critical to ensure good clinical care.* Many of your clients have had experiences of being exploited or betrayed by people in positions of authority and trust. This makes it imperative that you maintain the professionalism of the treatment in a way that safeguards both the client and you from interactions that could feel to the client like a repetition of earlier abuse or betrayal.

These boundaries do not need to be rigid, and it is often therapeutic for clinicians to demonstrate flexibility in reaching a mutually satisfactory agreement about the conditions of the clinical work. However, the boundaries do need to be *clear, explicit, and consistent.* While you are in training, you are required to adhere to the professional boundaries defined by your supervisor and training agency. It is likely that you will have some degree of latitude to establish boundaries that fit your personal preferences and style, which gives you valuable experience for practicing independently. While in training though, talk with your supervisor any time you change or consider changing a boundary, so you can examine your decision and ensure that you are maintaining the quality of care for your client.

Therapeutic Frame

One aspect of professional boundaries is the therapeutic frame. This refers to the *external structure for the clinical encounters between client and clinician,* including:

- When, where, for how many minutes, and how frequently you meet;
- How the treatment is funded and for what period of time;
- Under what circumstances you will have contact outside of scheduled sessions;
- What issues will be the focus of the treatment;

- What information about the client will be shared with others and under what conditions; and
- What conditions will lead to the termination of treatment.

These issues will be discussed in more detail in Chapter 3 in regard to establishing a treatment contract.

Self-Disclosure

Another aspect of professional boundaries is related to the issue of self-disclosure, or *information you share with the client about yourself, personally and professionally.* Clinicians vary regarding the amount and type of personal and professional information they feel is appropriate to disclose to clients. Due to the complex nature of decisions about self-disclosure, I recommend discussing this matter with your supervisor when you begin working at a new training site. Some of the variables to consider before sharing information with clients are

- The practices in your training setting,
- Legal and ethical requirements,
- The diagnosis and interpersonal style of the client,
- The type of clinical work you are doing, and
- Your own personal style and comfort with revealing personal information about yourself.

Reflect on and talk with your supervisor about your level of comfort in sharing personal information with your clients. Work to move toward the middle on the continuum of emotional expressiveness and reserve. If you tend to be expressive and self-revealing, practice more reserve. If you tend to be cool and self-protective, practice being more forthcoming.

Professional information. You will be required to share some professional information regarding your status as a clinician in training, and some clients may have additional questions about your professional training and experience. My style is to answer these questions briefly and factually. If the client presses for details, I usually comment on the purpose of the client's question. For example, if a client asks about how much experience you have, you can make a general statement like, "I've worked with families in a few other agencies and I've worked at this agency for four months." If the client asks for more detail, you can again answer briefly and add something like

> I wonder if you're concerned about my ability to help you. I find the best way for clients to find out whether I can be helpful is for us to begin to talk about what's going on in their lives. Can you tell me more about what led you to contact our agency?

Personal information. Decisions about how to respond to client questions for personal information are more complex. Keep in mind the client's welfare and the professional nature of the relationship. A useful guide in making decisions about self-disclosure of personal information is to ask yourself, "How do I share personal information in a way that respects and empowers my clients?" (Hays, 2008). This keeps the focus on your client's welfare and acknowledges that any answer to a question about yourself is a disclosure, even if you decline to provide the information the client seeks.

Some questions are relevant to the population or type of treatment you are doing, such as whether you are a parent or are in recovery. Others relate to aspects of the client's history or identity, such as whether you are a survivor of sexual abuse or are gay. Talk with your supervisor about questions that are likely to come up at your training site so you can anticipate the most common questions. You may want to prepare a standard response to these questions that includes acknowledgment of the similarities and differences between you and the client. For example, in response to a question from a client who has children about whether I have children, I might say, "Yes, I'm a parent, too. I'm sure we have had some similar experiences as well as some that are different." If I am asked whether I am in recovery, I might say, "I'm not in recovery, but I have an appreciation for how much courage and strength it takes to overcome an addiction. I also have some familiarity with the principles and practices of 12-step programs." Responses like these convey information about yourself and invite the client to share his experience with you.

I also recommend that you develop a *standard response to questions about personal information that you are not comfortable sharing* or that isn't relevant or appropriate to the treatment. An example is, "I can understand that you may be curious about my personal life, but I don't share that information with my clients. It's important that our discussions focus on you and how I can be helpful to you." Your supervisor can help you find a way to express yourself professionally while maintaining clear boundaries.

Initiating self-disclosure. At some point, you will probably consider sharing information about yourself or your personal life because it could be helpful to the client. *Be very cautious about this.* Most often the desire to initiate self-disclosure is prompted by a concern that you lack experience and knowledge and that sharing personal experience will compensate for this lack and will help the client feel more trusting of you. If you have overcome a problem similar to one facing your client, you may have a desire to speed up the client's process of change by helping him learn from your experience. Initiating self-disclosure in these instances is responsive to your needs rather than the client's.

If you find this situation occurring frequently in your work, practice restraint and reflect on the feelings that come about when you stay in a professional role, focusing on the client's experience and needs. Use supervision to explore your reliance on self-disclosure and to develop other interventions that can assist the client in taking his own steps toward change.

When you see similarities between your personal experience and the client's, it is possible to lose a degree of objectivity and become over-identified with the client. When this happens, *remind yourself of the balance between similarity and difference* that is present between you. Although you and your client may share the experience of raising challenging 5-year-old boys as a single mother, there are probably many aspects of your current life and past history that are different from your client's. Reminding yourself of the larger context will help you return to your professional role.

Summary

This chapter reviewed some areas of personal growth that begin during the early phases of clinical training. Self-awareness and self-reflection in these areas will maximize your effectiveness in your relationships with clients. Specific areas of growth are listed below.

1. Using yourself as an instrument of hope, change, and healing:
   a. Understand your motivations for becoming a clinician.
   b. Get support for personal growth.
   c. Examine cultural influences and identities.

2. Becoming confident in your authority and professionalism:
   a. Learn to maintain professional boundaries.
   b. Establish a therapeutic frame.

3. Developing interpersonal skills that strengthen the therapeutic relationship:
   a. Understand and know how to use the information from the client's transference and your countertransference responses.
   b. Use self-disclosure in ways that benefit and empower the client and maintain a focus on the client's welfare.

Case Example: An Introduction to Liz and Liz's Supervisor Dalia

I use a composite case example throughout the book to illustrate the areas of treatment described in each chapter. I have generated this composite from my experience as a therapist and supervisor working with numerous clients and clinicians in different settings. The purpose of using a composite rather than an actual clinical case is both to protect confidentiality and to illustrate the full range of issues that are present in a treatment, without the need to introduce multiple individual examples. *The client, clinician, and supervisor descriptions are all representative composites* drawn primarily from my work in clinical training settings.

In each therapeutic interaction, the interventions and responses in the case example represent one of many ways to approach the clinical situation. My choices reflect my preferred style and orientation to clinical work, but I do not mean to imply that the example is the only therapeutic response. In addition, I have chosen to describe the clinician using sound judgment and making thoughtful interventions rather than making some of the mistakes that are common for clinicians in training. I have found that learning is enhanced with examples of recommended therapeutic practice.

The case example describes psychotherapy with an individual adult; however, many of the principles apply to other types of clinical work, including case management, supportive counseling, and family therapy. This chapter will introduce Liz, the clinician, and Dalia, her supervisor.

Introduction to Liz

Liz is a graduate student who began practicum training at the Community Support Clinic 3 months ago. She did a prior year of training in a school-based program doing individual child therapy and family therapy. The Community Support Clinic offers outpatient individual, couple, and family therapy using a sliding scale based on family income.

Motivations. Liz's decision to enter graduate school and clinical training was influenced by her own experience in psychotherapy during college and also by volunteer experiences she had during high school and college at a homeless shelter and a crisis hotline for youth. She returned to psychotherapy in her first year of graduate school and has begun to explore some of the family dynamics that influenced her decision to become a therapist. Specifically, she has become aware that she played the role of mediator and peacekeeper in her immediate and extended family until her college years.

Support. Liz is currently in weekly psychotherapy and she has formed friendships with three members of her graduate school class. She and her friends work in different placements, but they get together every 2 to 3 weeks outside of work and school to talk about their training experiences, without sharing specific client information. Liz's placement also has a peer support group which she has attended since beginning her placement 3 months ago.

Cultural identities. Liz is a gay, single, 28-year-old Caucasian woman of middle class background, raised in a rural California town and currently living in the San Francisco Bay Area. Her father is Italian-American, and her mother is Irish-American. Both sets of her grandparents immigrated to the United States as young adults, and Liz's parents were born in the United States. Using the *ADDRESSING framework*, Liz is in the majority group in the areas of age, disabilities, European-American ethnicity and race, socioeconomic status, and indigenous and national heritage. She is in minority or non-dominant groups as gay and female. She was raised as a Catholic, which was a minority group in her home town; she currently has no religious affiliation. Liz views the fact that she is gay as her *primary cultural influence*. Her Catholic upbringing was in conflict with her growing recognition of her sexual identity during her late teens, and she experienced some teasing by peers in her high school due to her lack of interest in dating boys. There was significant family conflict when she came out in her early twenties after moving from her rural community to the San Francisco Bay Area for college. The family conflict has lessened somewhat in the subsequent years. Liz experienced little prejudice or discrimination related to her ethnicity, her religion, or her gender.

Introduction to Dalia

Dalia is a psychologist who has been licensed for 12 years and a supervisor for 8 years. She has been a supervisor at the Community Support Clinic for 5 years and supervised at another community mental health center before that. Dalia also sees clients at the clinic and has some administrative responsibilities.

Motivations. Dalia had a 7-year career in the public relations field before deciding to make a career change. Her decision was influenced by her personal experience of caring for her mother during her terminal illness. Dalia felt supported by the medical and social service professionals who provided care for the family through the local hospice. This led her to volunteer in a grief counseling program and enter graduate school. Her personal psychotherapy after her mother's death and during graduate school helped her become aware of her role as an emotional caretaker in the family prior to her mother's illness, and she continues to notice her tendency toward caretaking with clients and supervisees.

Support. Dalia has been in psychotherapy in the past, and she currently gets support through meeting with other supervisors at the clinic on a monthly basis and attending a consultation group outside the clinic. The consultation group is led by a senior clinician and members present psychotherapy cases and supervision dilemmas for feedback from the leader and other members. Dalia has had a daily meditation practice for 10 years and is part of a spiritual community that meets weekly.

Cultural identities. Dalia is a heterosexual, married 52-year-old Jewish woman of Middle Eastern descent. She was raised in Israel and moved to the United States to enter college on the East Coast. After graduation, she moved to the San Francisco Bay Area where she lives with her husband and two children. Dalia's parents moved from Lebanon to Israel in their early twenties where they opened a small business which Dalia's father still operates. Using the *ADDRESSING framework*, Dalia is in the majority group in the areas of age, disabilities, socioeconomic status, sexual identity, and indigenous heritage. She is in minority or non-dominant groups as Jewish, of Middle Eastern ethnicity, an immigrant, and female.

Dalia views her *primary cultural influences* as being Jewish, Israeli, and an immigrant. She views herself as a person of privilege due to her socioeconomic status who, nevertheless, has experienced prejudice and discrimination in a variety of settings. These experiences have heightened her empathy with clients who are members of non-dominant cultural groups.

Supervisory Interactions

Dalia and Liz meet weekly for individual supervision. In their first month of supervision, they discuss general issues related to clinical practice as well as Liz's specific client assignments and initial psychotherapy sessions.

Professional boundaries. Liz's volunteer work introduced her to the concept of professional boundaries, and she found it helpful to be clear about the difference between her interactions in personal and professional relationships. She talks with Dalia about some incidents in her school-based placement in which she was challenged by the casual nature of some requests from school personnel for information about her therapeutic work with children and families. Liz described the support she got from her supervisor and the way she handled these requests in order to maintain boundaries as well as collegial relationships.

Therapeutic frame. As Liz begins to see clients, she has questions about issues related to the therapeutic frame which Dalia discusses with her. Over several such conversations, Liz becomes familiar with the usual practices at Community Support Clinic.

- Weekly 50-minute sessions at the clinic offices with appointments scheduled by clinicians between 9 a.m. and 8 p.m.
- Open-ended treatment for clients paying on the sliding scale; time-limited treatment for clients funded by third parties, usually 10 to 25 sessions with a provision for renewal of authorization.
- Contact outside of scheduled sessions may include school observations of child clients and telephone contact with clients in crisis.
- Treatment is provided for a broad range of presenting problems and diagnoses, using individual, couple, and family therapy modalities.
- Confidentiality of all information about the client and the treatment is maintained, with exceptions for legally mandated situations of danger. Except in emergency or crisis situations, the client's permission is obtained for sharing of information that is legally permissible; e.g., coordination of care.
- Treatment generally ends when the client has met his goals or has made a decision to discontinue. Sometimes third-party funded treatment ends because of an expiration of funding. On other occasions, relatively rare, treatment may be ended by the clinician because of the client's lack of adherence to the recommended treatment plan or to clinic policies regarding safety.

Liz feels comfortable with these conditions of the therapeutic frame and is relieved to be clear about the structure so she can communicate clearly with her clients as needed.

Transference and countertransference. Dalia asks Liz in their first supervision session about her experience of and understanding of these terms. Liz says she was introduced to the terms transference and countertransference in a graduate school class but hasn't applied them to her clinical work. Dalia gives Liz a summary of the ways she talks with her supervisees about their countertransference and acknowledges that it sometimes feels emotionally challenging to talk openly with a supervisor about feelings that seem unacceptable or inconsistent with a therapeutic role. Dalia shares with Liz some examples of her own countertransference with clients and how she has used countertransference to make her work more effective. She asks Liz what feelings she would be most reluctant to share in supervision, and they talk about how Dalia can support Liz in sharing openly.

Self-disclosure. Dalia asks Liz about her experience with disclosing personal information to clients. Liz describes the difference between her work as a volunteer when she was encouraged to share some aspects of her personal life, and her practicum placement during which she shared more limited information. Dalia tells Liz that she will be expected to share information with her clients regarding her status as a clinician in training working under supervision. They then discuss some of the personal and professional questions clients often ask. Dalia helps Liz develop answers to some of the more common questions, and then asks Liz how she answered questions in the past about aspects of her personal life she didn't want to share. Liz talks about the response she developed with her supervisor's help the previous year, and Dalia agrees that Liz's response is appropriate.

The Next Step

Chapter 2 will describe additional preparatory steps for clinicians in training settings. The case example will introduce Susana, the client, and review the initial phone contact between Liz and Susana.

References

American Association for Marriage and Family Therapy. (2001). *Code of ethics.* Alexandria, VA: Author.

American Psychological Association. (2002). Ethical principles of psychologists and code of conduct. *American Psychologist, 57,* 1060–1073.

Barnett, J. E. (2011). Psychotherapist self-disclosure: Ethical and clinical considerations. *Psychotherapy, 48,* 315–321.

Cornish, J. A. E., Schreier, B. A., Nadkarni, L. I., Metzger, L. H., & Rodolfa, E. R. (Eds.). (2010). *Handbook of multicultural counseling competencies.* Hoboken, NJ: John Wiley & Sons.

Dressel, J. L., Kerr, S., & Stevens, H. B. (2010). Developing competency with white identity and privilege. In Cornish, J. A. E., Schreier, B. A., Nadkarni, L. I., Metzger, L. H., & Rodolfa, E. R. (Eds.). (2010). *Handbook of multicultural counseling competencies.* Hoboken, NJ: John Wiley & Sons.

Hanh, T. N. (2009). *Happiness.* Berkeley, CA: Parallax Press.

Hayes, J. A., Gelso, C. J., & Hummel, A. M. (2011). Managing countertransference. *Psychotherapy, 48,* 88–97.

Hays, P. A. (2008). *Addressing cultural complexities in practice: Assessment, diagnosis, and therapy* (2nd ed.). Washington, DC: American Psychological Association.

McWilliams, N. (2004). *Psychoanalytic psychotherapy: A practitioner's guide.* New York, NY: The Guilford Press.

National Association of Social Workers. (2008). *Code of ethics.* Washington, DC: Author. Retrieved May 4, 2012, from http://www.naswdc.org/pubs/code/code.asp.

Siegel, D. J. (2011). *Mindsight: The new science of personal transformation.* New York, NY: Bantam Books.

2

PROFESSIONAL PREPARATION

(Note: This chapter will use the female pronoun for supervisor, clinician, and client.)

Chapter 1 stressed the importance of self-awareness and personal growth as you become a behavioral health clinician. In this chapter, I will talk more specifically about how to prepare for your first session with your client. I begin with a discussion of information you need before contacting clients, and then describe a number of issues related to supervision—procedural, emotional, and interpersonal—ending with suggestions for your contact with the client that will set the stage for your therapeutic relationship.

Technical and Procedural Questions

Before your first contact with a client in a new training setting, I recommend that you become familiar with the *procedures related to the therapeutic frame and safety concerns*. Most training settings offer an orientation that may be more or less formal and may be quite lengthy or relatively brief. Some universal issues to be clear about before you begin your first clinical encounter are

- Where you will meet with your clients,
- How your sessions will be scheduled (by you or an administrative support person),
- How often you will meet with your clients and how long each session will last,
- What documentation you are required to complete during and after the session,
- Agency procedure for clinical emergencies (e.g., client danger to self or others, severe psychotic symptoms, intoxication, or other forms of acting out),
- Requirements and procedures for reporting abuse and neglect, and
- Provisions for emergency consultation or backup.

You may have additional questions based on the setting, population, and type of clinical work you are doing. If your orientation doesn't address all of these issues, check with your supervisor before contacting your first client. It is never possible to predict what may occur in an initial phone call with a client or to know when you will need to intervene in an emergency or crisis situation.

It is common to feel nervous when you begin working at a new training site, and learning about these practices will help you to calm your anxiety. You may need to use other supports if your anxiety is high, so you can step into the unknown of meeting with your first client and having your first clinical session. Remember that all of your professors, supervisors, and mentors were once in your shoes facing their first session in a new training site. The memories of those first encounters have stayed with many of us throughout our careers. We remember some of our fears and growing pains, and we want to do what we can to ease the path for others. When you share your anxieties with your supervisor, she can help you feel prepared for entering that first session.

Supervision

General Description

A key part of clinical training is the *mentoring, support, and guidance you receive* from your supervisors. The relationship you form with your primary supervisor will probably be the most powerful influence on the type and quality of professional growth you achieve in your placement. There is variability across different agencies in the role of supervisors, but they are generally licensed clinicians who have received some amount of specific training in supervision. The amount of post-licensure experience and training required to provide supervision is mandated by state licensing boards.

Supervisors may be employed by the training setting to do supervision only or to do clinical work in addition to training and supervision. They may also have administrative positions that overlap with their roles as supervisors. Many supervisors have an independent psychotherapy or consulting practice in addition to their employment and in some settings supervision takes place off-site in the supervisor's private office. Many training sites offer both individual and group supervision because of the unique learning opportunities in each. You may have one supervisor or several depending on the size of the agency, number of hours you are working, and different types of work you are doing.

Procedural Issues in Supervision

When you start in a new training setting, make sure your *weekly supervision schedule* is set as soon as possible to ensure that there is adequate time to discuss your new cases and that your hours will count toward your academic and licensure requirements.

In addition, I recommend that you clarify both your supervisor's expectations and availability for *contact outside of scheduled supervision* and the *procedures for emergency situations and backup* if the supervisor is not available in an emergency.

If you have more than one supervisor, one of them will be your primary supervisor. The *primary supervisor carries the legal responsibility* for the clients under your care, so you need to keep her informed of the progress of all of your cases, potential legal or ethical issues, and any changes in your treatment plans. If you receive advice on a case from a secondary supervisor or consultant that differs from your primary supervisor's perspective, talk with your primary supervisor before changing anything in your work with the client. Inform your primary supervisor immediately of any situation involving safety or legal issues.

Discrepancies in supervisors' perspectives. One reason you may get different feedback from different supervisors is based on theoretical orientation. This affects the supervisor's view of the case, and a secondary supervisor or consultant may make suggestions consistent with her theoretical perspective, which varies from your primary supervisor's advice. Another reason is that you may present a different description of the case to another supervisor, leading her to offer different feedback. *If you disagree with your supervisor's recommendations, discuss this disagreement openly with her.* Try to maintain an attitude of curiosity and interest in your supervisor's perspective as well as a willingness to be self-reflective about your point of view. Often disagreements among clinicians reflect the client's conflicts, and working through your differences with your supervisor is likely to create insight into the therapeutic relationship. See the *discussion of parallel process below* for a more extensive description of this phenomenon.

Professional Responsibility

Making the transition from the role of student to the role of professional clinician is part of clinical training. It is complicated by the fact that you are working under supervision; however, you make clinical judgments and decisions from the moment of your first contact with a client. One aspect of professionalism is *taking ownership of your training and growth*. If you are uncertain about something, ask your supervisor rather than waiting for her to tell you. If your school needs information from your training site, find out who can provide that information. If you feel unprepared or unable to meet the demands of the training, talk with your supervisor as soon as you identify the problem. If you need additional resources for managing a difficult client situation, ask your supervisor what is available. It is never too early to be proactive in charting your professional path.

You may be more comfortable either with being independent and autonomous or with being a beginner and asking for help. Clinical training requires you to *balance your growing ability to make autonomous decisions with the knowledge that your experience is limited.* If you are more comfortable with autonomy and independence, remind yourself that you are a beginner in clinical work, despite the expertise you have in other areas of your life. Your growing edge will be acknowledging your inexperience and your need for help and support. On the other hand, if you are more comfortable relying on others for help, you will need to take the risk of acting on your best judgment combined with your caring heart. Most supervisors are aware of the importance of balancing autonomy with the need for support, and they will encourage you to exercise the behavior that is less familiar to you. They will also help you to assess what decisions you are ready to make independently and what decisions require consultation.

Emotions Present in Supervision

Your training setting and supervisor may or may not explicitly encourage you to reflect on your emotional responses to your supervisor. Since these feelings often arise whether they are discussed openly, I believe the following insights will help you understand your interactions with your supervisor even if you don't talk about them directly.

Although the supervisory relationship is a professional and collegial one, the emotionally charged nature of clinical work means you will have strong emotional responses in supervision. Since we use ourselves as an instrument of healing, *we feel very exposed and vulnerable when we share our work with a supervisor*. In addition, the supervisor's role is to mentor, nurture, and support as well as to evaluate and give corrective feedback. It may be hard for you to be open and honest with your supervisor, knowing that she will evaluate your work. Supervisors also feel some tension in holding both sides of the supervisory relationship. However, clinical growth requires that you develop an accurate picture of your strengths and limitations, and that can only happen when you are honest with your supervisor and receive constructive feedback. I encourage you to be open about your clinical work and to use your supervisor's supportive and corrective feedback to further your growth.

You may notice strong *positive and negative feelings toward your supervisors* that are based partially on experiences with parental and other authority figures. Personal psychotherapy can help you to differentiate the emotional reactions to your supervisor from feelings about your parents and others who are or have been in positions of authority. Because of the strong feelings that are evoked in supervision, supervisees may feel confused about the similarities and differences between supervision and other close relationships. Some helpful distinctions to bear in mind are that supervision is friendly but is not a friendship and that supervision can be therapeutic but is not therapy.

Parallel Process

A common phenomenon in supervision is that *interactions between the supervisor and supervisee begin to mirror interactions between the supervisee clinician and the client*. This phenomenon, called parallel process, has been described extensively in the psychoanalytic literature about supervision (Frawley-O'Dea & Sarnat, 2001) and is recognized across theoretical orientations (Tracey, Bludworth, & Glidden-Tracey, 2012). Parallel process is especially likely to happen when your clinical work with the client is complicated by an intense and unpleasant set of interactions that you are unable to describe consciously and verbally. When faced with this struggle, you may unintentionally relate to your supervisor as the client is relating to you, and the problematic exchange is repeated in supervision. When this repetition can be recognized and talked about openly, it provides one of the most useful sources of information about the clinical relationship. The discussion in supervision can then focus on the nature of the client's interactions with others and the therapeutic stance that will be most effective.

Effective Use of Supervision

You may be unsure how to use supervision effectively when you begin at a new training site. Your case load may be large, your clients may have complex needs, and supervision time is usually not sufficient to allow discussion of every aspect of every case in detail. Talk with your supervisor at the beginning of the training year about *different ways to present cases* so that supervision will be effective in facilitating your clinical growth. Examples of variations in presenting cases are (a) reviewing a number of cases briefly versus one or two cases in depth, (b) using transcripts or recordings versus clinician notes and summaries, and (c) discussing administrative versus clinical aspects of the work.

I recommend that clinicians in training come to supervision with *questions and concerns in order of priority* so that the supervision discussion can focus on the issues that are most salient and urgent. Review all of your cases with your supervisor periodically, so that she is up to date on the progress in each case. You may do this during the supervision hour or by providing written notes or summaries. Supervision is a time to talk about cases that are going well, although it is sometimes difficult to make time for this. Your professional growth is enhanced when you talk about cases that are improving, as the insights you gain help you understand what contributes to your effectiveness. It is usually best to start with crisis or safety concerns, followed by new cases, then clinical questions or concerns in ongoing cases.

Dissatisfaction in Supervision

Supervision is the most influential component of training for most clinicians, and it can be painful to feel you aren't getting the support you need from your supervisor. You may be uncomfortable discussing your dissatisfaction with your supervisor directly, but avoiding this discussion will detract from the quality of your training experience.

The *first step toward resolving any difficulty in supervision is to discuss it directly* with the supervisor, as clearly and respectfully as possible. This may mean getting support and advice from other mentors outside the agency, from other clinicians in training, and from personal psychotherapy. I recommend stating directly what you would like to be different in supervision, while making a request for what you need from the supervisor. Include some specific examples of what you would find helpful. It will be easier for your supervisor to respond to your request if you state what you would like rather than dwelling on what isn't working. Assume that your supervisor wants to be helpful to you and will do her best to be responsive to your requests.

If this discussion doesn't lead to an improvement, it may be helpful to *request a meeting with an administrator or training director* to discuss your concerns and requests. Although it is painful to work through conflicting or disappointing supervisory experiences, many clinicians report that doing so was a valuable contribution to their learning.

Initial Contact with the Client

You may think of your initial phone conversation with the client as a time to simply schedule an appointment. However, I recommend that you think about this first contact as *the first step in establishing the therapeutic frame and the therapeutic relationship*. In most training settings, you will contact your client by telephone or email to schedule the first face-to-face session. If sessions are scheduled by administrative staff or if you see clients on a drop-in basis for an initial intake interview, your first contact will also be your first session, which is discussed in Chapter 3.

When you call to schedule an appointment with a client who is assigned to you, you may have only a name and phone number or you may also have a more detailed description of the client's demographics (i.e., age, gender, ethnicity), living situation, and reasons for seeking help or reasons for referral by a third party. I recommend that you make this first phone call at a time when you are free from distractions and other pressures so that you can be fully engaged with the client. It is possible that another person will answer the phone or that your call will go to voice mail, so be prepared for those scenarios before you call.

I prefer scheduling appointments in a live telephone conversation, as this gives me an opportunity to experience the client's style of interacting. However, it is sometimes difficult to speak to the client directly. Alternatives are to leave a voice mail message in which you offer two or three appointment times and ask the client to leave you a message about which time is best. If your agency practice allows it, you can also schedule an appointment by email. Talk with your supervisor about the agency practice and options if you are unsuccessful in reaching your client by phone. See the following section for additional tips when working with a child, couple, or family.

The initial telephone call with a client sets the tone for your future relationship with her. You are establishing the therapeutic frame and beginning a therapeutic relationship, which means conveying a combination of professionalism, collaboration, and understanding. The *essential elements of an initial conversation* are

- Introducing yourself by name, including your role and the agency or organization where you are working (note that in some states you are required to inform the client of your status as a clinician in training in the initial contact);
- Briefly summarizing the information you have (e.g., "I understand you are looking for help with your depression");
- Scheduling a first appointment in a welcoming way (e.g., "I'd like to schedule a time to meet you and talk about how we might work together");
- Clarifying the payment arrangements and what documentation and payment the client needs to bring to the appointment (e.g., check, cash, or credit card; insurance card; proof of income; identification);
- Confirming the location of the appointment, being explicit about where you will meet the client, and asking whether the client needs directions or information about public transportation, if she is coming to the agency office; and
- Giving the client your name again with your phone number and asking her to call you if she can't keep the appointment for any reason.

As you prepare for calling the client, take some time to *think about what you know about her and how she may feel about entering treatment.* More often than not, your clients will have feelings of shame and inadequacy about the circumstances that have led them to ask for help. They often fear rejection and criticism, they hope for understanding and answers, and they may expect disappointment and frustration. Your client has taken a big step in acknowledging that her life isn't meeting the expectations she has of herself and/or that others have for her, and her emotional state is probably fragile. Common questions and concerns include:

- Can I rely on you to help rather than hurt me?
- Will you try to dominate and control me?
- Will you see me as worthless in the way others see me?
- Is there any reason to hope for my life to be better?

These questions are usually unspoken, but they influence how the client enters the therapeutic relationship.

Your primary goal in making contact with the client is to schedule a first appointment, and this is more likely when you take a therapeutic approach by being aware of the client's emotional vulnerability. *Combining a welcoming and accepting attitude with a tone of professionalism and confidence is most effective.* For example, you might say, "I'm looking forward to meeting you and learning more about how we might work together," or, "It sounds like it's taken a lot of strength to cope with everything you're facing and this seems like a good time to get help."

I generally end my first call with a client by asking her if there is anything else she would like me to know or anything she would like to ask me before we meet in person. This establishes a collaborative tone to our relationship and gives her an opportunity to feel heard by me. I generally limit calls to 10 minutes, so I keep my responses brief and redirect the client to the first appointment if she begins to go into a lot of detail. A simple statement like, "I can see there's a lot going on for you and I look forward to being able to talk more about these things when we meet on Tuesday," is usually sufficient. If not, I am more explicit by saying, for example, "I'm sorry I don't have more time to talk now, but I'll plan to see you on Tuesday at 3." Similarly, if the client asks me one or two simple questions about my background or approach to treatment, I will answer them briefly and redirect her to our first appointment after that.

Child, Couple, and Family Clients

When your client is a child, couple, or family, the *initial contact is somewhat more complicated*. Some training settings offer individual, couple, and family treatment while other settings use only one modality. Being assigned a case for child, couple, or family treatment may be a matter of the client's preference, the presenting issue, the practice in your training agency, or the requirements of a funder. Even when the modality of treatment seems clear, I recommend preparing for the possibility that additional information may come in your initial contact or that there may be some confusion or question about who will be involved in the treatment. Examples of these possible situations are discussed next.

When you begin with *a request for service for a child under 18*, there are several options to consider. Your first session may be scheduled in one of several ways, depending on the theoretical orientation of your organization, the setting (office, home, or school), the age of the child client, and the presenting issues that led the parents and other adults to seek treatment for the child. The first session might be held:

- With the whole family including parents and siblings as well as the client,
- With the parent or parents alone, or
- With the child alone.

Check with your supervisor before you make the first call so you can *be clear with the parent about who should attend the first session*. Also check with your supervisor about the agency policy regarding the involvement of both parents if they are separated or divorced. You may need to talk with both parents by phone before seeing the child, for legal as well as clinical reasons.

When you begin with *a request for couple or family treatment* or if you work in a setting that uses a family systems model in working with children, you will usually ask both members of the couple or all family members to attend the first session. Family therapy most often begins with the parents and children in the household and may include extended family members who live in the household or are closely involved in the daily life of the family. Check with your supervisor about who you should talk with before scheduling a first appointment with a couple or family. I usually talk with both partners of the couple and each adult and adolescent in the family before the first session. This practice may not be a requirement of your training setting, but I find it is clinically useful in establishing an equal relationship with the adult and adolescent participants in treatment. Having these conversations will give you a chance to ask about each person's involvement in seeking help, to explain the importance of everyone's attendance at the first session, and to answer questions anyone may have.

Emergency Situations

Sometimes the client discloses *information in the first call that requires action on your part.* This rarely happens, but being prepared for the possibility of an emergency situation will help you intervene most effectively. Examples of information that may require *further assessment and potential action* on your part are suicidality, other forms of danger to self or others, and psychotic thinking that severely impairs judgment and safety. Your state law may also require reporting an incident of abuse or neglect of a child under 18, or an elder, or dependent adult. Be clear on your agency procedures for situations of danger and reporting obligations.

If the client gives you information in the first phone call that requires action, *proceed thoughtfully and explain your concern and obligation to the client* in a calm manner so that you can maintain a therapeutic relationship. If you aren't clear about your obligation, tell the client you need to consult with your supervisor. An example of how to speak to a client in such a case would be

> I'm concerned about the suicidal thoughts you've been having, even though you've told me you don't plan to act on them. I'd like to consult with my supervisor to make sure we've done everything we can to ensure your safety. Would it be okay for me to call you back today or tomorrow after I talk with her?

I recommend that you role play some potential emergency situations with your supervisor or a more experienced colleague so your responses foster the therapeutic relationship.

Lack of Response from Clients

Every clinician has had the experience of contacting a client who has asked for help but does not respond to follow-up calls. Some of the clients who are assigned to you will not respond to your attempts to contact them, and others will schedule an initial appointment but not keep it. This is frustrating, especially when you come to a new agency and are eager to begin the work. It is useful to examine your initial interactions with clients and get feedback from your supervisor and colleagues who can share effective techniques for engaging reluctant clients.

There are a *number of reasons clients have difficulty following through* on their initial requests for treatment.

• Many of the individuals and families you see during your training are living in stressful, somewhat chaotic circumstances. The state of crisis that prompted the initial call may have passed by the time you call the prospective client to schedule an appointment.

• The client may have felt coerced by a family member or professional to make the initial call and is not ready to engage in treatment.

• Asking for help puts a person in a position of vulnerability, and the client's shame and fear may interfere with scheduling or keeping an appointment.

Most agencies have a *standard practice regarding the number and type of outreach contacts to make* before discontinuing your efforts, and your supervisor can give you this information. My recommendation is to make three calls at different times of day and different days of the week within a 2-week period. If you receive no response to the second call, let the client know the third call will be your last. For example, "I haven't heard back from you about making an appointment, so you may have changed your mind. If I don't hear back from you by next Tuesday, I will assume you are no longer interested in treatment here." I use a similar guideline if a client responds with a message but doesn't schedule an appointment or doesn't keep a scheduled appointment. My experience is that setting a deadline often results in the client making contact or coming in for an appointment. If not, you have kept a therapeutic frame by being clear about your respective roles in the treatment.

You may feel your time has been wasted if the client doesn't come in to begin treatment, especially if it takes more time than you anticipated for your caseload to build. However, *these experiences are rich in information about yourself and your patterns of engagement with others.* You may notice that you feel rejected when the client doesn't respond and that you are tempted to give up after only one call. On the other hand, you may feel invested in reaching the client and have a hard time letting go even after multiple attempts. Reflecting on these patterns provides useful knowledge about what you bring to your therapeutic relationships.

Summary

This chapter reviewed several aspects of practice that are relevant to your first contact with clients, as you begin to establish a therapeutic relationship. I also discussed the emotional and interpersonal issues inherent in the supervisory relationship. Your investment in preparing for your initial contact with clients and in examining your clinical challenges in supervision will bring rewards in professional growth. Specific areas of preparation are listed below.

1. Using yourself as an instrument of hope, change, and healing:

    a. Recognize the sources of strong emotions in your supervisory relationships, based on personal experiences and client relationships.

2. Becoming confident in your authority and professionalism:

    a. Clarify procedures related to therapeutic frame, safety, and supervision.
    b. Take ownership of your professional growth, including balancing autonomy with reliance on supervisors and experienced colleagues.

3. Developing interpersonal skills that strengthen the therapeutic relationship:

    a. Talk openly about discrepancies and disagreements in supervisory perspectives and about dissatisfactions in supervision.
    b. Prepare to establish the therapeutic frame and therapeutic relationship in the initial client contact by anticipating questions, concerns, and emergencies.
    c. Use self-reflection and feedback to improve your skill in client engagement during the initial contact.

Case Example: An Introduction to Susana and Initial Contact

Introduction to Susana

Liz is assigned to work with Susana in her third month of placement. She is given the following information from a short telephone screening, which is the practice at Community Support Clinic as the first step for individuals who request services.

Susana is a 36-year-old single mother of three. She requested services for herself after an incident 2 weeks ago in which her 15-year-old daughter called 9-1-1 during an argument between Susana and Susana's live-in boyfriend. Susana reported that her boyfriend moved out after the incident, which involved police visiting her apartment but not taking any action against her or her boyfriend. In the telephone screening, Susana said she had been depressed and was finding it hard to get out of bed in the morning to go to work. She also said she was angry with her daughter for over-reacting and causing the boyfriend to leave.

Liz's Reactions to Screening Information about Susana

When Liz looks over the screening information, she has a number of thoughts and questions. She wonders if the relationship between Susana and her boyfriend included physical violence at any point and what role that might have played in the daughter's emergency call. She notices that there is no information about the other two children, and that the 15-year-old daughter seems to have assumed a somewhat parental role. Liz wonders about the severity of Susana's depression and whether she has been depressed before. She feels concerned about Susana's performance on her job as well as her ability to take care of her children. She feels annoyed with Susana for what appears to be a lack of empathy and concern for her daughter, since Liz assumes the daughter must have been quite frightened to call for emergency help.

Liz's Initial Supervision Discussion

Liz tells Dalia about her new case assignment and her concerns and questions about Susana. Dalia comments on Liz's annoyance and asks Liz to imagine the situation from Susana's point of view. Liz wonders if Susana's anger toward her daughter is related to feelings of guilt and embarrassment about the police visit. She also notices that Susana is reporting being angry with the daughter, and Liz is feeling annoyed with Susana. Liz thinks about the similarity in their feelings and wonders if she can learn from noticing how she feels toward Susana. Dalia encourages her to reflect on the presence of feelings of anger in the case before Liz has talked with Susana. As Liz imagines how Susana felt when her daughter called the police, she notices that her annoyance decreases. This leads Dalia to suggest that Susana has been unable to view the argument between herself and her boyfriend from the daughter's point of view and that Susana continues to feel angry because she has not been able to empathize with her daughter. Dalia encourages Liz to focus on her therapeutic relationship with Susana by being empathic with her experience, since that will be required before Susana will be able to think about her daughter's feelings and perspective.

First Phone Conversation

Liz leaves two phone messages before reaching Susana in person. They then have the following conversation:

Liz: Hello, Ms. Rodriguez. I'm glad I was able to reach you in person. My name is Liz Matthews. I'm an intern in training at the Community Support Clinic. I understand you called because you've been feeling depressed. I'd like to set up a time for us to meet and talk more about what's going on for you.

Susana: I'm actually feeling better today so I have decided I don't need to come in after all.

Liz: It sounds like there is lot going on in your family. Don't you think it would be a good idea to come in and talk about it?

Susana: No, I don't think talking changes anything. Things are better so I'll just handle it on my own. I'm sorry for taking up your time.

Liz: There's no need for an apology. I hope you continue to feel better and you can call if that changes.

Susana: I don't think it will, but thank you for the offer.

Second Supervision Discussion

After this conversation, Liz makes a note of Susana's decision and returns the intake information to the administrator who assigns cases. In her next supervision session, Dalia asks Liz about the case, and Liz tells her about their conversation stating that Susana doesn't seem to want help. Dalia detects irritation in Liz's voice and asks about her countertransference feelings. Liz expresses frustration that, like another client who recently ended treatment abruptly, Susana seems to be unable to help herself or her children. Dalia empathizes with Liz, and she points out that most of the agency clients are ambivalent about treatment, expecting judgment and rejection instead of help. She wonders if Liz may have given up too quickly because of her frustration with the other client, and she comments on their previous discussion about the case containing feelings of anger and annoyance, both between Susana and her daughter and between Susana and Liz. As they discuss Liz's feelings and Susana's situation, Liz softens and decides it would be best to call Susana again. Liz and Dalia discuss how Liz can open the conversation in a way that is likely to minimize Susana's feelings of guilt and shame and to encourage her to take the risk of coming for an initial session.

Second Phone Conversation

A few days later, Liz reaches Susana again by phone.

Liz: Hello, Ms. Rodriguez. This is Liz Matthews again. I'm an intern in training at the Community Support Clinic. We spoke last week.

Susana: I told you I was feeling better then and didn't want to come in.

Liz: Yes you did, but I wanted to check in with you again. People often find that depression comes and goes a bit, and I wanted to see how you've been feeling in the last week. It sounds like a lot has been going on for you lately, and when people are going through a lot of stress they sometimes find their feelings can change pretty quickly.

Susana: It is true that this week has been harder. I've been kind of depressed again. You say that's normal with depression?

Liz: Each person is different, but it is common that depression can be better and worse depending on circumstances and stress.

Susana: I'm still not sure talking will do any good.

Liz: I can understand that. I can't tell for sure how it might help for us to talk, but I wonder if you'd be willing to come in once so we can meet and talk some more about what is going on for you and your family?

Susana: I guess I could try it once.

Liz: I'm glad you're willing to do that. It looks like you told the person on the phone that you'd need to come after work. Would Tuesday at 5 be possible?

Susana: I think so. Where should I come?

Liz: Our office is at 59 Central Street, on the second floor. There's parking in front of the building and we have a lobby on the second floor where I'll meet you at 5 o'clock.

Susana: OK. I think I know where that is. My friend Judy sees a therapist there and she showed me the building one time when we were in that neighborhood having dinner.

Liz: Good. I'm glad you're familiar with it. The charge for the first visit will be $40, and we ask everyone to pay at the time of the session. Will that be possible for you?

Susana: Money's pretty tight right now, but I can manage it once at least. Can I bring a check?

Liz: Yes that's fine. When we meet, you'll have a chance to decide if it seems helpful to talk about what's been going on for you and whether you want to come again. Is there anything else you'd like me to know or like to ask me?

Susana: Judy thought maybe I should bring my daughter Maria with me. I've been really mad at her, and right now she won't talk to me.

Liz: For now I'd like to meet with you alone. If you decide to continue coming in, we might decide that it would be helpful for you to bring Maria but I think it would be best to start with you by yourself.

Susana: OK.

Liz: So I'll see you Tuesday at 5 o'clock at 59 Central Street in the lobby on the second floor. Our session will last 50 minutes. If anything comes up that you can't make it, you can call me at the same number you've been using. I look forward to meeting you.

Susana: I'm pretty sure I'll be able to come on Tuesday and if I can't I'll let you know.

Liz: Good. I'll see you then.

Review of the Initial Contact

In their first phone conversation, Liz was put off by Susana's ambivalence and took Susana's decision at face value, in part because of her frustration about another case and in part because of her countertransference feeling of irritation, which was a feature of the case even before Liz talked directly with Susana. Dalia helped Liz identify her emotional reaction and move beyond her countertransference to a more empathic stance. Once Liz could identify the risk Susana might feel in revealing the distressing events and emotions in her life, she was able to reach out again. In their second conversation, Susana was more open to Liz, perhaps because she was more depressed and perhaps because Liz's persistence communicated her care and understanding. Liz expressed a welcoming attitude while acknowledging Susana's option to schedule an appointment. She also talked about the decision to schedule an appointment as being based on Susana's desire for help. This conveyed that the focus of Liz's attention was on Susana's well-being, which Liz knows is an unfamiliar experience for many clients who have spent years relating to friends, family members, and professionals on the basis of meeting the needs of the other person while neglecting or sacrificing their own needs.

Another way Liz responded to Susana's ambivalence was to focus on setting a time for the first appointment rather than talking about weekly psychotherapy. Framing the first session as the beginning of weekly psychotherapy might have increased Susana's ambivalence and led her to not schedule or not keep the first appointment. In order to reduce Susana's anxiety and uncertainty about Liz's expectations, Liz also provided clear, complete information about the time, place, and length of the first session as well as payment information. Offering this information establishes the professional nature of the encounter and the therapeutic frame for their relationship.

Toward the end of the conversation, Liz provided an opening for Susana to tell or ask her more. When clients express uncertainty about treatment or aren't forthcoming about their reasons for seeking treatment and their feelings about treatment, it is especially helpful to ask a general question as Liz did. In this case, Susana provided important information regarding her concern about her daughter as well as her friendship with Judy who seems to be a supportive presence in Susana's life.

Susana's question about bringing her daughter Maria to the first session is one that might be handled differently in different settings. In this example, Liz suggested that Susana come in alone and left open the possibility of bringing Maria into a later session. This response is based on the importance of Liz maintaining a consistent frame regarding Susana's original request for help for herself and the likelihood that Susana's question is another manifestation of her ambivalence about seeking help. In a setting where family systems theory is the primary orientation, the phone conversation might have begun with Liz encouraging Susana to come to the first session with her daughter Maria as well as the other two children. Alternatively, in a setting that has a primary mission to serve the needs of children, Liz might have asked Susana more questions about her daughter earlier in the conversation in order to make a joint decision about who should come to the first session.

The Next Step

Chapter 3 will describe the tasks and goals of the first session of behavioral health treatment. The case example will describe the first session between Liz and Susana.

References

Frawley-O'Dea, M. G., & Sarnat, J. E. (2001). *The supervisory relationship: A contemporary psychodynamic approach.* New York, NY: The Guilford Press.

Tracey, T. J. G., Bludworth, J., & Glidden-Tracey, C. E. (2012). Are there parallel processes in psychotherapy supervision? An empirical examination. *Psychotherapy, 49,* 330–343.

3
FIRST SESSION

(Note: This chapter will use the male pronoun for supervisor, clinician, and client.)

This chapter discusses the goals and tasks of the first session with your client. I view the primary goal of a first session to be the creation of a relationship that is respectful and collaborative and in which you offer your knowledge and expertise to support the client to make changes in his life. There are a number of tasks you need to accomplish in a first session, and I will illustrate how you can approach these tasks in a way that also fosters the therapeutic relationship.

Greeting the Client

Your emotional state when meeting a client for the first time is a powerful influence on the quality of the therapeutic relationship. Most clinicians in training feel somewhat anxious before their first session with a client and may wonder whether they can even be helpful to their clients. After you are comfortable in the clinician role, your anxiety will decrease overall, but it may resurface when you go to a new training site, when you see a new type of client, or when you learn a new treatment modality or approach. *Connect with your genuine desire to understand the client and to be helpful*, and remember that many clients have little or no experience relating to others who are interested in helping them. Entering the session with a focus on the client's needs and well-being sets the stage for a strong relationship.

I do my best to go into the first session with an *intention to communicate my interest in working collaboratively with the client*. This intention is reflected both in my choice of words and in my style of relating. For example, I generally use the term *we* when I describe the treatment, such as saying, "as we get to know each other," or, "how we will work together." I also give the client options when possible by saying, for example, "I know you originally called because you were concerned about your depression. Would you like to start with that or is there something else more pressing today?" When I need to introduce something that may be more related to my agenda than to the client's, I explain the reasons and ask the client's permission. For example, I might say, "I usually find it helpful to talk with the psychiatrist who is prescribing your medication. That makes it more likely that he and I will be working in a consistent way. Would you be willing to sign an authorization for me to speak with him?"

In the midst of the complicated emotions that often enter into your initial interactions with the client, it can be difficult to adopt a collaborative style. Due to your own anxiety and the client's enactment of familiar relationship patterns, *you may feel pulled at times into being directive or passive rather than collaborative*. Monitoring your initial response to the client will give you information about yourself and about the client's habitual ways of relating to others. I recommend talking with your supervisor about the interpersonal style and feeling of your first session as well as the content to identify the ways you are pulled away from a collaborative stance.

Remember to be cognizant of the *client's cultural background* as a factor in his experience of the therapeutic relationship. While European American culture places an emphasis on equalizing power differences as a means of connection, other cultures place greater emphasis on mutual respect (Hays, 2008). If your client is not in the dominant cultural group (e.g., is an older adult, a person of color, a woman, an immigrant, or a person with a disability), address the client formally in your first contact. For example, it is more respectful to say *Mr. Garcia* or *Ms. Hall* than *Jose* or *Roberta*. As you get to know the client better, he may ask you to use his first name or you may ask his preference.

Establishing a Treatment Contract

Informed Consent

Your therapeutic relationship begins with you *informing the client about the nature and limits of treatment* and obtaining the client's agreement before he shares more about his life and concerns. This is a legal and ethical obligation and is called *informed consent* (AAMFT, 2001; APA, 2002; NASW, 2008). When you begin to work in a new training setting, review the informed consent procedures and documents before you meet with your first client. Be prepared to review and summarize the documents with the client. Many clients do not read the documents carefully, so your oral review and summary is particularly important. A collaborative therapeutic relationship is grounded in the client's informed consent.

The issues most often included in the process of informed consent are

- The general purpose and limitations of the treatment;
- How you and other agency staff will use and protect confidential information that is part of the treatment, possibly including a statement or separate document regarding electronic communication;

- The circumstances in which you are required to break confidentiality;
- Your status as a clinician in training working under supervision, as required by state law;
- The expectations and limitations regarding payment for services by the client or a third party;
- Policies regarding cancellation of appointments;
- Conditions under which treatment may be discontinued by the clinician; and
- The process for registering a complaint if the client is dissatisfied, if required by a funder or accrediting organization.

The information that is part of the informed consent process may be contained in one document or in several documents.

Child, couple, and family treatment. If you are working with a couple or family, each adult consents individually to the treatment so each adult signs the consent forms. If a child is the primary client, you will need consent from one or both parents before seeing the child alone. When the parents are separated or divorced, you may need the consent of both parents before seeing the child, depending on state laws and organization policies. Check with your supervisor about this issue before holding your first session with a child client.

Treating a child without parental consent is permissible under some conditions, based on state laws and organization policies. Check with your supervisor about the circumstances permitting treatment of children without parental consent.

When working with children and adolescents in individual or family therapy, you should review and summarize the informed consent documents with the child or adolescent directly, using developmentally appropriate language, in addition to obtaining the parents' legal consent. I usually ask adolescents to sign the informed consent documents in order to foster a sense of ownership and investment in the treatment.

Introducing informed consent forms. Your first session should begin with reviewing the informed consent forms and getting the client's agreement and signature. Most clinicians in training feel the informed consent process is a distraction from establishing rapport and giving the client a chance to tell his story, and many clients view the required paperwork as a distraction from their primary reason for seeking help. You may be tempted to wait until the end of the first session to present the informed consent forms, but this choice is problematic in that *you do not have a treatment relationship with the client until he has signed the informed consent documents.* If the client gives you information that meets one of the conditions requiring you to break confidentiality before you have informed him of these conditions, he is likely to feel betrayed and may not return. If the client is unwilling to agree to some of the agency policies and requirements, you cannot proceed with treatment, and it is better to address the situation before you and he have begun the session.

Rather than waiting until the end of the session, it is preferable to *review and summarize the documents with clinical sensitivity*. This approach is consistent with the fact that the informed consent process is the first step in defining your therapeutic relationship and communicating your desire to work collaboratively. For example, you can say

> I'm interested in learning more about you and the concerns you have. Before you tell me more about yourself, though, I need to go over some aspects of our working relationship so that we have the same understanding of how we'll be working together.

If the client begins to talk about his presenting issues anyway, you can respond with something like

> I can see you have a lot to talk about today and I'm really interested to hear about what's going on for you. Can we take a few minutes first to talk about some things that are important for you to understand before we begin? After we do that I'll be able to fully concentrate on what you want to tell me.

Confidentiality. Issues related to confidentiality and sharing of information are part of the informed consent process and must be reviewed in the first session. You can begin with a *general statement about protecting confidential information* and the circumstances under which you are required or permitted to break confidentiality. An example of such a statement is

> I am obligated to keep all information about your treatment confidential, with certain exceptions. If I believe you are a danger to yourself or others or if you tell me about a child or older adult who is in danger, I am obligated to notify authorities. Some information about your treatment will be available to other staff at the agency for billing and administrative purposes, but not the details of what you share with me. Otherwise, I will not share information without your permission.

If your organization provides multiple services, you should discuss *how information is shared within your organization* among the different service providers. Sometimes you will ask in the first session for the client's permission to exchange information with family members, health care professionals, or others involved in the client's life. See Chapter 6 for further discussion of using information from others in your assessment. Be aware of special protections of confidentiality that apply to treatment for substance use disorders, described in more detail in Chapter 12, and check with your supervisor about agency policies if you are working with clients who have substance abuse diagnoses.

When working with *couples and families*, I recommend addressing one additional issue of confidentiality in the first session. One member of the couple or family may share information with you outside of your couple or family session and ask you to withhold it from the others. A request like this puts you in a clinically untenable position, and for this reason, many clinicians have a policy of *"no secrets."* Check with your supervisor to see if your agency has a document for this purpose. If so, you would tell the couple or family as part of the informed consent process that you may share anything disclosed by one family member with other family members, usually after encouraging the family member to talk about the matter himself in the couple or family session. When the family members understand and agree, you ask for their signatures on the agency document.

Fostering a Therapeutic Alliance

The therapeutic alliance refers to a sense of collaboration between you and the client, so that there is a *shared feeling of working together toward the same goal.* This quality of the therapeutic relationship has been shown to be a primary factor related to psychotherapy outcome (Norcross, 2010; Shedler, 2010). Some of the ways you can facilitate the development of this alliance are to

- Instill hope,
- Communicate empathy and understanding of the client's experience,
- Balance warmth and professional boundaries, and
- Address obstacles to the therapeutic alliance.

Your clients may have years of experience in relationships that involve violence, betrayal, or neglect, and therefore, the therapeutic alliance will develop gradually over a number of weeks or months. Being attuned to the client's needs and his responses to you will help him to feel safe and to begin to view you as a source of support.

Instilling Hope

One of the most important factors that determine whether clients return to treatment after the first session is the degree of hope they feel. Clients need to leave the first session with *confidence that working with you will enable them to make positive changes in their lives.* The mental health recovery movement has emphasized the importance of instilling hope regarding the client's ability to overcome obstacles and direct the process of growth (Clay, 2012; Copeland, 2002). Development of hope has also been shown to be one of the common factors in psychotherapy outcome across different theoretical orientations (Snyder, Michael, & Cheavens, 1999).

Your client is likely to feel hopeful when you *hold and communicate a belief in his strengths and capacity for growth* despite the current challenges in his life.

Commenting on the client's strengths throughout the session helps to counter his feelings of inadequacy and disempowerment. Statements like, "I see that you're managing to get to work every day even though you're feeling really anxious," or, "It sounds like you have some really good insights into yourself and what you need to do to improve your life" affirm the client's capacities and let him know that you see more than his struggles and symptoms.

Communicating Empathy and Understanding

The cornerstone of a therapeutic alliance is the client's experience of your empathy and understanding of his emotional distress (Elliott, Bohart, Watson, & Greenberg, 2011; Teyber & McClure, 2011). You communicate empathy and understanding by *listening to the client and reflecting his subjective experience*. This is sometimes difficult because it requires setting aside judgments or reactions you may have to the way he tells his story or relates to you. The goal of empathy is to understand what it feels like to be the client. To move toward this goal, you focus on being guided by the client into an exploration of his emotional experience and world view. Through this dialogue, you incorporate the client's feedback to develop an accurate view of his thoughts and feelings.

Developing empathy for the client is not always an easy process. *Examining your countertransference responses to the client* can help you understand what makes it difficult for you to feel empathic. Examples of insights that can come from countertransference examination are as follows.

- He may remind you of someone in your past or some unwanted aspect of yourself.
- He may be accustomed to interacting with people who are judgmental and rejecting and consequently relate to you in a way that reenacts that familiar relationship.
- His experience may feel foreign to you and require that you let go of your familiar assumptions.

One way to communicate empathy is to *reflect your understanding of the client's central feeling* (Teyber & McClure, 2011). For example, if the client says, "I don't know why I keep messing up my relationships," you might reflect, "It seems like you feel responsible when things don't work out with your partners." This statement names the feeling of responsibility that gives rise to the client's self-criticism about his relationships.

Another way to convey empathy is to *describe themes or meanings related to the client's emotions*. For example, if the client has told you about the death of his mother when he was ten and later describes feelings of confusion and loss after a relationship breakup three months ago, you might say, "I can imagine you feel lost and confused now like you felt when your mother died and there was no one to comfort you." This statement includes a reflection of the client's subjective experience of confusion and loss while providing a broader context to understand the depth of his feelings.

Balancing Warmth and Professional Boundaries

Most clinicians feel more comfortable with communicating warmth than with maintaining boundaries, but both sides of the therapeutic role are important. *Your clients will develop a sense of safety and trust when these roles are balanced,* but they may relate to you in ways that make it easy for you to emphasize one behavior over the other. In this situation, you are likely to choose the role that is more comfortable for you.

You may notice that you are more relaxed about professional boundaries with clients who seem to long desperately for warmth and acceptance. You sense that they need to be reassured that you care and understand their pain. However, failing to establish a balance between warmth and maintenance of boundaries often leads to an increase rather than a reduction in the client's expression of need. When this happens, it will become necessary to establish a clear, consistent framework for your work together. Be sure to talk with your supervisor any time you change an aspect of the therapeutic frame or rely on self-disclosure as a clinical intervention. He can support you to understand the meaning of your shift and to return to a balanced position.

At the other end of the spectrum, you may have clients who seem unresponsive to your warmth and compassion, leading you to become cool and detached. In these cases, supervision can help you understand your reaction and regain access to feelings of compassion in order to provide the optimal balance for the client.

Addressing Obstacles

With some of your clients, you will identify obstacles in the first session that interfere with developing a therapeutic alliance. Causes of obstacles include:

- External factors and cultural differences inherent in treatment,
- The client's familiar strategies for coping with painful feelings, and
- The clinician's feeling of being endangered by the client (which rarely happens).

Talk with your supervisor about how to address these obstacles or adapt your therapeutic style so you can foster the collaboration necessary for an effective treatment.

Some obstacles are due to *external factors and cultural differences* inherent in the treatment. Examples are treatment that is mandated by a third party or treatment by a client who is different from you in age, gender, race, or ethnicity. Initiating a conversation about these potential obstacles in the first session is often the best way to lessen their impact. Statements like, "I expect it may be hard for you to see any personal benefit to coming here, when your probation officer says you have to be in treatment or return to jail" or, "I recognize that my experience as a white woman is pretty different from yours as an African American man," invite the client to talk about his full range of feelings in a genuine way rather than hiding his ambivalence and distrust. Clients do not always respond immediately to statements like these, but these openings lay the groundwork for a later conversation. They also communicate to the client that you are aware of and interested in discussing things that make it hard for him to trust you.

Other obstacles are presented by the *client's familiar strategies for coping with painful feelings*. In your first session with the client, he is likely to be worried about and expecting some degree of rejection, to feel vulnerable and ashamed about seeking help, and to be in a heightened state of emotional distress about the issues that led him to seek help. Many of the coping strategies used for dealing with these painful feelings involve avoidance and alteration of the feeling or the situation. For example, a client may be rejecting of you to avoid feeling vulnerable to your judgment or rejection. Alternatively, he may report a series of traumatic events in his past but deny any emotional impact, in order to maintain a view of himself as strong.

Obstacles related to the client's coping strategies are generally difficult to address directly in the first session because these strategies protect him from being overwhelmed by the intensity of his emotions. He needs to use them until he can develop trust in your ability to help and can learn more adaptive ways of coping with emotional pain. A first step in addressing these obstacles is to identify your countertransference responses. For example, you may withdraw, become confrontational or punitive, or feel inadequate. Once you identify these responses, examine their meaning in supervision in light of what you know about the client's internalized relationships and work to adjust your therapeutic style. You need to be open and collaborative without challenging the client's protective strategies.

On rare occasions, an obstacle to the therapeutic alliance occurs when *the clinician feels endangered by the client*. Safety for both clinician and client is essential and must be established before treatment can proceed. If you are assigned to work with a client who has a history of violence toward others, talk with your supervisor in advance about protective measures that are available to you in the event that the client escalates during a session. Follow the agency procedures regarding volatile or dangerous situations, and schedule your sessions at a time when others are in the building. You may need to set specific limits on the client's behavior from the beginning of treatment to create conditions of safety for both of you.

Hearing the Client's Concerns

Facilitating Engagement

The collaborative attitude and focus on the client's concerns in your first session set the tone for what the client can expect in the therapeutic relationship. You want to invite him to talk about the issues that led him to seek treatment and what changes he wants to make in his life. After reviewing the informed consent documentation, look to facilitate the client's active engagement in sharing his concerns and goals with you. One way to do this is to *solicit the client's questions about the treatment and encourage his feedback* about his experience as you work together. You can encourage the client's active participation with questions like, "Is there anything I haven't covered or any questions you have about what we've discussed so far?" and statements like, "As we go along, I hope you'll let me know if I seem to be off track or if there's anything about our work together that doesn't fit for you."

Assessment Process in First Session

If you are required to complete an assessment in the first session, it may be difficult to do this while also establishing a collaborative relationship in which the client has an opportunity to guide and direct the discussion. If you approach the assessment process in the first session by asking a number of questions about the client's life circumstances and history, the client will feel passive and disengaged rather than active and emotionally involved.

One strategy for addressing this dilemma is to *ask the client to begin the discussion by focusing on his area of primary concern.* Introduce the assessment and your desire to hear the client's concerns with a statement like, "During our time together today, I'll need to ask you questions about a number of areas of your life, but I'd like to start with what you feel is most important for me to know." After the client has talked about what is uppermost in his mind, you can move to getting other information you need to complete the assessment.

You can also *begin with an open-ended question and use the client's answers to guide the order and type of questions you ask* in the assessment. Begin with a question like, "How would you like to start our discussion of the issues that bring you here?" or, "What do you feel is most important for me to know about your situation?" If the client begins by talking about his depression, you could first ask about the symptoms, earlier episodes of depression, and family history. The client's answers to these questions are likely to lead naturally to other areas of assessment like substance use, medical history, current psychosocial stressors, and relationship history.

When you complete an assessment in the first session, I recommend telling the client that you will be more directive in this session than in the future. This gives the client an explanation for your style and prepares him for a change in the interactional pattern in future sessions.

Assessment Process over Several Sessions

If your assessment can be completed in several sessions, you can be less directive and can follow the client's initiative in approaching different topics, with the exception of prioritizing issues related to safety. Open the discussion of the client's concerns with a question like, "Can you tell me more about how I can be helpful to you?" or "Where would you like to start in telling me what brings you here?" These kinds of questions convey your wish to be led by the client in defining the issues you will address and choosing the way you will work together. *Begin the discussion with an open-ended question so the client can choose where to start in revealing himself to you.* He may choose to begin with a different issue from the one he talked about in his initial contact with the agency. I prefer to focus on the client's leading concern rather than assuming I know what is most important to him or what he is ready to talk about with me. His circumstances may have changed, or he may need to develop more safety and trust before talking about an area of vulnerability.

I strive to *maintain an attitude of curiosity* when a client tells me about his concerns and goals in the first session. I convey my curiosity by asking clarifying questions, reflecting my understanding, and asking for his feedback rather than assuming I understand his initial response. For example, I might follow a client's statement, "I'd like to be less depressed" with the question, "Can you tell me what that would look like for you?" This question allows the client to tell me what aspects of his life are impacted by his depression and what is most important to him. The answer might be that he would enjoy playing with his kids, or that his sexual relationship with his partner would improve, or that he would have more energy. By asking the question, I learn what "less depressed" means for this particular client.

Difficulties in Exploring Client's Concerns

The exploration of the client's concerns is difficult when the *treatment is mandated by a third party* rather than being initiated by the client. However, if you bring an attitude of collaboration and curiosity to the session, the client may be able to recognize your desire to work together in a way that will bring him personal benefit. For example, if a client identifies a need to meet probation requirements as his primary concern, you might say, "I understand you want to get through this period of probation as quickly as possible and without extra hassle. Is there a way I could help you with that?" or "Is there anything that will be hard for you in meeting the requirements of your probation that could be a focus of our attention?" Chapter 7 contains further discussion of working in mandated treatment.

Another difficulty with some clients is that they begin with *a lengthy, unfocused account of numerous issues from the past and present.* In these cases, conveying a collaborative attitude means providing direction and focus so that you can be helpful rather than get caught in the client's confusion and turmoil. You can provide this direction by making summarizing comments or asking more focused questions. It is sometimes necessary to interrupt the client's narrative to bring some structure and order to his story. You can also suggest what issues seem to be most important to him. For example, you might say

> I understand you're concerned about how your childhood abuse has affected your life in many ways, but you also said you're in danger of losing

your job because you're so depressed you can't get up in the morning. Can you tell me more about your depression, so we can think about things that will help you get to work on time?

When establishing priorities, it is important to let the client know that you hear his other concerns, to acknowledge the significance of those concerns, and to assure him that you will incorporate them in your work together if possible.

Developing Questions for Assessment

During the first session, the client may refer to *past events or aspects of his present life that you believe are relevant to the treatment,* but you may choose to defer discussing them until a later session. Reasons to defer discussion include the time constraints of a single session and your sense that the client is reluctant to give more detail about a particular event or life circumstance. I suggest making note of these questions and issues so you can refer back to them in your assessment with the client. As you learn more about him, you will continue to identify areas of his history and present life that need follow-up attention and exploration. Make note of these issues in your personal notes rather than in the formal documentation of the session, so that you will remember to return to them in a future session. See Chapter 10 for more discussion of documentation and personal notes.

Your understanding of the client integrates two perspectives: the client's subjective experience and the client as observed and experienced by others, including you. Questions for follow-up in the assessment may come from your efforts at understanding the client from one or both of these perspectives and from discrepancies between these perspectives. For example, you may observe the client to be lethargic, pessimistic, and hopeless, but he may object to a description of himself as depressed. Another client may describe himself as sociable and having many close relationships, but you may experience him as being irritable and unpleasant. In both of these cases, you would need to use the assessment period to integrate your observation of the client with his subjective experience. Other situations in which you would question the validity of the client's report include symptoms suggesting cognitive impairment, psychotic thoughts and behavior, and legally mandated treatment. In cases like these, you may need to incorporate information from others in order to develop an accurate assessment.

Outcome of the First Session

Quality of Client Interactions

One way to evaluate the first session is to examine the quality of your interactions with the client. In the first session, you discover how the client relates to you, and you test ways of working with him most effectively. It helps to *notice variations throughout the session in the client's presentation* of himself and his concerns: open or guarded, focused or vague, collaborative or adversarial. Tracking these variations during the session is difficult, but you can often identify subtle shifts in the interpersonal process when you reflect on the session after it occurs, on your own or in supervision.

Clients give clearer descriptions of themselves and disclose more information when they feel accepted and safe (Weiss, 1993). When you identify which interventions were followed by clarity and openness in the client, you gain important information about what helps him feel safe. Because each client has a unique history of being cared for at times and neglected or disappointed at others, you will need to adapt your clinical approach based on the client's way of relating to you as well as on direct statements he makes.

Closing Summary

Ending the first session with a summary fosters the therapeutic alliance. The summary should reflect *your understanding of the client's primary concern and your ideas about how you can help him address this concern.* An example of a summarizing statement is

> I understand that you're primarily concerned about the panic attacks you've had for the last few months, since they're getting in the way of socializing with your friends. I think we can develop a plan for approaching those situations slowly and in small steps so that you have fewer panic attacks and can do more of the things that are important to you.

Ask the client what he thinks about your summary, and fine-tune it until he feels you have correctly understood his concerns. For example, after the summarizing statement above, the client might clarify that the panic attacks also interfere with talking to his boss at work. You would then need to restate your summary until the client agreed that your statement was an accurate reflection of the issue he wants to address in treatment. If he has questions about the treatment approach you recommend, you will need to modify the plan until you have a mutual understanding about how you will proceed. This agreement is the basis for a formal treatment plan, which you may develop in the first session or after several sessions, depending on your agency and funder requirements. See Chapter 9 for more discussion about treatment planning.

Child, Couple, and Family Treatment

When working with a child, couple, or family, I recommend that you also *share a closing summary after the first session.* Use language that is developmentally appropriate for the child clients. If you use a couple or family therapy treatment approach, the nature of your summary after the first session will reflect your understanding of the presenting issue and your plan to meet with the couple or family as a whole to address their concerns. If you are seeing a child individually as your primary client, you will share your treatment approach with the parents and child together or separately including your expectation of how the parents will be involved in the treatment.

An example of *a summary for a couple case* is

> You have talked about how hard it is for you to communicate with each other and resolve disagreements. It seems you both want to work on better communication, and I think we can practice some tools here that will help both of you feel heard and understood.

Ask each member of the couple if they feel you have described their concerns and if they would like to work with you to improve their communication. As with an individual client, modify your summary until both partners have agreed.

An example of *a summary for a family case* is

> I understand that mom and dad are concerned about Luke's grades in school and that there has been a lot of conflict at home recently. It seems like Luke started having more trouble at school when his baby sister was born, and I think it might be helpful for us to meet together and talk about this change in your family.

Follow this summary by checking with each family member to get their feedback and agreement.

An example of a *summary for the parents of a child treated individually* is

> I understand you're concerned about Luke's grades and you've noticed he began having trouble in school after your daughter was born. I'd like to meet with Luke alone next week and then with all of you together. It would probably be helpful for me to talk with his teachers also, if you are willing to give me permission to do that. Then I'll be able to talk with you about how I think we can address your concerns about Luke's grades and the changes in your family.

In this case, you would update the parents after the individual and family sessions and after consulting with Luke's teachers, giving them a more complete description of your view of Luke's issues and how you would work with him and them.

Summary

This chapter discussed the goals and tasks of the first session with a new client. I illustrated ways to accomplish the necessary tasks of a first session while establishing a strong therapeutic relationship. Conveying a collaborative attitude and communicating your interest in and understanding of the client are the foundation of a therapeutic alliance, which is necessary for treatment to continue. The important features of the first session are summarized below.

1. Using yourself as an instrument of hope, change, and healing:

    a. Pay attention to your emotional state as you prepare for the first session.
    b. Examine your countertransference responses when it is difficult to be empathic or when there are obstacles to the therapeutic alliance.
    c. Reflect on the client's clarity and openness with you at different points during the session.

2. Becoming confident in your authority and professionalism:

    a. Review and summarize informed consent documents at the beginning of the session with particular attention to confidentiality.
    b. Recognize and develop strategies for obstacles to the therapeutic alliance.
    c. End the session with a closing summary.

3. Developing interpersonal skills that strengthen the therapeutic relationship:

    a. Foster a therapeutic alliance by:

        i. Expressing a belief in the client's strengths and capacity for growth,
        ii. Communicating empathy by listening and reflecting the client's experience,
        iii. Balancing warmth and professional boundaries, and
        iv. Addressing obstacles that could interfere.

    b. Facilitate active engagement by encouraging the client to identify concerns and priorities.

Case Example: Liz's First Session with Susana

On the day of their first appointment, Liz has three clients scheduled in the hours leading up to her appointment with Susana. She feels somewhat rushed, but she takes a moment to read the information from Susana's telephone screening and their initial telephone conversation before she goes to meet Susana in the lobby. Liz notes that she wants to follow up on Susana's current level of depression, her relationship with her daughter Maria, and what contact she has had with her boyfriend since the incident. She has 60 days to complete her assessment so she plans to start with Susana's primary area of concern and use that as a starting point for learning more about Susana's current life and past history.

Susana arrives in the lobby about 5 minutes late and she and Liz have the following interchange:

Liz:	Hello. I'm Liz Matthews.
Susana:	I'm Susana Rodriguez. Sorry I'm late. My supervisor asked to talk with me just as I was getting ready to leave, and it made me late leaving work.
Liz:	I'm glad you're here. We'll go this way to the room we'll be using for this evening.

After they get to the room, Liz introduces the informed consent documents.

Liz:	I'm interested in hearing more about how things are going for you and how I can be helpful. Before we do that, I'd like to go over some information with you about our work together. You may have seen documents like these when you've gone to your doctor or if you've seen a counselor in the past.
Susana:	OK. Do you need me to sign those?
Liz:	Yes, I do, but first I'd like to go over some of the important issues in them so you understand what you're signing. Is that all right?
Susana:	OK.

Liz covers the highlights of the informed consent documents, including a general description of mental health treatment, protection of confidential information, exceptions to confidentiality, Liz's status as a clinician in training, and expectations regarding payment. She does this in a conversational style and asks Susana if she has any questions about each document before moving on to the next. She gives Susana a copy of the documents and keeps the original for the treatment record.

Liz:	Thanks for taking the time to look at these documents. I also like to take care of payment at the beginning of the session, if that's all right with you. I find it's easier to get it out of the way at the beginning rather than doing it at the end. Did you bring payment with you?

Susana gets out her checkbook. She confirms the amount of $40 and the name of the clinic as the payee on the check then gives the check to Liz.

Liz:	Thank you. Now, can you tell me more about what led you to call the clinic and how I might be helpful to you?
Susana:	I think I told you on the phone about my daughter Maria calling 9-1-1 when my boyfriend and I were fighting. I was pretty mad at her but we've started talking to each other again. The main thing I'm worried about is that my boyfriend Carlos moved out the next day, and I haven't heard from him. At first I was glad he was gone because we had been fighting a lot, but now I really miss him and I don't know where he is. I've called a couple of his friends and his brother, but they either don't

know or they won't tell me. I just want to know he's okay and to let him
know I'm sorry about Maria calling the police.

Liz: So after being relieved at first, you now find you're missing him and
maybe wanting to see him again?

Susana: I don't know if I want to see him, but I'd like to talk to him and apologize. He was really upset that the police came. I want him to know
I'm sorry and that I told Maria she shouldn't have done that. The fight
wasn't that bad so there really wasn't any reason for her to call. When
he left, he said he didn't want to risk having the police around, so he
wouldn't be coming to see me anymore. At first I thought, "Good rid-
dance," because we hadn't been getting along that well, but after a few
days I started feeling lonely. I miss having someone to talk to after my
little one goes to bed, and he helped pay some of the bills so it's hard
financially to make it without his help.

Liz asks Susana more about missing Carlos and about her loneliness. Susana
describes having trouble falling asleep which makes it hard to get up in the
morning. She says she missed a few days of work during the 2 weeks after the
9-1-1 call but has gone to work every day since then. She talks about feeling tired
all the time, not being able to concentrate, and not enjoying anything even her
favorite television shows. Liz follows up on Susana's statement that she wants to
apologize to Carlos and as Susana describes her thoughts, Liz reflects that Susana
seems to be feeling guilty.

As Susana talks more about her feelings, Liz comments that Susana seems
depressed. Susana agrees and says she started feeling depressed a few months ago
and that it's been worse since the 9-1-1 incident. Liz asks if she has had similar
times of depression in the past. Susana describes feeling depressed in her fresh-
man year of college, which led her to drop out after the first semester. As Liz asks
about this, Susana reveals that she made a suicide attempt by taking an overdose of
her roommate's anxiety medication. She was hospitalized for a week and felt too
embarrassed to return to school. Liz asks Susana about current thoughts of suicide
or self-harm, and Susana says she would never hurt herself now because her kids
rely on her. Liz asks Susana if she can agree to let Liz know if she has any thoughts
about suicide or hurting herself, and Susana says she'll do that. They then have the
following exchange:

Liz: It sounds like you've been having a hard time and I'm wondering how
you've been coping with your depression and loneliness. What have you
done to try to help yourself?

Susana: I tell myself I don't have it that bad. Lots of people have worse.

Liz: I see. You compare your situation to others', and does it seem like you
shouldn't feel bad? Like there isn't a good reason for your feelings?

Susana: I guess everyone feels bad after a breakup, but I just tell myself not to wallow in it. I need to get over it and move on with my life.

Liz: I sense you may feel a little impatient with yourself and also that you may not know exactly what you can do to feel less depressed.

Susana: When I was depressed before, I just moved back home from college and got a job, and then I married Antonio and pretty soon Jorge was born. I wasn't depressed anymore because I was so busy with the baby.

Liz: It sounds like this time your situation is really different, so I understand why you might be wondering how you'll get out of your depression. Do you have people in your life that you can talk to about what happened with Carlos and how you're feeling?

Susana: My friend Judy always asks me how I'm doing. We usually go out on the weekends. We meet at a bar and have a couple drinks. That helps. After a couple drinks I don't care so much about Carlos.

Liz: So you talk to Judy and have a couple drinks with her on the weekends. Are there other people you talk to?

Susana: Not really. I have other friends but I don't talk to them about what's really going on. We talk about our kids and jobs but nothing more than that.

Liz: It sounds like you're pretty alone, so I'm not surprised you've been missing Carlos since he left. Are there other things you've tried to help with the loneliness?

Susana: I don't really know anything else to do. I've had other men leave me, so I know I'll get through it. I just tell myself it will get better. But this time seems harder than the others. That's why I called the clinic. I don't know what's wrong with me.

Liz: I think you made a good decision in calling for help. I wouldn't say there's something wrong with you exactly, but it sounds like you want to understand why you're feeling so bad. I imagine you'd like for us to figure out how you can feel better.

Susana: Do you think that's possible?

Liz: I do. I think if we put our heads together, we can come up with some ideas about why this breakup has been so hard for you and what might help you feel less depressed.

Liz goes on to ask Susana more about her pattern of drinking, introducing the topic by saying that drinking sometimes contributes to depression, even though it may seem like a way to feel distracted from loneliness and other painful emotions. Susana says she doesn't drink during the week since Carlos left, because she doesn't think it's good for her kids to see her drinking. She says her older kids are with their friends on the weekends and her youngest daughter visits her dad, so she only drinks on the weekends when they're gone. She says she usually stops after two drinks with Judy on the weekends. She acknowledges that she drank more than that on the weekend after the 9-1-1 incident, and that she decided to take a cab home because she didn't think she should drive. Then Susana quickly says:

Susana: But it only happened that one time because I was really upset. It hasn't happened again.

Liz: I'm glad to hear you made the decision to not drive when you felt you'd had too much to drink. Can you tell me more about why you aren't drinking during the week now? You said you think it's better for your kids.

Susana: My dad was an alcoholic. He died a few years ago, but I remember when I was a kid it really upset me to see him drinking every night. Sometimes he would get angry, and other times he just didn't seem to notice I was there. I don't want my kids to feel that way.

Liz: You really want to be consistent with them and you know drinking makes you act differently toward them. Can you tell me more about your kids? I think you said when you called the clinic that Maria is 15. You also mentioned Jorge and a younger daughter.

Susana: Jorge is my oldest. He's 16, Maria is 15, and Amelia is 7. Antonio left when Maria was 5, and then I met Devon who is Amelia's dad. We were together for 5 years, although we didn't get married. He left when Amelia was 2, but she sees him on the weekends. Antonio went back to Mexico a couple of years ago so I haven't seen him for awhile.

Liz: You've talked about your feelings of depression and loneliness since Carlos left. How have your kids been affected by him leaving?

Susana: They all said they were glad he left. They had been telling me for months that I should make him leave. We fought a lot, although it was usually at night after they were in bed. But I guess they could hear. Amelia asked me yesterday if Carlos was coming back and I told her I didn't think so. She said, "That's good, Mommy."

Liz: Do you have a sense of why she thinks that?

Susana: All I can think of is the fighting, but she was usually asleep. Maybe she wants me all to herself. She always seemed a little jealous of Carlos. She's been that way with the other men I've been with too, even if they weren't living with us. Jorge and Maria don't really care. They're out so much with their friends, and when they're home they just watch TV or use the computer. I was surprised when they both said they thought I should make Carlos leave. That was about 6 months ago. I didn't think they even noticed he was there.

Liz asks Susana more questions about her children and learns Susana feels somewhat rejected by her older children, although she knows it is usual for teenagers to focus on their friends and social activities. She expresses sadness that Amelia, whom she calls her baby, is less interested in cuddling and spending time together as she gets older. Liz asks about Susana and Maria talking again. Susana says Maria just started talking to her again a few days ago, and she's glad things seem better. Liz asks if Susana has talked with any of her children about the 9-1-1 incident since that night. Susana says she has been afraid to bring it up, since she was so angry with Maria then. She thinks it is better to forget about it now that Carlos has moved out. Susana then talks more about her loneliness, missing Carlos, and wanting to meet another man before Amelia becomes more independent like the older two children.

With about 5 minutes left in the session, Liz says:

Liz: It's getting close to time for us to end for today. You've let me know about your loneliness, depression, and concerns you have about your relationship with your kids as they get older. I've noticed that you seem to feel pretty alone and that you can be kind of hard on yourself, taking responsibility for Carlos leaving and thinking there's something wrong with you because you're having a hard time with the breakup. If you decide to continue our work together, I think we can get a better understanding of what makes this breakup so hard for you. I'd also like to see if we can come up with some ways you can help yourself when you feel lonely. Are you interested in coming back again to talk about these things some more?

Susana: I think so. Do you think talking about problems can help? I'm not sure.

Liz: I have found that it can help, but I understand it's new for you and you may need some time to find out for yourself whether this can be helpful to you. Are you willing to give it a try again next week? I have this time open if it would work for you.

Susana: Yes, I can do that. Is there anything I should do before then?

Liz: You don't have to do anything, but if you're interested in trying an experiment you might think about times in your life when you liked yourself and what qualities you liked.

Susana: Right now I can't think of anything. That will be hard.

Liz: It's pretty different to think of liking yourself, but it might be interesting to see what comes to you if you put your mind to it.

Susana: OK. Maybe I'll ask Judy what she likes about me or ask my kids.

Liz: Good idea. I'll plan to see you again at 5 next Tuesday.

Liz gives Susana a business card with her name and contact information and shows Susana out to the lobby.

Liz's Reflection on the First Session

After the session, Liz takes time to reflect on the session and her impressions of Susana. She notices that she feels very sad, which she infers is a reflection of the depth of Susana's depression. She also feels worried about Susana's children because Susana seems limited in her ability to have empathy for their experience of the recent events. Liz is relieved that Susana agreed to come for another session because the emotional tone of their interaction was somewhat reserved and tentative. She wonders whether Susana's lateness to the session reflects the overall ambivalence she feels about seeking help, but she also believes Susana's explanation about talking to her boss. Liz notes that Susana has difficulty prioritizing her own needs and this pattern probably extends to her work relationships.

Liz is struck by Susana's focus on Carlos throughout the session, and she begins to think Susana may have a pattern of looking for security and validation in relationships with men who are unreliable and possibly abusive. She notes that Susana didn't identify many positive resources for coping with her depression and loneliness, although Liz also appreciates Susana's strength in surviving some challenging circumstances in childhood and her adult life. Liz is also surprised to notice that she neglected to comment on or ask about Susana's cultural background. Since this is usually something she does in the first session, she is curious about why she didn't address this with Susana.

Liz identifies a number of questions for further assessment. More information about Susana's history of relationships with men and about her family of origin will shed light on patterns that may have been established in childhood that Susana has repeated in her adult life. Liz notes that Susana described her father as alcoholic and suggested that Carlos may have had a problem with alcohol. Liz wants to learn more about Susana's history of depression, including the episode in college, and her history of and risk for self-harm. She will also do a more extensive assessment of Susana's current and past use of alcohol and other drugs because Susana acknowledges potential abuse and has a family history of alcoholism. Susana's general reticence leads Liz to think that Susana is probably under-reporting the seriousness of her alcohol use as well as her depressive symptoms. Liz also wants to ask more about Susana's children to assess the impact of current and past relationship disruptions on them. She wonders whether Susana's focus on her own needs and lack of empathy with her children is a general pattern or a consequence of her current depression. Liz will put a priority on identifying coping strategies that Susana has used in the past, which can be strengthened and expanded. She will also learn more about Susana's cultural background as a context for her current and past difficulties and her view of herself.

Review of the First Session

Liz took a few moments to prepare and ground herself before meeting with Susana, even though she felt rushed. This helped her to connect with Susana before meeting her in person.

Liz established a treatment contract with Susana by reviewing the informed consent documents with her at the beginning of the session and by indicating her preference to handle payment at the beginning of the session. Establishing this pattern allowed Liz to discuss any issues regarding payment at the beginning of the session rather than at the end when there is likely to be inadequate time to discuss any problems regarding lack of payment.

Regarding the therapeutic alliance, Liz was empathic in identifying Susana's feelings of guilt and loneliness, and Liz reflected her understanding that Susana tends to be self-critical. These are examples of ways to foster the alliance. It was relatively easy for Liz to balance her expressions of warmth with maintaining professional boundaries because Susana didn't present as either needing excessive reassurance or being unresponsive. Several features of Susana's interpersonal style and way of coping with painful feelings were apparent and important for Liz to consider as potential obstacles to the alliance. Susana is dismissive of her feelings, seems to have little experience of care and support from others, and uses alcohol to avoid and numb her pain. This suggests that Liz will need to approach emotionally charged issues at a pace that allows Susana time to develop the sense of safety and the trust required to recognize and experience the full extent of her emotions. Because Susana is disengaged from her feelings, Liz may find it difficult to maintain her own emotional engagement and compassion with Susana.

Liz gave Susana an opportunity to talk about the issues of primary concern to her. She maintained a collaborative approach, asked open-ended questions, and followed Susana's lead in addressing different areas of her life. She was also able to follow-up on the areas of concern that Liz identified from their telephone contact.

The outcome of the first session is that Susana agreed to meet with Liz again. Because of Susana's tentativeness, Liz asked only about meeting again the following week. She assessed the quality of their relationship as generally positive and collaborative and noted that Susana seems most responsive to Liz being curious and affirming Susana's feelings. She is curious to see how Susana responds to Liz's suggestion to identify things she likes about herself.

The Next Step

Chapter 4 will discuss issues related to cultural identities, cultural influences, and cross-cultural dynamics in behavioral health treatment. The case example will describe a discussion of cultural issues in the second session between Liz and Susana.

References

American Association for Marriage and Family Therapy. (2001). *Code of ethics*. Alexandria, VA: Author.

American Psychological Association. (2002). Ethical principles of psychologists and code of conduct. *American Psychologist, 57,* 1060–1073.

Clay, R. A. (2012). Yes, recovery is possible. *Monitor on Psychology, 43,* 53–55.

Copeland, M. E. (2002). *Wellness recovery action plan®* (Rev. ed). West Dummerston, VT: Peach Press.

Elliott, R., Bohart, A. C., Watson, J. C., & Greenberg, L. S. (2011). Empathy. *Psychotherapy, 48,* 43–49.

Hays, P. A. (2008). *Addressing cultural complexities in practice: Assessment, diagnosis, and therapy* (2nd ed.). Washington, DC: American Psychological Association.

National Association of Social Workers. (2008). *Code of ethics.* Washington, DC: Author. Retrieved May 4, 2012, from http://www.naswdc.org/pubs/code/code.asp.

Norcross, J. C. (2010). The therapeutic relationship. In Duncan, B. L., Miller, S. D., Wampold, B. E., & Hubble, M. A. (Eds.). *The heart and soul of change: What works in therapy* (2nd ed.). Washington, DC: American Psychological Association.

Shedler, J. (2010). The efficacy of psychodynamic psychotherapy. *American Psychologist, 65,* 98–109.

Snyder, C. R., Michael, S. T., & Cheavens, J. S. (1999). Hope as a psychotherapeutic foundation of common factors, placebos, and expectancies. In Hubble, M. A., Duncan, B. L., & Miller, S. D. (Eds.). *The heart and soul of change: What works in therapy.* Washington, DC: American Psychological Association.

Teyber, E., & McClure, F. H. (2011). *Interpersonal process in therapy: An integrative model* (6th ed.). Belmont, CA: Brooks/Cole.

Weiss, J. (1993). *How psychotherapy works: Process and technique.* New York, NY: Guilford Press.

4

CULTURAL CONSIDERATIONS

(Note: This chapter will use the female pronoun for supervisor, clinician, and client.)

This chapter discusses issues related to cultural identities, cultural influences, and cross-cultural dynamics in treatment. Your client's cultural background is central to her development and experience of herself in the world, and you need to think about the cultural influences that are present for you and your client from the beginning of treatment. Similarities and differences between you and your client shape the meaning of your interactions and provide the context for all of the verbal and nonverbal exchanges that occur between you. Cultural competence means developing self-awareness of your own cultural context, obtaining knowledge about cultures different from your own, and implementing skills in working with diverse individuals (Metzger, Nadkarni, & Cornish, 2010). It also means designing your treatment plan and choosing your interventions in collaboration with the client and based on her preferences, some of which may be culturally based (LaRoche & Christopher, 2009).

Aspects of Cultural Identity

The ADDRESSING framework (Hays, 2008) was presented in Chapter 1 as an introduction to examining your own cultural identities. This tool is also a useful way to think about your client's cultural identities.

- Age and generational influences
- Developmental disabilities
- Disabilities acquired later in life
- Religion and spiritual orientation
- Ethnic and racial identity

- Socioeconomic status
- Sexual orientation
- Indigenous heritage
- National origin
- Gender including gender identity

Like you, your client probably experiences some of her cultural identities as more important than others as they affect her sense of self. As you get to know her, you will learn how these factors shaped her view of herself and others, and how her ideas about relationships have been affected by cultural variables. It is important to *learn about the client's individual experience of her cultural identities* because each person develops a unique set of beliefs, values, and interpretations of the relationships and events in her life related to culture. Find ways to learn about the meaning of the client's cultural identities within her cultural group as well as within the dominant culture so that you can understand the full context of her experience.

Some of the client's cultural identities may be more prominent at the beginning of treatment, while others emerge later. For example, in working with a 25-year-old woman who immigrated to the United States from Mexico 6 months ago and is living in poverty because of the difficulty of finding work, you may identify the immigration, ethnic, and class factors as primary influences on her symptoms and ways of relating to you. After establishing a therapeutic relationship and working together to reduce her symptoms, you may learn that she has questioned her sexual identity since adolescence, which is in conflict with her Catholic identity. Her religious and sexual identity influences will then emerge as themes for exploration and understanding.

The *influence of cultural identities in the therapeutic relationship* is fluid and dynamic, and you are likely to notice changes in your awareness of cultural similarities and differences between you and the client at different times. You may also notice changes in the way she relates to you and in your feelings toward her that accompany these shifts. Talking with your supervisor about these changes will help you understand the shifting influence of cultural factors.

Consultation with another experienced clinician and research regarding a particular community are resources you may need to use at times. Your client is the only person who can educate you about the unique meanings and nuances of her cultural experience, but it is your ethical and clinical responsibility to become knowledgeable about the general aspects of the cultures to which your clients belong. Consultation and research are especially valuable when a client's cultural background is unfamiliar to you or when you face a clinical dilemma related to cultural factors.

The Impact of Discrimination

Many racial, ethnic, and other non-dominant communities have a history of being targeted by racism, prejudice, discrimination, and oppression. Unfortunately, these toxic forces continue to be present in many social and interpersonal contexts. You may have experienced various forms of discrimination, and these experiences increase your awareness of this factor in your clients' lives. Regardless of your own experience, be aware that any client who is a member of a minority or other non-dominant community is likely to have experienced discrimination and disrespect in a number of situations and will have developed strategies for anticipating and coping with these painful interpersonal interactions.

Diagnosis and Assessment

The impact of discrimination must be considered carefully in your diagnosis and assessment. Identify potential social or environmental factors contributing to the client's symptoms, and describe the origin and adaptive function of the client's coping strategies as well as the obstacles they present in her present life. This is especially important in evaluating your client's suspicion and mistrust of others, a belief that she is being targeted or singled out by authorities, or reports of unprovoked attacks. These symptoms could be associated with paranoia, or they could be an accurate description of the client's experience. When you are unsure, you can use a provisional diagnosis while you assess the cultural context of the client's symptoms. The *relationship between cultural factors and diagnosis is complex*, and a client may have paranoid symptoms as well as cultural experiences of discrimination. The best strategy is to do a thoughtful and thorough assessment and to consult with your supervisor and others if needed. This process will ensure that you have considered all factors in assigning a diagnosis and that you are not repeating the client's past experience of negative stereotyping and misinterpretation.

In considering cultural factors and discrimination in diagnosis, be aware of the risk of minimizing the client's difficulties. You will provide the most effective treatment when your view of the client is accurate in identifying the impairment and disruption associated with her presenting problems and symptoms. Some helpful strategies are to compare her behaviors, beliefs, and symptoms with norms in her cultural community; to identify the cultural context for expression of the identified symptoms; and to assess the balance of adaptive and disruptive functions of behaviors (Hays, 2008). For example, a client who believes she is visited by the spirit of her grandmother may be part of a cultural community that considers communication with the spirits of ancestors to be meaningful and helpful. She may have had and observed many such manifestations of spirits in her family, and she may feel comforted by experiencing her grandmother's presence. Your interpretation of this phenomenon would be different if the client reported the experience of communicating with her grandmother's spirit as unfamiliar in her cultural community, as having a recent onset with no other experiences by her or anyone in her family, or being accompanied by feeling anxious or endangered.

Treatment Goals

It may be hard for you to develop treatment goals with clients who have regular, ongoing experiences of discrimination. You may feel hopeless in the face of societal and interpersonal forces that aren't impacted by your treatment interventions. You may be concerned that the client will interpret your focus on changing her behavior as your belief that she is responsible for her mistreatment. These reactions are valid, and it is important to move beyond them in order to help the client effectively.

An effective treatment approach in this situation is to *acknowledge the client's experience of discrimination* where it occurs—at work, in her family, and/or in society at large—and to affirm that the client isn't responsible for the behavior of others. You can then *explore with the client what responses related to this discrimination she is able to change.* These responses could include overcoming her internalized racism or other form of self-hatred, engaging in effective self-advocacy, and taking steps to leave toxic situations.

Access to Health Care

Many members of cultural minority communities have had limited access to health care and other preventive services. Some of your clients may have had serious emotional and behavioral symptoms for a long period of time before seeking treatment. Do not assume that a lack of prior mental health treatment means your client's symptoms were mild or nonexistent in the past or that this is the first time she has experienced this presenting problem. If your client is a child who has been symptomatic for a long time, do not attribute the delay in seeking treatment to a deficit in parenting. The pragmatic and social obstacles to seeking treatment are very challenging for families in minority cultural communities.

The experience of limited access to care may also lead a client to enter treatment with an expectation of receiving minimal care from you. When discussing her options for continuing treatment, it may be helpful to be clear about the full extent of services that are available and to express your belief that continued treatment will be effective. Communicating a warm and welcoming attitude is especially important with someone who has been denied care or whose care has been substandard.

Views of Symptoms and Treatment

Meaning and Origins of Symptoms

Our cultural context shapes our sense of identity and world view, which includes ideas about the meaning and origin of psychological symptoms. *A careful exploration of the client's understanding of her symptoms* is needed when the client's cultural background is different from yours or unfamiliar to you. A client may describe and explain her panic attacks very differently depending on whether she is of Japanese American, Central American, or Eastern U.S. descent, and whether she is part of an evangelical Christian, Catholic, or Muslim community.

Views of Effective Treatment

Our views of effective treatment for distressing and disruptive emotions and behaviors are influenced by cultural experiences and beliefs. Part of an initial assessment with all clients is an inquiry about what steps the client has taken to improve her symptoms and what other treatment she has tried. With clients from non-dominant cultural communities, ask what they believe or have been told will be helpful, so you can explore culturally based views of effective treatment. Your inquiry should include alternative medicine or healing practices and healers from the client's cultural and religious communities. You need to support cultural healing practices that the client has found helpful, and *talk about your approach to treatment in a way that is consistent with her cultural beliefs.* For example, a depressed client from an evangelical Christian community who believes she has strayed from God because she no longer feels comforted by prayer may be helped by an explanation of depression as having a physiological basis and a suggestion that treatment of the depression may enable her to regain her familiar, comforting experience of prayer.

As you begin to discuss treatment goals and interventions with the client, you will find *her preferences are influenced by her cultural identities and may be different from your beliefs and assumptions.* If the client's cultural beliefs are different from your recommended treatment, you will need to find an initial area of common ground in order to engage the client and establish a therapeutic relationship.

Treatment Planning

Respect for the client's cultural beliefs and a desire to collaborate in developing a plan for working together on the client's concerns are essential elements of a therapeutic alliance. Be aware of your desire for control and for recognition of your expertise and remember that treatment can only be effective in partnership with the client. This is especially true when you represent the majority cultural group and may hold unexamined assumptions of privilege. For example, an African American client may object to taking medication for her depression because of historical incidents in which African Americans were subjects in medical experiments without their consent and in which they were sedated in institutional settings to suppress legitimate protest. It would not be appropriate for a white therapist to attempt to override her objections, since this would repeat a relationship of power and domination. Instead, your response should affirm the client's role as decision maker and communicate your desire to be a partner in her healing process. An example of this type of response to a client concern is, "I can certainly understand your concern about medication, given your knowledge of these abuses of power. Are there other ways we might address your depression that you think could be useful?"

Cross-Cultural Dynamics in Treatment

Cross-cultural dynamics exist in all treatment relationships, since there are always differences in cultural identity between you and the client. Cultural differences are also present within couple and family relationships. Whether you are treating an individual, couple, or family, be aware of how cultural differences are related to the presenting issues. The cross-cultural dynamics between you and your supervisor also have an impact on your discussion of cases and your experience of supervisory feedback.

Cross-Cultural Issues Between Clinician and Client

The cross-cultural issues that are most important to address at the beginning of treatment are those *areas in which there is a majority/minority disparity between you and the client.* Some clients may be uncomfortable discussing cultural issues early in the treatment relationship, before they have established trust, so I prefer to bring up the topic initially in the form of a statement rather than a question for the client. An example is

> Since I'm Caucasian and you're Chinese American, those differences in our background may affect how you feel about our work together. I hope we can talk about that as we get to know each other over the next few weeks.

Before making a definitive statement about the client's racial or ethnic background, however, it is important to get information from the client directly rather than making assumptions based on the client's name or appearance. If you do not have that information, a more general statement would be appropriate, such as:

> I'm aware of differences in our age and race that may affect how you feel about our work together. I hope we can talk about that as we get to know each other over the next few weeks.

Requesting information. A common way for a professional to request information from a client is to ask her questions. However, *in some cultural communities asking questions is considered impolite or intrusive.* In addition, the inherent imbalance of power between a clinician representing a dominant cultural group and a client representing a minority cultural group can be amplified through this kind of interaction. In discussing a client's cultural background and/or issues that are sensitive, ask a more general question or make a statement that invites the client to share whatever information she feels is important. Examples are as follows:

- What do you feel is important for me to know about your cultural background and how you identify culturally?
- Many people have religious and spiritual practices that are important to them, and I wonder if you'd be comfortable telling me about what role religion and spirituality play in your life.

Privilege. Societal privilege, or a set of unearned benefits and advantages (Dressel, Kerr, & Stevens, 2010), is conferred on the majority or dominant cultural group. *Be sensitive to your assumptions and stereotypes as well as to the impact of cultural influences* in the areas in which you are a member of the dominant group. With clients who are members of a non-dominant group, be aware that they may be deferential because of having received discriminatory and disrespectful treatment in other contexts or because they feel that challenging someone with expertise and authority is rude or unwise.

If you are a member of a dominant cultural group, recognize that it will *take time to establish trust and rapport* with a client who is in a non-dominant group. In your eagerness to be helpful, you may have a desire to show the client that you will treat her differently from what she fears and has experienced in the past. Your eagerness can exert subtle pressure on her to confirm your trustworthiness and can work against establishing an authentic therapeutic alliance. Instead, acknowledge the potential obstacles and be open in expressing your desire to provide a different experience. You might say,

> Given your experience of being turned down for promotion when white co-workers were promoted, I can imagine there may be times in here when you wonder if I can really understand you. I hope we'll be able to talk about that when it comes up.

Working to be empathically attuned to the client's experience within and outside the clinical relationship will promote a sense of safety and support her in building trust (Mishne, 2002).

Non-dominant cultural group membership. In areas where you are not part of the dominant cultural group, there will be different cross-cultural dynamics present between you and the client depending on whether the client is part of the majority, the same minority group, or a different minority group. Work to *develop comfort and openness in talking about these cross-cultural dynamics,* which are influenced by your own experiences of stereotyping and discrimination and the degree to which you are identified with the values of the majority group in conflict with those of your own cultural group (Mishne, 2002). Self-reflection and discussion with your supervisor and other colleagues help you (a) become more aware of the interplay between your personal and professional experiences, (b) notice your reactions to clients of different cultural groups, and (c) gain confidence to engage with clients in discussing your cultural similarities and differences.

Self-awareness and examination. Ultimately, the most important factors in addressing cross-cultural dynamics between you and your client are self-awareness and willingness to examine the impact you have on her whether intended or unintended. Explore your cultural biases and assumptions, the presence of privilege associated with your cultural background, and the influence of your cultural identities. This exploration will enhance your openness in discussing the ways in which cultural similarities and differences affect your therapeutic relationship.

Child treatment. When working with children, *cross-cultural issues will arise differently at different developmental stages.* Younger children are likely to comment on concrete aspects of your appearance such as skin color, hair style, or age while adolescents are more likely to be exploring their own cultural identifications and may be interested in cross-cultural differences from that perspective. Engage with the child or adolescent's question and the meaning it has for her at her stage of development. "Answer the question that is asked" is a good rule of thumb.

Couple and family treatment. The cross-cultural dynamics are more complex when you work with couples and families because you may have *different areas of similarity and difference with each member of the family.* The same attitudes of building trust, communicating respect, and engaging in self-reflection described above are the best tools for addressing these complexities.

Cross-Cultural Issues in Couple and Family Relationships

Cultural differences. The concerns that bring individuals, couples, and families to treatment are often related to cultural differences within couple and family relationships. Identifying these differences and acknowledging the impact on relationships are ways to help the clients begin to understand and have respectful negotiations about their disagreements. Often cultural assumptions about relationship roles, communication, and parenting are implicit and can become sources of conflict. In addition, immigrant parents often feel ambivalently about their children adopting the values and customs of the new culture. This can lead to intergenerational conflict, and the process of acculturation can contribute to mental health problems for immigrant and bicultural youth (Bacallao & Smokowski, 2005). When you encourage direct acknowledgment and discussion of these unspoken assumptions and feelings, family relationships are likely to improve.

Cultural values in parenting. An important cross-cultural issue in family relationships is the *cultural value of respect for elders.* The dominant cultural value in the United States is more egalitarian in role expectations for parents and children than in many other cultures. When you are working with children and families representing non-dominant cultural groups, be aware of these differences and refrain from advocating for values that are different from the family's values. Your role is to help the family come into alignment with their values rather than impose your own. You need to communicate respect for the parents and to partner with them in order to engage the family in treatment. In addition, you can encourage discussion and negotiation when there are conflicts between parents and children or between parents.

Definitions of child abuse and neglect. If you work with families who are recent immigrants, *use clear communication about the laws related to child abuse and neglect and reporting obligations.* My colleagues who are experienced in this area are very specific in talking with parents about what is considered child abuse and neglect according to state law. They acknowledge that local laws may be different from laws in the parents' country of origin and describe it as an issue of ensuring children's safety. Often the parents experienced childhood physical and sexual abuse, and you have an opportunity to acknowledge the lack of protection of the parent during childhood and the mixed feelings the parent may have about the laws in the United States. This can be a fruitful discussion with the parents of a child client or in a family session.

Cross-Cultural Issues in Supervision

Cultural identity provides a context for the relationship between you and your supervisor as it is a context for your treatment with clients. The degree to which you explicitly explore areas of similarity and difference in cultural identities will vary in different settings and with different supervisors. It may be difficult to bring up the subject of cultural differences with your supervisor because of her role in evaluating your clinical work, but I encourage you to do so in the service of your professional growth.

Developing self-awareness about the *influence of your cultural identities on your reactions to supervisory feedback* will expand your understanding of your relational patterns with clients as well as supervisors. Issues related to disagreement and authority for decisions are often particularly salient in cross-cultural supervisory relationships. If you and your supervisor can discuss cross-cultural dynamics in supervision, it will contribute to your learning and understanding of clinical work, but you can also benefit from your own self-reflection if that isn't possible. You will probably find that the meaning of cultural differences with your supervisor fluctuates depending on the cultural identity of the client you are discussing. For example, if you are an African American clinician working with a Caucasian supervisor, you may respond differently when discussing African American and Caucasian clients.

If you are a member of a cultural minority group, it may be helpful to work with a supervisor who is a member of the same cultural minority group. Your needs and preferences for specific supervisory experiences will evolve during your training, so the salience of a cultural match may be greater at one time than another. If you are unable to work with a supervisor who has a similar cultural identity, seek out teachers, consultants, or experienced clinicians as mentors.

Summary

In this chapter, I reviewed issues related to cultural identities, cultural influences, and cross-cultural dynamics in treatment. Cultural factors are central in the sense of self, social and interpersonal experiences, views of symptoms and treatment, and the therapeutic relationship. Specific aspects of these cultural factors are listed below.

1. Using yourself as an instrument of hope, change, and healing:

    a. Notice cultural similarities and differences between you and your clients, especially regarding dominant cultural group membership and privilege.
    b. Reflect on the impact of cultural influences on your responses to supervisory feedback.

2. Becoming confident in your authority and professionalism:

    a. Gain knowledge about cultural groups different from your own.
    b. Recognize the impact of discrimination as you prepare a diagnosis, assessment, and treatment plan.

3. Developing interpersonal skills that strengthen the therapeutic relationship:

    a. Understand the client's experience of cultural identities and notice changes during different phases of treatment.
    b. Explore the client's culturally based views of symptoms and treatment.
    c. Recognize and encourage discussion of cultural differences in couple and family relationships.

Case Example: Cross-Cultural Issues for Liz and Susana and for Liz and Dalia

Before Liz met Susana for their second session, Liz reflected on the fact that she had neglected to ask Susana about her cultural background in their first session. She decided that doing this would be a priority during her second session with Susana, and she spent time thinking about the information she had about Susana from the intake screening and her first session.

Based on the intake screening, Liz knows that Susana is a 36-year-old Latina with a lower middle class income. Susana's physical presentation does not indicate any disabilities. Tentatively, Liz identifies Susana as in the majority group in age, disabilities, and sexual identity, and in minority groups in ethnicity, socioeconomic status, and gender using the ADDRESSING framework. Liz is lacking information regarding Susana's indigenous and national heritage and her religious identification. Liz is curious about how Susana will describe her cultural background, although Liz's impression is that Susana's ethnic identity as a Latina is probably the most relevant cultural factor for the initial phase of treatment.

Liz has several friends who immigrated to California from Mexico and Central America, which has given her some knowledge of those cultures and issues related to immigration and acculturation.

When Liz begins the second session, she has several things in mind in addition to learning about Susana's cultural background. She wants to follow up on her suggestions at the end of the first session that Susana think about times in her life when she liked herself and to think about qualities she likes in herself. Susana had said she couldn't think of anything and might ask her friend Judy or her children for ideas. Liz also wants to learn more about various areas of Susana's life as part of her initial diagnosis and assessment process.

Most importantly, Liz wants to begin the session with an invitation for Susana to set the tone and agenda, in order to foster an atmosphere of collaboration. Liz is aware that Latino culture includes respect of and deference to authority, and Liz has had the experience of Latino clients being hesitant to express their desires and preferences regarding the direction of treatment due to their view of the therapist as an expert. She wants to communicate explicitly her desire for her treatment with Susana to be a partnership.

Second Session

Susana is again 5 minutes late for the session and apologizes as she did before, saying that she was unable to leave work on time as happened last week. Liz greets her and leads her back to the office.

Liz: I'm happy to see you again. Where would you like to start our conversation today?

Susana: I remember you asked me to think about times I have liked myself and I wasn't sure I could think of anything.

Liz: Yes, you thought you might ask Judy or your kids what qualities they liked about you.

Susana: But I did think about it, and I realized that I like myself most when I am with a man and he's happy with our life together. I like to make people happy, especially my husband or boyfriend, and I like myself when I can do that.

Liz: That's an important thing to know about yourself. I appreciate you giving thought to my question. It helps me understand why you've been feeling so bad, so depressed, since Carlos left. It seems like it's hard for you to feel good about yourself when you're not with a man or when you're with a man who is unhappy. Maybe it's hard for you to know how much of his unhappiness is related to you and how much is about other things.

Susana: I always think it's my job to help him feel good and that it's my fault if he's upset.

Liz:	It sounds like you take a lot of responsibility in your relationships with men. Has that always been the case for you? Did you feel responsible for happiness in your family growing up?
Susana:	I don't really remember much about that when I was a kid, but definitely when I met Antonio and we got married I figured that was my job.
Liz:	Sometimes the ideas we have about relationships and responsibility are related to messages in our culture as well as in our own families. I'm interested in knowing more about your cultural background. Could you tell me how you identify culturally?
Susana:	Well, I'm American if that's what you mean. I'm not illegal.
Liz:	I actually wasn't asking about that, but it sounds like other people may have assumed you were here without papers and that's been upsetting to you.
Susana:	At my kids' school, the teachers always tell me not to worry about whether I have papers, and I tell them I'm an American citizen. It's insulting because my parents worked really hard to bring us here, and we were very proud when we got our citizenship. I don't even have much of an accent but people assume I don't belong here.
Liz:	I can understand why that would feel hurtful, and I'm sorry it sounded like I was questioning your citizenship. The reason I asked about your cultural background is that I find that different cultural factors, like the fact that you came to the United States from another country and are proud of being a citizen, are important in our thoughts and feelings about ourselves and other people. I'm interested to know more about this when you're willing to share more with me, but we can also move on to other issues if you'd prefer.
Susana:	I guess I'm pretty sensitive about it, and it's been an issue in my relationships too. Two of the men I've been with were illegal, including Carlos. That's why he left after my daughter called the police. I was so mad at her for doing that because she knew he could be deported if the police thought he had done something wrong. They didn't ask for his papers when they came out to our apartment, but I was really scared they would. When he left, he said he couldn't stay with somebody who might get him sent back to Mexico.
Liz:	So the issue of being a citizen and being with someone who isn't has been a conflict with Carlos and with another relationship. Was that Antonio or someone else?
Susana:	Yes, Antonio was illegal, too.
Liz:	Maybe that's related to the way you've felt responsible for their happiness. It also sounds like the fact that Carlos didn't have papers created more conflict between you and your daughter than might be there if you hadn't been worried about Carlos getting deported. Could you tell me more about how you came to the United States?

Susana:	I was born in El Salvador and my parents came here to California when I was 7. The war had been going on for about four years and my brother was 10. My parents were worried he would be taken by the soldiers to fight in the war so they arranged for all of us to leave—my parents, my brother, little sister, and me. We went first to Los Angeles, and then came here to San Francisco after we got our citizenship when I was 13.
Liz:	I understand why you said your parents worked hard to bring you here. It sounds like it was a really frightening time for everyone, and they were especially worried about your brother's safety.
Susana:	Yes, my cousin had already been taken by the soldiers when he was 12. When that happened, my parents said we couldn't stay. We were the first in the family to leave. After we got here, my parents tried to get my aunts and uncles and cousins to come, but most of them stayed. I only have two cousins who live in Los Angeles. Everyone else is still there, at least the ones who didn't get killed in the war.
Liz:	Did you lose a lot of family members in the war?
Susana:	Three cousins and one of my uncles were killed in the fighting. Another aunt and cousin were killed when the village was burned. It went on for a long time, you know. I was in high school by the time it was over.
Liz:	That was most of your childhood then. Have you been back to visit your family since the war ended?
Susana:	Only once. My parents took us back there about 10 years ago after they thought it was safe again. They weren't sure for awhile whether it was safe to go back. It was a really sad trip because our village was completely different. All the houses had been bombed or burned and had to be rebuilt so nothing looked the same. I wish I hadn't seen it because now it's hard to remember it the way it was. My grandparents had died, which I knew, but I missed them more when I was there and couldn't see them. My dad said he wished we hadn't gone back. He kept saying that over and over until he died.
Liz:	So going back really brought up a lot of loss for your family: that your village wasn't the way it was when you lived there, your grandparents weren't there, and other family members had died during the war. Are there other things about El Salvador that you miss? You were very young when you left, so I don't know what you remember about that time.
Susana:	It was nice to live in a village with family all around—my grandparents, aunts, uncles, cousins. Everyone else seemed like family because the village was small, and everyone knew each other and had lived there for several generations. Sometimes I'd stay at one of my cousins' houses overnight or even for a couple nights, or they'd stay with me. All the adults took care of all of the kids. I was only 3 when the war started, so I don't remember a time before the war. We never knew when the

fighting would come close to us or when the soldiers would come for the boys. I don't miss that, but I do miss the close family. I wish my kids had that. My brother moved back to Los Angeles to work after he graduated high school and my sister, too. Then after my dad died, my mom decided to go back there to be closer to them. They all keep asking me to move, but I have a good job and my kids are in good schools here. Also, every time I've thought about moving I've met a man who wants to stay here and that's kept me from leaving.

Liz then asks Susana about her children, to learn more about how they seem to be progressing developmentally and to assess the degree of impact on them of Susana's early exposure to trauma and loss as well as her pattern of placing the emotional needs of her male partners above her own, and possibly above the needs of her children. Liz learns more about Susana's history of depression, beginning with the episode in college which included a suicide attempt and continuing throughout her adult life coinciding with the end of an intimate relationship. She also asks Susana about her current symptoms of depression, and Susana reports that she feels about the same as she did the previous week.

At the end of the session, Liz wants to raise the issue of meeting on a weekly basis, which she has deferred because of Susana's initial ambivalence.

Liz: It's time for us to end for today. I'm really struck by how much you've been through in your life. It sounds like the war took a big toll on you and your family, and even though it was a good decision to come here to escape the war, you also gave up the close ties you had with your family and neighbors in El Salvador. That type of trauma and loss can certainly contribute to depression, so I'm not surprised that you've struggled with that for a number of years. I'm also impressed at the strength it has taken for you to make a life for yourself and your children here and at your courage to come here and talk about what's troubling you. I know we've talked about a lot of difficult things today. How are you feeling?

Susana: I feel okay. I haven't thought about El Salvador and the family back there for a long time. When you asked me about it, I realized how much I miss them and how I wish my kids had more family around here. I guess it's too late to do anything about that now.

Liz: I think knowing what you want is the first step to figuring out whether you can find ways to make it happen. I'm glad you feel okay after what we've talked about today. Sometimes it's a relief to put things into words that have just been thoughts and feelings inside for a long time. I think it would be a good idea for us to meet weekly so we can understand more about your depression and come up with some ideas of how you can begin feeling better more of the time. What do you think about that? I know you weren't sure initially whether you could manage it.

Susana: I've liked meeting with you, and I do want to be less depressed. Do you mean we'd meet at this time every week? What if one of my kids is sick or I have to work late?

Liz reviews the agency policies regarding cancellation and the degree of flexibility she has to reschedule appointments. Susana agrees to meet weekly and asks if she should do anything in particular during the week. Liz asks her what she feels might be helpful, and Susana says she'd like to look at some of the photos she took on her visit to El Salvador 10 years ago to remember the family she saw during that visit. Liz says she'll be interested to hear about whether Susana decides to look at the photos and what it is like to remember her family in El Salvador.

Liz's Reflection on the Second Session

After the session, Liz reflects on what she has learned about Susana's cultural background and the cross-cultural dynamics between them. She now knows that Susana's ethnicity as Salvadoran is a source of interpersonal conflict for her. Liz empathizes with Susana's sensitivity around others' assumptions that she is undocumented, in part because of her own experience of being teased as a gay adolescent, certain other painful experiences within her family, and other instances of discrimination related to her sexual identity. She also notes that Susana's experience in El Salvador was laden with the trauma of the civil war and probably led her to have an ambivalent attachment to her country of origin. Liz wonders if this ambivalence is related to Susana's choice to identify strongly as American and to stay in her current home rather than moving to Los Angeles with the rest of her nuclear family.

Another factor Liz thinks about is Susana's current socioeconomic status, which is lower middle-class based on her income. Liz wonders about the family's socioeconomic status before immigration and whether there was a change in their status after immigration. Liz remembers hearing her own grandparents describe what they left behind to come to the United States and how they valued the freedom and opportunity in the United States that offset their material and emotional losses. She wants to know more about Susana's experience of immigration and the losses that accompanied the family's move.

Liz reflects on Susana's initial reaction to her question about cultural identity, and notes that Susana is vulnerable to feeling shamed or disrespected when she feels she is being treated as inferior. Liz felt in the session that she was able to repair the rupture she inadvertently caused with her question, and she felt that Susana was less sensitive when Liz asked about other areas of Susana's life. She does make note of the importance of explicitly supporting Susana's strengths and being respectful especially when asking about anything related to Susana's experience as an immigrant. Liz also remembers that Susana said in the first session that her father was alcoholic and had died a few years earlier. She wonders about the onset and duration of his alcoholism and how it was related to the family's immigration and the trauma of war.

Liz feels pleased that Susana is willing to commit to weekly sessions. She also notes that the extended family and close relationships in Susana's village in El Salvador seemed to offer a protective, comforting experience of security despite the uncertainty and trauma of the war. She is interested that Susana's idea about the week ahead is to look at her photos, and she is curious about Susana's reactions to looking at the photos.

Supervision After the Second Session

Liz meets with Dalia a few days after the second session. She shares how Susana responded to Liz's initial question about cultural identification and what Susana told her about her life in El Salvador and her family's immigration. She asks Dalia for her feedback and Dalia discloses to Liz that she immigrated to the United States from Israel in her early twenties and that she lived with war and the threat of war there. She tells Liz that Susana's response to Liz's question about cultural identification is understandable given her status as a Central American immigrant, though Dalia feels differently about her own immigration and citizenship.

Dalia adds to Liz's reflections about the session by noting that Susana and her family do not seem to have a community connection with other Salvadorans or Central Americans. Dalia sees this as somewhat unusual based on her personal experience as an immigrant and her work with Central American immigrants. Dalia also comments on Susana's tension regarding legal status in two of her intimate relationships and wonders how that is related to the trauma of war, immigration, and lack of community after immigration.

Liz thanks Dalia for her self-disclosure and her perspective on Susana's immigration experience. She says this gives her another context for understanding Susana's depression and her sense of responsibility for her intimate partners.

Review of the Second Session

Susana's response to Liz's suggestion at the end of the first session (to think about times she likes herself) provided important information about her relational pattern of prioritizing the needs of others over her own. Liz recognized that Susana seems unable to identify her own strength or to feel self-affirming outside of being able to please her intimate partner. She saw this pattern as significant in Susana's recurring depression, while recognizing it as a culturally normative role for women in Latino culture. Liz chose to defer exploring this issue in more depth, instead using it as an opening to her explorations about cultural identity.

There are numerous times in each session when there is a choice to explore an issue in depth or to move to another issue. During the initial assessment phase of treatment, it is often necessary to move between different areas of the client's life in order to be comprehensive in gaining information and understanding. However, it is important to stay with an issue that has emotional content long enough for the client to feel heard and understood. Liz did this with her exploration of Susana's experiences related to immigration and her return visit to El Salvador as an adult. It is also important to follow the client's lead if she seems reluctant to engage in a particular issue in depth or if she seems to need to stay with an issue to reach some resolution or insight. Susana's comments at the end of the session suggest that she benefitted from this discussion, and her willingness to commit to weekly sessions confirmed that she experienced the session with Liz as helpful.

The Next Step

Chapter 5 will discuss the process of identifying a diagnosis that describes the client's symptoms and provides some guidance for the treatment. It also will review how to talk with the client about the diagnosis. The case example will describe how Liz developed a diagnostic description of Susana and how she discussed this diagnosis with her.

References

Bacallao, M. L., & Smokowski, P. R. (2005). "Entre dos mundos" (between two worlds): Bicultural skills training with Latino immigrant families. *The Journal of Primary Prevention, 26,* 485–509.

Dressel, J. L., Kerr, S., & Stevens, H. B. (2010). Developing competency with white identity and privilege. In Cornish, J. A. E., Schreier, B. A., Nadkarni, L. I., Metzger, L. H., & Rodolfa, E. R. (Eds.). *Handbook of multicultural counseling competencies.* Hoboken, NJ: John Wiley & Sons.

Hays, P. A. (2008). *Addressing cultural complexities in practice: Assessment, diagnosis, and therapy* (2nd ed.). Washington, DC: American Psychological Association.

LaRoche, M. J., & Christopher, M. S. (2009). Changing paradigms from empirically supported treatment to evidence-based practice: A cultural perspective. *Professional Psychology: Research and Practice, 40,* 396–402.

Metzger, L. L. H., Nadkarni, L. I., & Cornish, J. A. E. (2010). An overview of multicultural counseling competencies. In Cornish, J. A. E., Schreier, B. A., Nadkarni, L. I., Metzger, L. H., & Rodolfa, E. R. (Eds.). *Handbook of multicultural counseling competencies.* Hoboken, NJ: John Wiley & Sons.

Mishne, J. (2002). *Multiculturalism and the therapeutic process.* New York, NY: The Guilford Press.

5
DIAGNOSIS

(Note: This chapter will use the male pronoun for supervisor, clinician, and client.)

This chapter describes the process of diagnosis, which is part of the assessment that takes place in the beginning of treatment. Diagnosis is a way to describe, in standardized form, the client's presenting symptoms, other behavioral health conditions, and related health concerns. This chapter includes a discussion of how to assign an accurate diagnosis; how to use the DSM-5, the diagnostic manual that is most commonly used in behavioral health settings; how to develop a comprehensive diagnostic description; and how to approach a conversation about diagnosis with your client.

Assigning an Accurate Diagnosis

Usefulness of a Diagnosis

Many clinicians in training question the reasons for assigning a diagnosis to a client. I will review some of those concerns below, but first will discuss the ways a diagnosis can be used to further treatment. An accurate diagnosis serves to:

- Summarize the client's symptoms and other related conditions,
- Aid in communicating with the client, family members, and other professionals,
- Guide treatment goals and interventions, and
- Enable billing to a third party.

First, a diagnosis *summarizes the client's symptoms and other related conditions*. Diagnostic labels condense multiple pieces of information into one term, which allows you to organize your knowledge of many aspects of the client's thoughts, feelings, and behavior and understand the client's difficulties as part of one condition.

For example, symptoms of low mood, feelings of hopelessness, lethargy, sleep and appetite disruption, difficulty concentrating, and irrational guilt are combined into a diagnosis of Major Depressive Disorder.

Because a diagnosis uses standardized categories to summarize the client's symptoms, it *aids in communicating with the client, family members, and other professionals.* The section "Discussing the Diagnosis with the Client" describes an approach to communicating with the client. When communicating with family members, you can share both the diagnostic name and the symptoms that are characteristic of that diagnosis. You will often find that family members are relieved to know the client's symptoms are understandable, and they may recognize the diagnosis as a condition shared by other family members. Communications with other professionals are aided by the use of diagnostic terms because they are shared and understood by most professionals in the behavioral health, medical, educational, and social service fields. These professionals have different approaches to working with clients, but it is easier to collaborate in the client's care when you begin with a common language.

Identifying the client's diagnosis often serves to *guide your treatment goals and interventions.* You would use a different treatment approach with a client whose symptoms of lethargy and lack of motivation are part of a diagnosis of Major Depressive Disorder than one with the same symptoms whose diagnosis is Schizophrenia. Your treatment is likely to be more effective if you use interventions for symptoms within the context of the diagnosis.

Finally, assigning a diagnosis will *enable billing to a third party,* which is often required for the client to access treatment. Third parties such as public or private insurance or a governmental agency generally require a primary behavioral health diagnosis, and will not fund treatment without it.

Concerns About Diagnosis

Like many beginning clinicians, you may be concerned that assigning a diagnosis will stigmatize the client or limit his eligibility for benefits related to health or life insurance. You may also object to the medical model underlying the diagnostic process as lacking in consideration of client's strengths, the social context for his current difficulties, and his cultural background. You may feel uncomfortable with the level of responsibility associated with assigning a diagnosis and question your qualifications to make that professional decision.

I recommend that you *talk with your supervisor about your concerns* related to diagnosis when you begin a new training placement. He can tell you about the agency practices regarding diagnosis and help you develop strategies for using the diagnostic process to enhance the quality of your treatment. If your concerns are related to diagnosis of a client in a non-dominant cultural group, assess the degree to which his behavior deviates from the norms of his cultural community and the degree to which his behavior is more or less adaptive (Hays, 2008) to identify the most appropriate diagnosis.

Accuracy of Diagnosis

Review the diagnoses of all of your clients with your supervisor who can assist you in choosing a diagnosis that is the best description of the client's symptoms and current functioning. In the early stage of training, it can be difficult to differentiate among different conditions that have overlapping symptoms. Your supervisor's input will help you develop this skill. Your concerns about the implications of assigning a diagnosis may lead you to assign a diagnosis that underestimates the severity of the client's condition, and your supervisor can guide you in identifying an accurate diagnosis. It is a valid practice to use the least severe diagnosis that accurately describes the client's symptoms, but it is not in his interest for you to assign a diagnosis that minimizes his condition or the disruption it may be causing to his life.

Billing Practices

If your client's treatment is funded by a third party, you *may be required to assign a primary diagnosis at the time of your first visit* with the client. Often you have insufficient information to be certain about the client's diagnosis after only one visit, and you may feel uncomfortable or uncertain about how to meet this requirement. Your supervisor will advise you of the practice that is used at your training placement, which will include some of these options:

- Assign a diagnosis with *Provisional* following the diagnostic term.
- Use a diagnosis given to the client by another professional within or outside your agency.
- Use an Other Specified or Unspecified diagnosis that falls within the category of the client's primary symptoms (as described in "Using DSM-5 for Diagnostic Purposes" below).

After you complete your assessment, you can revise the diagnosis based on the full picture of the client's current difficulties and history.

Be aware that some insurance companies have a limited list of diagnoses that are eligible for reimbursement. This list is usually found in medical necessity guidelines which outline the conditions under which treatment will be reimbursed. Check with your supervisor about the requirements of third parties that fund your clients' treatment.

Using DSM-5 for Diagnostic Purposes

Most behavioral health settings use the Diagnostic and Statistical Manual of Mental Disorders (DSM) for diagnosis, which contains alphanumeric codes from the International Classification of Diseases (ICD) and diagnostic criteria developed by a professional working group convened by the American Psychiatric Association. At the time of this publication, third-party billing in the United States requires ICD-10-CM codes (Contexo Media, 2013), which are listed in the DSM-5 (American Psychiatric Association [APsyA], 2013). The following discussion and the case example use the DSM-5 as the basis for diagnosis.

Primary Diagnosis

The primary diagnosis is defined as the *purpose of the client's initial visit or ongoing treatment* and is used by third parties as the basis for reimbursement. The DSM-5 lists mental health and substance use disorders in various categories as well as other conditions or circumstances that may lead someone to seek behavioral health treatment. Often, the clients you see during your training will meet the criteria for more than one behavioral health disorder and may have one or more other conditions related to treatment. Many clients also have medical conditions that are directly or indirectly related to mental health and substance use.

In determining the client's primary diagnosis, *consider the focus of your treatment.* For example, you might see a child with Attention Deficit/Hyperactivity Disorder whose parents are going through a divorce and request services for his low mood and withdrawal. The primary diagnosis for this child's treatment would be related to his low mood and withdrawal since that is the focus of your treatment. Another example is a client with a history of alcohol abuse in recovery for a year who presents with symptoms of anxiety and panic attacks. Your primary diagnosis would be the anxiety disorder rather than the alcohol use disorder.

Organization of DSM-5 Diagnoses

The DSM-5 does not use a five-axis descriptive system to record different aspects of the client's behavioral health, medical, and psychosocial functioning, as was used with the DSM-III and DSM-IV. A DSM-5 diagnosis begins with the primary diagnosis (the reason for treatment) followed by other mental health and substance use disorders, psychosocial and historical conditions affecting treatment, and medical conditions. These are listed sequentially rather than labeled on different axes.

The behavioral health disorders of DSM-5 are *grouped into categories with several specific diagnoses listed in each category.* Each diagnosis lists a series of behavioral symptoms that are either reported by the client or observed by others, with specification of the minimum number of symptoms required for that diagnosis to be assigned. Some clients do not meet any specific diagnosis within a category even though their symptoms fall in that category. In these cases, there is a provision for designation of Other Specified or Unspecified within the category. For example, if a client's primary symptoms are depressive but he doesn't meet the criteria for a specific depressive disorder diagnosis, you could use a diagnosis of Other Specified

Depressive Disorder or Unspecified Depressive Disorder. More detail about the use of these diagnoses and examples of clinical presentations appropriate for the diagnoses are provided in the DSM-5.

Review and Summary of DSM-5 Behavioral Health Categories

To identify the primary diagnosis that best fits a client's symptoms and general clinical condition, begin with the type of symptoms that are most prominent in the client's presentation, and then look within that category for the specific diagnosis. There are 19 categories in the DSM-5, described next.

Neurodevelopmental disorders. Deficits, disability, or difficulties in intellectual, communication, social and motor behavior, attention, and learning are included in this category. These diagnoses are not treated with psychotherapy or counseling, but specific behavioral interventions may be effective in symptom management. Clinicians may be of assistance in advising parents, teachers, and other caregivers about interventions for managing and improving behaviors associated with these disorders. In addition, individuals with these conditions may have co-occurring disorders that can be treated with psychotherapy and counseling.

Schizophrenia spectrum and other psychotic disorders. Psychotic symptoms include delusions, hallucinations, and disorganized speech or behavior. Clients with schizophrenia also may show a decrease in emotional expression and self-initiated action, and such behaviors are called negative symptoms. This category is used when psychotic symptoms are prominent or when the client is taking medication to manage psychotic symptoms which are reported by the client or others who have observed the client closely.

Bipolar and related disorders. These disorders are characterized by episodes of elevated mood, reflected in feelings of expansiveness and/or by irritability along with a heightened level of energy. There are often sudden changes in the tone of responses to others as well as the sense of self, ranging from agitation to elation. The client may have depressive episodes in addition to manic or hypomanic episodes.

Depressive disorders. Clients with these disorders have a sad, hopeless, or irritable mood, sometimes accompanied by changes in sleep patterns and appetite, feelings of guilt and worthlessness, and a decreased interest or pleasure in most activities. Irritable mood as an indicator of a depressive disorder is more common in children and adolescents than in adults.

Anxiety disorders. The client's clinical presentation is dominated by excessive fear and anxiety, leading to tension and/or avoidance of things or situations that are feared or unpleasant. Cognitive distortions or preoccupations are often associated with the states of anxiety.

Obsessive-compulsive and related disorders. These disorders are characterized by intrusive thoughts and/or repetitive behaviors that are excessive and persistent. The preoccupation with these thoughts and behaviors can be time-consuming and/or interfere with aspects of the client's life.

Trauma- and stressor-related disorders. The client's symptoms develop after the occurrence of a traumatic or stressful event. In order to apply these diagnoses accurately, the report of the client or others should indicate that there was a change in functioning following the event. It can be difficult to identify the onset of symptoms after the event when the client reports repeated traumatic experiences in the distant and recent past. In these cases, consult with your supervisor about the client's history, and consider multiple diagnoses.

Dissociative disorders. Dissociation refers to a lack of integration in the cognitive, affective, and behavioral aspects of experience. These disorders are usually related to traumatic experiences, but they are listed in a separate category.

Somatic symptom and related disorders. These disorders describe clients whose somatic or physical symptoms are predominant and a source of distress. These individuals are more likely to present in a medical setting, but they may be referred to behavioral health treatment if medical treatment doesn't alleviate the cognitive and emotional symptoms of distress.

Feeding and eating disorders. These disorders describe a disturbance in eating behavior that interferes with physical or psychosocial health.

Elimination disorders. Enuresis and encopresis are included in this category and are usually first diagnosed in childhood.

Sleep-wake disorders. These disorders are generally treated in medical settings.

Sexual dysfunctions. These disorders are generally diagnosed and treated in specialized treatment settings that include evaluation of medical conditions related to the dysfunction.

Gender dysphoria. This diagnosis has separate criteria for children and for adolescents and adults, reflecting the changes in the experience and feelings related to gender at different developmental stages.

Disruptive, impulse-control, and conduct disorders. The central feature of these diagnoses is difficulty with self-control of behavior and emotion, resulting in violations of the rights of others or significant conflict with societal norms and authority.

Substance-related and addictive disorders. This category includes disorders related to the use of 10 classes of substances accompanied by significant substance-related problems, as well as a disorder related to problematic gambling behavior. Substances and behavioral addictions often serve to numb or mask psychological distress and pain, and they may represent an attempt to self-medicate the symptoms of another disorder. Therefore, clients with substance-related diagnoses often have co-occurring mental health diagnoses.

Neurocognitive disorders. The core feature of these diagnoses is cognitive impairment due to acquired rather than developmental conditions. As with the neurodevelopmental disorders, clinicians may be involved by advising caregivers and by using behavioral interventions to assist in managing problematic behaviors associated with these disorders. In some cases, psychotherapy and counseling can be adapted to alleviate symptoms of co-occurring disorders.

Personality disorders. These disorders describe maladaptive patterns that deviate from cultural expectations, are inflexible, and occur in a broad range of situations. These patterns are generally first evident in late adolescence or early adulthood.

Paraphilic disorders. These sexual disorders are generally diagnosed and treated in specialized treatment settings.

After you have identified the category that describes the most prominent feature of the client's clinical presentation, you will need to *identify the diagnosis within that category that describes his specific symptoms*. This diagnosis is associated with an alphanumeric code derived from the International Classification of Diseases (ICD). The DSM-5 lists codes from the ICD-9-CM and ICD-10-CM since it was published during a transition period for billing codes. The case example uses ICD-10-CM codes because those codes are currently required for third-party billing in the United States.

For some diagnoses, there are additional specifiers that may be reflected in the alphanumeric code. These specifiers include information about the severity, type of episode, clinical presentation, and remission of symptoms. These additional specifiers are described in the narrative explanation of the diagnosis, so it is important to read the full section and include any additional information that may be required for the diagnosis you assign to the client.

Additional Categories

The DSM-5 includes two additional categories that are not behavioral health diagnoses but may be coded if they are relevant to the client's presentation, history or current functioning.

Medication-induced movement disorders and other adverse effects of medication. These disorders are associated with the use of psychotropic medications prescribed for mental health disorders.

Other conditions that may be a focus of clinical attention. These conditions may be the focus of treatment in addition to or in the absence of another diagnosis. Third-party funders generally require a behavioral health diagnosis as the primary reason for treatment, but these codes can be useful in providing a context for some of the client's difficulties. There are codes for different types of relational problems, abuse and neglect, and other psychosocial circumstances and stressors.

Developing a Comprehensive Diagnostic Description

Initial Primary Diagnosis

Begin to develop a diagnosis in your first session with a client because thinking in diagnostic terms will organize your thoughts and observations of him and his description of his symptoms and concerns. Your comprehensive diagnostic description is part of the assessment, which may take place over multiple sessions (discussed in

Chapter 6), but the treatment will be more focused if you make an initial primary diagnosis in the first one or two sessions. The additional information you gather in the process of assessment may lead you to revise your primary diagnosis, and it is good clinical practice to review your diagnosis at least every 6 months throughout treatment as the client's symptoms change and as you learn more about him.

Clients with Prior Diagnoses

You are likely to work with a number of clients who are or have been in treatment with other clinicians or have had prior psychiatric treatment. These clients often report one or more diagnoses that they have been given by other professionals. This is helpful information but does not substitute for your *independent assessment of the client's current symptoms, presenting issues, and functioning.* If your diagnosis is different from one given in the past, it is often useful to talk with the other professionals or review records from prior treatment. This helps you identify whether the client's presentation and symptoms have changed or if you have a different interpretation of the same presentation. Your supervisor can help you evaluate the meaning of a discrepancy in diagnostic impressions.

Multiple Diagnoses

As you complete a full assessment of the client, you will often identify several behavioral health diagnoses, psychosocial conditions, and medical conditions that are present. Since all of these are relevant to the client's overall health and functioning, your comprehensive diagnostic description should *list multiple DSM-5 diagnoses and conditions, in order of the focus of treatment.* The primary diagnosis or reason for treatment comes first, followed by other behavioral health diagnoses, any relevant psychosocial conditions in approximate order of their relevance to the current treatment, and medical conditions reported by the client.

It is sometimes difficult to determine which diagnosis is primary, especially with clients who have *co-occurring mental health and substance use disorders.* Often the symptoms of one disorder interact with symptoms of another, and providing integrated treatment for co-occurring mental health and substance use conditions has become the standard of care (Substance Abuse and Mental Health Services Administration, 2009; Mangrum, Spence, & Lopez, 2006). Consult with your supervisor about the practices in your organization for designating a primary diagnosis to guide your decisions.

Diagnostic Issues in Child, Couple, and Family Treatment

When the *child is the primary client* or when the child's behavior and symptoms are the main reason for the family entering treatment, you will probably be required to assign a primary diagnosis to the child. Most of the DSM-5 mental health and substance use diagnoses can be considered for children, but it is important to note that the criteria for some diagnoses describe differences in the clinical presentation of children and adolescents compared with adults. When you begin working with children, reading the diagnostic criteria carefully will help you to become familiar with these differences.

In *couple and family treatment*, the clinical focus is often related to the quality of the relationships and the patterns of communication. The DSM-5 Other Conditions section contains diagnostic codes for relational problems, which are not considered behavioral health diagnoses, and these can be used in addition to or in place of another behavioral health diagnosis.

It is often *clinically useful to identify behavioral health diagnoses* that are applicable to members of the couple or family. Some of the individuals may be in treatment with another clinician or psychiatrist, and I recommend asking the client for authorization to speak with the other treating professional. This gives you diagnostic information as well as facilitating coordination of care, further described in Chapter 12. The diagnosis and individual treatment are part of the context for the relationship and communication difficulties in your couple or family treatment, and you can choose more effective interventions when you have diagnostic information.

I also recommend spending some time considering a behavioral health diagnosis when the individuals are not in concurrent treatment. The couples and families you see during your clinical training often have *complex presenting issues* with histories of trauma, mental health and substance use problems, and psychosocial stress. Taking time to consider individual diagnoses may lead to referrals for adjunct treatment that will enhance the couple or family treatment.

If the couple or family is relying on third-party reimbursement, you probably will be required to assign a behavioral health diagnosis to the member of the couple or family who is considered the primary client for billing purposes. If this is the case, formulating a diagnostic impression of each person will help you maintain an evenhanded view of the contribution of each family member to the difficulties in the relationship.

Cultural Formulation in Diagnosis

Include a description of the client's cultural influences in your assessment, in addition to considering cultural factors in identifying DSM-5 diagnoses. The DSM-5 contains an outline for a cultural formulation that you can use for this purpose. It includes cultural identity, cultural conceptualizations of distress, psychosocial stressors and cultural features of vulnerability and resilience, cultural features of the relationship between the individual and the clinician, and an overall cultural assessment related to diagnosis and treatment. There is a 16-question Cultural Formulation Interview that you may use as a guide for your assessment (APsyA, 2013).

Psychodynamic Diagnostic Manual

The Psychodynamic Diagnostic Manual (PDM; PDM Task Force, 2006) complements the DSM-5 and is particularly *valuable as a way to understand the whole person.* The diagnostic framework of the PDM is a listing of three axes:

- Personality patterns and disorders (P axis)—personality patterns and disorders that organize the client's ways of relating to self and others and that have implications for choosing an effective treatment approach;
- A profile of mental functioning (M axis)—examples of different levels of functioning in nine cognitive, emotional, and interpersonal capacities, which reflect the client's strengths and challenges; and
- The subjective experience of symptom patterns (S axis)—the subjective experience of the behavioral symptoms associated with the DSM mental health and substance use disorders, which is valuable in developing both cognitive and emotional insight into the client's inner world and will help you develop an empathic description and understanding of the client's distress.

The manual has different sections that describe the application of these three axes to adult mental health disorders and to child and adolescent mental health disorders. The 2006 edition of the PDM is linked to the DSM-IV-TR and ICD-9-CM codes.

Discussing the Diagnosis with the Client

Reasons to Discuss Diagnosis

Like many clinicians in training, you may be reluctant to share diagnostic information with the client, fearing he will respond negatively. Your questions concerning the meaning of diagnosis and your level of confidence in your competence to assign a diagnosis will also contribute to your reluctance to have this discussion.

I believe that withholding diagnostic information from the client is inconsistent with the spirit of collaboration that forms the foundation of a therapeutic alliance and of effective treatment. I have found *therapeutic value in discussing the client's diagnosis openly* because it can facilitate his awareness and understanding of symptoms that are confusing or frightening. For example, a client who fears he is "going crazy" because he has violent nightmares after being physically assaulted will be relieved to learn that his symptoms are characteristic of posttraumatic stress disorder rather than an indication of a psychotic break.

Guidelines for Discussing Diagnosis

Follow the guidelines below to prepare for discussing diagnosis with your client in a clinically useful way that will enhance the therapeutic alliance and promote therapeutic progress.

- Discuss your apprehension or discomfort in supervision so you can understand your feelings and be prepared to have an open conversation with the client. Consider doing a role play with your supervisor if you are concerned about the client's response.

- Talk about diagnosis when the client asks for an explanation of his symptoms, when you are sharing your treatment recommendations, or when you are developing a treatment plan together. The diagnostic information then is part of your discussion about how treatment can be helpful in addressing his symptoms and concerns.

- Remind the client what he has told you about his symptoms, current functioning, and life history, and then introduce the diagnosis as a way to understand his experiences.

- If the diagnostic label is one that the client may find objectionable (e.g., borderline personality disorder, bipolar disorder, delusional disorder), you can follow your review of the client's symptoms with a statement that mental health professionals understand these symptoms as part of a pattern or syndrome. You can then go on to say what this pattern is called if the client seems interested or come back to the conversation in a later session when the client may be more ready.

- Ask for the client's reactions to hearing this diagnosis applied to him and correct any misconceptions he may have. For example, many clients are upset by a diagnostic label because they believe it means they will never be able to live a normal life, they are defective or flawed, or there is no hope of getting better.

Discussions in Child, Couple, and Family Treatment

When the *child is the primary client* or when the child's behavior and symptoms are the main reason for the family entering treatment, your discussion about diagnosis may take place with the parents and child separately or in a family session. The inclusion and participation of the child in the discussion depends on his developmental age and the family dynamics related to the child's diagnosis, according to the following guidelines.

- Separate discussions with the child and parent are preferable when you are seeing the child individually and:

    - You believe the parents may have concerns or reactions to hearing about the diagnosis, or
    - The child is pre-adolescent and your discussion with the parents would not be developmentally appropriate for the child.

- A joint discussion with the child and parents together is preferable when:

    - You are doing family therapy and all members of the family attend each session, or

- You are seeing the child individually and believe there would be therapeutic value in having a diagnostic discussion with the child and parents together. If the child is an adolescent, it might be clinically appropriate to talk with the adolescent about his diagnosis before the joint session.

In all discussions of diagnosis with children, you should use language and terminology that is appropriate to the child's developmental level.

In *couple and family treatment*, discussion of diagnosis will be needed in some cases and not in others. The diagnosis of one or more members of the family is relevant when:

- The treatment is funded by a third party and you are required to assign a diagnosis for reimbursement,
- The diagnosis impacts the treatment goals and interventions, or
- You recommend additional treatment or resources for one or more member's symptoms.

In these cases, your discussion would address the interactions between the individuals' diagnoses and the couple or family treatment. For example, in family treatment with a presenting issue of the child's anxiety symptoms after the death of a maternal grandparent, you might identify symptoms of depression in the mother. You would discuss the goal of family therapy as increasing the family members' sense of closeness by sharing their feelings of grief and loss. You might also recommend that the mother get additional grief counseling support for her symptoms.

Another example is couple treatment in which one member has a diagnosis of bipolar disorder that is not managed with medication. Your discussion of this diagnosis would include the fact that the benefit of couple treatment will be limited unless the individual seeks a medication evaluation to manage the symptoms that are disruptive to the couple's relationship and communication.

Summary

This chapter reviewed the process of diagnosis including assigning an accurate diagnosis, using DSM-5, developing a comprehensive diagnostic description, and discussing diagnosis with clients. Diagnosis is a standardized language for understanding and communicating about the client's symptoms and functioning. Specific areas of professional growth related to diagnosis are listed below.

1. Using yourself as an instrument of hope, change and healing:

    a. Explore your concerns and discomfort about assigning a diagnosis as a part of treatment.

2. Becoming confident in your authority and professionalism:

    a. Understand the use of diagnosis as a clinical tool.

    b. Become familiar with the DSM-5.

    c. Supplement the DSM-5 diagnostic labels with cultural formulation and understanding the whole person (aided by the PDM).

3. Developing interpersonal skills that strengthen the therapeutic relationship:

    a. Make diagnostic observations from the beginning of treatment.

    b. Discuss diagnosis with clients in a clinically useful way.

Case Example: Liz's Comprehensive Diagnostic Description of Susana

After Liz's first session with Susana, she begins to think about the DSM diagnosis that best fits Susana's symptoms. The agency requires clinicians to assign a primary diagnosis after the first session, and Liz has found this practice orients her thinking about her client's clinical presentation. It enables her to begin her case formulation, identify additional assessment information that she needs to clarify the diagnosis, and develop initial treatment interventions that may lead to symptom relief.

Review of Presenting Symptoms

Susana's presenting symptoms follow the incident of the 9-1-1 call, so Liz begins with the Trauma- and Stressor-Related Disorders section of the DSM-5. She looks at the criteria for Adjustment Disorders, which refers to symptoms that develop in response to a stressor, and which seems to describe Susana.

The first two criteria for Adjustment Disorder are met in that Susana's symptoms developed within three months of onset of the stressor and are clinically significant. The fourth criterion, that the symptoms do not represent normal bereavement, is also met. The third criterion is that the symptoms do not meet the criteria for another disorder. Liz's impression is that Susana's depression isn't severe because she is able to work and care for her children. Also, Liz felt Susana was more engaged in the session than other depressed clients with whom Liz has worked.

Liz looks next at the Depressive Disorders category to confirm her initial impression of an Adjustment Disorder diagnosis. The only diagnosis in this category that could fit Susana's symptoms is *Major Depressive Disorder*. The first criterion is the presence of five or more of nine symptoms during a 2-week period, representing a change from previous functioning. As Liz reviews the symptoms, she recognizes that Susana has described five that have been present for more than two weeks: depressed mood, diminished pleasure, insomnia, fatigue, and diminished concentration. Liz also noticed Susana's excessive guilt related to the breakup with Carlos, which is a sixth symptom.

Provisional Primary Diagnosis

Liz is surprised to see that Susana meets the criteria for Major Depressive Disorder and recognizes that she has minimized the severity of Susana's condition. Liz notices that she has joined with Susana's tendency to neglect herself and to consider her needs as unimportant. This is an important insight into the power of Susana's interpersonal pattern and leads Liz to recognize the importance of carefully examining her intuitive impressions of Susana before making treatment decisions.

After confirming the symptoms for a diagnosis of Major Depressive Disorder, Liz sees that there are specifiers for single or recurrent episode and for severity. Susana acknowledged being depressed in college and although Liz didn't ask about the specific symptoms that were present at that time, the fact that Susana made a suicide attempt suggests that her symptoms would meet the criteria for Major Depressive Disorder. Therefore, Liz assigns a *provisional diagnosis of F33.0 Major Depressive Disorder, Recurrent Episode, Mild*. She sees that there are further specifiers for that diagnosis, none of which are present in Susana's presentation. She recognizes that she will need to ask Susana about past symptoms of a manic episode to confirm this diagnosis and rule out the presence of a bipolar disorder. She also plans to get more information about the severity of Susana's symptoms in the college episode and any other episodes of depression.

Review of Primary Diagnosis

During subsequent sessions over the next 6 weeks, Liz learns more about Susana's current life and history and develops her full DSM-5 diagnosis. Liz administers the Beck Depression Inventory (BDI-II; Beck, Steer, & Brown, 1996) in order to confirm the diagnosis and provide additional information about the severity of Susana's symptoms. Susana completes the BDI in the third session, and her score is 18, which is in the mild range. Liz learns that Susana had two additional episodes of depression between the initial episode in college and the current episode. Both of these followed the end of her intimate relationships. Although it was difficult to verify that all of these episodes met the full criteria for Major Depressive Episode, Susana said her current symptoms were familiar to her and seemed about the same as those accompanying the prior periods of depression.

When Liz asked about symptoms of manic episodes, she learned that Susana remembered times at the beginning of her intimate relationships in which she felt "high" even though she wasn't using any substances. These episodes were accompanied by a decreased need for sleep, racing thoughts, and taking on new work or volunteer projects. None of these episodes resulted in any impairment in Susana's ability to work or care for her children, and they lasted a few months before her mood and energy level returned to normal. This information leads Liz to *consider a diagnosis of F31.81 Bipolar II Disorder, Current Episode Depressed, Mild*.

Liz consults with Dalia about Susana's manic symptoms, and Dalia advises that the presence of manic symptoms only when starting an intimate relationship does not warrant a diagnosis of Bipolar II Disorder. She suggests that Major Depressive Disorder is the most appropriate diagnosis and recommends that Liz continue to monitor the emergence of manic symptoms or additional reports of manic or hypomanic episodes in the past.

Additional Diagnoses

As Liz completes her assessment, she considers *secondary diagnoses* that fit Susana's symptoms and history. Susana's exposure to the war in El Salvador for 5 years before she and her family immigrated to the United States could have led to the development of *posttraumatic stress disorder*, but Susana does not report symptoms of re-experiencing or avoidance that are characteristic of this diagnosis.

Liz also evaluates the presence of an *alcohol use disorder*, but Susana's report of her drinking does not meet the criteria for this diagnosis. The results of the Alcohol Use Disorders Identification Test (AUDIT; Babor, Higgins-Biddle, Saunders, & Monteiro, 2001) indicate that Susana's use of alcohol is problematic, and this is an area that Liz will address in the treatment even though Susana does not meet the diagnostic criteria for alcohol use disorder.

Liz then moves to consider the *personality disorders* category of the DSM-5. Based on her assessment, Liz does not find that Susana meets the first criterion for a personality disorder diagnosis, which is "an enduring pattern of inner experience and behavior that deviates markedly from the expectations of the individual's culture" (APsyA, 2013, p. 646). Susana's pattern of putting the needs of others, especially her male partners, ahead of her own is consistent with cultural expectations. In addition, since this pattern is present primarily in Susana's intimate relationships, the second criterion of a personality disorder is not met. This criterion describes the pattern as "inflexible and pervasive across a broad range of personal and social situations" (APsyA, 2013, p. 646).

Finally, Liz looks at the section for Other Conditions that may be a Focus of Clinical Attention to identify *areas of psychosocial and historical stressors*. She lists three conditions to reflect Susana's conflict with her daughter Maria, her recent breakup with Carlos, and her exposure to war in childhood.

Liz asks Susana about her *physical health and medical conditions* as part of the assessment and learns that Susana is under medical care for recurring migraine headaches. This was confirmed when Liz consulted with Susana's primary care physician.

Comprehensive DSM-5 Diagnosis

Liz enters the following DSM-5 diagnosis in her assessment report:
    F33.0 Major Depressive Disorder, Recurrent Episode, Mild
    Z62.820 Parent-Child Relational Problem
    Z63.8 Disruption of Family by Separation or Divorce
    Z65.4 Exposure to Disaster, War or Other Hostilities
    Recurring migraine headaches

Psychodynamic Diagnostic Manual

Liz also looks at the PDM (PDM Task Force, 2006) for additional insight into Susana's diagnosis. On the *P axis* related to personality patterns and disorders, Susana fits the description of the depressive personality type at the neurotic level of severity. Liz has noticed Susana's sensitivity to experiencing loss and rejection and her tendency to feel guilt and shame, which are part of the depressive personality type. The PDM description also suggests that Susana may unconsciously believe she is bad and that others who know her will reject her. Liz notes that people whose personality organization is at the neurotic level of severity generally develop a therapeutic alliance fairly quickly and are helped by open-ended exploration of current feelings and behavior, as well as past events.

Liz observes mild impairments in Susana's functioning as outlined in the *M axis*, the Profile of Mental Functioning. The areas that seem most problematic for Susana are her level of confidence and self-esteem, restriction of emotional expression, and self-reflective capacity. Liz identifies these capacities as areas that can be improved through their treatment.

Liz consults the descriptions of depressive episodes on the *S axis* of the PDM, since she has identified Major Depressive Disorder as Susana's primary diagnosis. The description of the experience of a depressive episode indicates that Susana is likely to feel helpless and inadequate, to fear being abandoned, and to have difficulty expressing anger. She is also likely to believe herself guilty of wrongdoing, have low self-regard, and be either clinging or antagonistic toward others. Liz also notes that depression is often accompanied by somatic pain including headaches, for which Susana has received medical care.

The information from the *PDM is useful to Liz in building a clinical formulation.* She infers that Susana developed a negative view of herself based on experiences of loss and rejection. This negative view of herself contributes to her vulnerability to depression when an intimate relationship ends and some hypomanic symptoms when she enters a relationship. Liz will use this insight, combined with the extensive assessment data she has obtained, to construct a case formulation to guide her treatment approach. She is aware that Susana's view of herself in relation to intimate relationships is consistent with the cultural image of *marianismo* (de Rios, 2001).

Discussing the Diagnosis with Susana

Liz has a discussion with Susana about her diagnosis in the fourth session, after getting sufficient information from Susana's report of her symptoms and history and from the BDI-II. Their discussion proceeds as follows:

Liz: I'd like to talk with you about my understanding so far of the difficulties you've been having recently—with feeling down and not enjoying things, having trouble sleeping and concentrating, and not feeling good about yourself. We've talked about this as depression, and from what you've told me and the answers you gave on the questionnaire I asked you to fill out, it does appear that you are in an episode of depression.

Susana: I was afraid of that. I know it's happened before, and I guess I just have to expect this will happen when men leave me.

Liz: You told me that you've been depressed before, and I think we can understand more about how and why the end of a relationship triggers that for you.

Susana: If I'm having an episode of depression, do you think I should take medication?

Liz: Medication can be helpful for people in relieving depression, but I think you said your internist had suggested it and you didn't want to take anything. If you feel differently about it at some point, we could talk about the next step of getting more information from a doctor. It's usually helpful to see a psychiatrist who has more specialized knowledge about prescribing for psychological conditions.

Susana: I still don't feel ready to take a pill to make me feel better. I think I told you my mom has taken pills ever since we came here from El Salvador. I don't think she even knows anymore what everything is for. She takes four or five different things.

Liz: I understand you don't want to consider medication now. If that changes, we can talk about finding a psychiatrist who would give you more information about different medications that might be helpful to you. Do you have any questions about what I've told you regarding your diagnosis?

Susana: Is this something I'll have for the rest of my life?

Liz: Many conditions, including depression, seem to have a physiological or genetic component, but they're usually triggered by an event or other change of some kind. It seems like you've figured out that your episodes of feeling up and down happen at the end of your relationships with men and that your feelings about yourself depend on what your partner thinks or how he behaves toward you. As we continue working together, we can talk about building confidence in yourself and developing other supportive relationships that will help you stay more stable when your intimate relationships are changing.

Susana: That's hard to imagine, but I'd like to try.

Liz then encourages Susana to reflect on her feelings before, during, and after her relationships and asks how she has felt when she has been alone for short periods of time. This discussion leads to exploration of Susana's relationships with her parents and the family environment as she remembers it before immigration and after.

The Next Step

Chapter 6 will discuss the process of assessment, beginning with integrating the assessment with a therapeutic approach and reviewing the steps to completing a comprehensive assessment. The case example will describe how Liz compiled information for her assessment, including a sample assessment report.

References

American Psychiatric Association. (2013). *Diagnostic and statistical manual of mental disorders* (5th ed.). Arlington, VA: Author.

Babor, T. F., Higgins-Biddle, J. C., Saunders, J. B., & Monteiro, M. G. (2001). *AUDIT: The alcohol use disorders identification test* (2nd ed.). Geneva, Switzerland: World Health Organization.

Beck, A. T., Steer, R. A., & Brown, G. K. (1996). *BDI-II: Beck depression inventory* (2nd ed.). San Antonio, TX: The Psychological Corporation.

Contexo Media. (2013). *International classification of diseases,* (10th Revision, Clinical Modification). Salt Lake City, UT: Author.

de Rios, M. D. (2001). *Brief psychotherapy with the Latino immigrant client.* New York, NY: The Haworth Press.

Hays, P. A. (2008). *Addressing cultural complexities in practice: Assessment, diagnosis, and therapy* (2nd ed.). Washington, DC: American Psychological Association.

Mangrum, L. F., Spence, R. T., & Lopez, M. (2006). Integrated versus parallel treatment of co-occurring psychiatric and substance use disorders. *Journal of Substance Abuse Treatment, 30,* 79–84.

PDM Task Force. (2006). *Psychodynamic diagnostic manual.* Silver Spring, MD: Alliance of Psychoanalytic Organizations.

Substance Abuse and Mental Health Services Administration. (2009). *Integrated treatment for co-occurring disorders evidence-based practices (EBP) KIT: The evidence.* Retrieved January 18, 2016, from http://store.samhsa.gov/shin/content//SMA08-4367/TheEvidence-ITC.pdf.

6
ASSESSMENT

(Note: This chapter will use the female pronoun for supervisor, clinician, and client.)

This chapter presents the assessment process, which generally takes place in the first one to eight sessions of treatment. Assessment is most effective when it is integrated with the establishment of a therapeutic relationship, and in this chapter you will learn how to approach this integration. I will also introduce the goals, elements, and outcome of an assessment as well as guidelines for sharing assessment results with the client.

Assessment as Part of the Therapeutic Process

Description of Assessment

An assessment involves *gathering information about the client's current life, symptoms, stressors, and historical events*. Most clinical work, including psychotherapy and case management, requires an initial assessment at the beginning of treatment, which you document in a narrative report or a structured form. You may have access to other professional assessments as background or as a supplement to the information you collect directly.

In adult treatment, the client is the primary source of information for your assessment, although you may also contact family members or other professionals who work with her, after getting her authorization to do so. When a child is your primary client, a full assessment always includes information from parents and teachers.

The amount of time allotted to complete an assessment varies among training settings. You may be expected to complete the assessment in the first session, with some additional information from family members and other professionals added as it is available. Some strategies for doing an assessment and establishing a therapeutic alliance in the first session are contained in Chapter 3. Other agencies allow as many as six to eight sessions over 2 months or more to conduct an assessment. The following guidelines apply regardless of the amount of time allotted.

Integrating Assessment with Developing a Therapeutic Relationship

Clinicians in training often view the process of assessment as separate from developing a therapeutic relationship with the client. Being empathic and attuned can feel incompatible with getting information, and you may feel you have to choose between the two. However, *treatment is most effective when you integrate the skills that enhance the therapeutic relationship with the skills that lead to a comprehensive assessment.* I share some strategies to help you approach these tasks as complementary rather than contradictory.

As a starting point, recognize that *your client is likely to appreciate your thoroughness and comprehensiveness* in your examination of her current life and past experiences. This approach conveys your seriousness and dedication to understanding your client as fully as possible. When you engage her in the process of diagnosis and assessment early in treatment, she generally feels more seen and understood rather than less.

Collaboration in the Assessment Process

Assessment involves *asking questions about issues the client hasn't raised herself* and asking for information that she hasn't volunteered. You may worry that the client will feel pressured or put off, or that she may feel you're diverting attention from her agenda to yours when you take the initiative in directing your conversation. Many clients are, in fact, particularly sensitive to interpersonal power and control due to their prior experiences of rejection, exploitation, and criticism.

Ways to *establish an atmosphere of collaboration* while gathering information for an assessment are to:

- Explain the purpose of your questions,
- Ask the client's permission to inquire about a sensitive issue,
- Let the client know these questions are asked of all clients in your agency, and
- Ask open-ended questions about cultural identities.

When you *explain the purpose of your questions*, you communicate openness and respect for the client as a participant in treatment. An example of a general statement introducing the assessment is

> I want to understand you and your life as completely as possible in order to be effective in helping you with the issues you have mentioned. I've found that learning about the different areas of my clients' lives helps me develop the best ideas about how we can work together.

An example of a more specific statement about the relationship between the areas you are exploring and the client's primary concern is, "Researchers have found that depression can be related to physical health and medical conditions, so I'd like to ask you about your medical history."

When you *ask the client's permission to inquire about a sensitive issue*, the client will feel less shame and fear of criticism. Your statement should include letting the client know she can defer answering. An example is

> I'd like to ask you some questions about the incident with the police you mentioned earlier. If I ask about something you don't want to tell me, you can just let me know you're not ready to talk about that today. Is that all right with you?

Approaching sensitive topics in this way gives the client an experience of the therapeutic relationship that is different from her relationships with other professionals and authorities.

When you approach other sensitive issues that are part of the standard assessment, *let the client know these questions are asked of all clients in your agency*. This minimizes her feeling singled out. An example is

> Since alcohol and other drugs can have an impact on mental and physical health, we ask all of our clients here about their use. Would you be willing to tell me about your drinking and use of prescription and other drugs?

Last, *ask open-ended questions about cultural identities*, including sexual and gender identity. This is especially important if you are a member of a dominant cultural group and the client is not (Hays, 2008). Examples of open-ended questions are, "Could you tell me about your cultural background?" or, "Could you tell me about your sexual and gender identity?"

Influence of Clinician's Emotional State

You will find that when you are comfortable with and clear about the importance of assessment, your clients will be comfortable responding to your questions. Resolving your feelings of conflict about the requirement for assessment will enable you to experience the assessment process as enhancing rather than detracting from establishing the therapeutic relationship.

You can *increase your confidence by practicing aspects of assessment* in supervision and with colleagues in your academic program or training site. Hearing yourself and others ask questions or introduce issues in different ways can help you settle on the wording, style, and tone that feels best to you. You will discover a balance between leading and following the client and between asking for information and listening to the client's concerns. Your ability to achieve this balance will evolve as you gain experience.

Taking Notes

Some clinicians find it helpful to take notes during the session, especially in the early sessions of treatment when you hear details about the client's current and past life experiences that are important to remember. Other clinicians find it distracting to take notes during sessions and prefer to allocate time immediately following the session, although this can be difficult if you are doing sessions in consecutive hours. Talk with your supervisor about the recommended practice in your training site. You may want to experiment with both styles to see what allows you to be most engaged with the client while retaining the information you need to understand her and develop an effective treatment plan. If you do take notes during the session, explain what you are writing and why. An example is, "I'm going to take some notes while we're talking, which will help me remember the details of what we talk about today and think about ways we can work together on the issues that brought you here."

Goals of Assessment

A thorough assessment helps you to accomplish the following goals:

- Understand the context for the client's current presenting problem,
- Identify strengths and earlier periods of higher functioning,
- Increase empathy for the client's difficulties and coping strategies,
- Develop a direction for treatment, and
- Structure the sessions when the initial presentation is scattered or volatile.

The information you gather in the assessment helps you *understand the context of the client's current presenting problem.* Clients often enter treatment in a state of crisis and distress that narrows their focus to their immediate symptoms and stressors. When you ask about the client's life history and different areas of her current life circumstances, patterns often emerge that bring order to the client's chaotic feelings and confusion. For example, one client may have experienced recurring periods of depression following loss or disappointment in relationships. Another client may have symptoms of anxiety that coincide with her daughter reaching the age at which the client was sexually abused by a family member. It is reassuring for the client to be able to put her current difficulties in a larger context, and feel less confused and overwhelmed by her current situation.

The assessment also helps you *identify the client's strengths and earlier periods of higher functioning.* As you learn about her past history, her earlier strategies for coping with earlier adversity, and her past successes, you are able to reflect her strengths and capacities. This is useful and validating for the client who is overwhelmed by her current circumstances and feels discouraged by a sense of failure.

The process of assessment generally results in *increased empathy for the client's difficulties and coping strategies*. It is easier to have empathy for the client when you understand the larger context of her life. For example, you may have a client who has three children by three different men and has no contact with any of the fathers. With this information alone, you may feel judgmental of her choices. However, your assessment may reveal that she grew up witnessing domestic violence from her father to her mother, and that she ends relationships when she begins to feel angry with her partner because she fears her anger will precipitate violence from him. With this information, you can understand the client's behavior as an attempt to protect her children and her partners, and you can feel compassion for her dilemma rather than judgment about her life choices.

Another function of the assessment is to assist in *developing a direction for treatment*. After you gather the assessment information about the client's current symptoms, life circumstances, and past history, you are ready to develop a clinical case formulation explaining the factors that contribute to the client's symptoms. The case formulation guides your treatment plan, which consists of goals and interventions and is the basis of your agreement with the client about how you will work together. Chapters 8 and 9 provide detailed descriptions of case formulation and treatment planning.

An assessment can also serve to *structure the sessions when the initial presentation is scattered or volatile*. In these situations, a structured assessment process helps contain the client's chaotic presentation and reduces the client's anxiety as well as yours. The structure communicates your expectation that the client can manage her distress more adaptively, and it builds a sense of physical and emotional safety which is required in order for you and the client to focus on her needs for help.

Elements of an Assessment

An assessment combines information obtained in the following ways:

- Clinical interview with the client (and family members if clinically indicated),
- Behavioral observations,
- Questionnaires or tests, when necessary to validate or clarify the diagnosis, and
- Information from other professionals who have current or past knowledge of the client.

After gathering the information for the assessment, you create a report or complete a form that summarizes the client's current difficulties, life circumstances, strengths, and past history. The format of the report may be primarily narrative, primarily checklists, or some combination of the two.

Familiarize yourself with the assessment format at your training site before you begin your assessment so you are efficient in collecting the information you need. If your assessment period spans several sessions, begin writing sections of the narrative and complete some of the checklists after each session. Writing an assessment report can be a daunting task, and you will have an easier time if you break it up into sections. When you work on it after each session, you will also be able to identify the additional information you need to obtain in future sessions.

Consult with your supervisor as you gather information for your assessment so she is aware of your progress and can suggest whether to include additional sources of information. Let her know if you have any difficulties obtaining information from the client or others, if you question the accuracy of your client's report, or if you receive contradictory information from different sources or from the client at different times.

Clinical Interview

A comprehensive clinical interview is extensive and is difficult to complete in one session. If your assessment is due after the first session, prioritize the issues that are most relevant to your client and defer asking about the other issues until a future session. That information can be entered in your progress notes and/or a follow-up review of the assessment or treatment update. The following areas of the client's current life and history are included in the clinical interview portion of an assessment:

- Psychological symptoms including the severity, duration, and frequency of the current symptoms and previous episodes of similar symptoms;
- Primary presenting problem or issue, including the history of this problem and current context;
- The impact of the symptoms on overall health, interpersonal relationships, daily living skills, and work or education (often called the degree of functional impairment);
- Risk factors including suicidal and homicidal ideation and impulses, violence toward others, and exposure to violence in the family, home, or community;
- Substance use, both current and past, including alcohol and both prescription and non-prescription drugs;
- Cultural influences and how these cultural influences affect the client's ideas about mental health, wellness, and treatment (using the ADDRESSING framework discussed in Chapter 4, the Cultural Formulation Interview in the DSM-5, or another framework);
- Coping strategies, strengths, and resources, including strengths and supports related to the client's cultural communities and identities;
- Expectations of treatment and desired outcomes;
- Current life circumstances including family and other interpersonal relationships, work or educational involvement, housing and financial status, and legal involvement;

- History of mental health and substance use treatment including involvement in 12-step groups and the use of non-traditional or non-Western healing practices;
- Physical health, medical conditions, and history of medical illness and treatment; and
- Family and developmental history including significant losses or disruptions, trauma and abuse, achievement of developmental milestones, current and past mental health symptoms and treatment in other family members, and substance use and abuse in other family members.

Child treatment. When your primary client is a *pre-adolescent child*, it is generally best to interview the parents without the child to discuss the presenting problem, current situational factors, and historical events. Also talk with the child about her symptoms, distress, and understanding of treatment using developmentally appropriate language.

In working with *adolescents*, it is often helpful to have an initial session with an adolescent, after getting written consent from the parents, to discuss the presenting issues and views of treatment. Doing this helps to build the therapeutic alliance with the adolescent when the decision about treatment is made by parents or teachers. You may meet with the parents without the adolescent for a clinical interview or hold a family session to discuss the relevant history and current situation.

Couple and family treatment. With couple and family treatment, it is the usual practice to gather relevant information for your assessment in a couple or family session. At times there may be clinical reasons to meet with family members individually, but check with your supervisor before doing so. Notice the similarities and differences in the views of different family members regarding the symptoms, presenting problem, and expectations of treatment, because they may be related to the communication and relationship difficulties you are addressing in treatment.

Family members of adult clients. Sometimes it is helpful to interview family members of an adult client as part of your assessment. Some examples are when your client (a) relies on family members for support in basic living skills, (b) lives with or is financially dependent on her parents, and (c) has a diagnosis and symptoms that make self-report unreliable. You are required to obtain the adult client's consent before interviewing family members, unless the client is under guardianship. Be prepared to talk with the client about how it will be useful to the treatment for you to get information from family members.

Observations

While you and the client are talking about her life, you will *observe different aspects of how she interacts with you and how she responds to the treatment setting and to you.* At times you also may observe the client outside of the treatment setting. Outside observations are usually included in the assessment when working with children and sometimes with adults enrolled in a residential or day treatment program. Variations in symptoms and behavior in different settings are common, and observations in the client's home, school, or work can expand your understanding and contribute to setting treatment goals that are relevant to different areas of the client's life.

Your assessment report should make *clear distinctions between what you directly observe in the client's behavior and what you infer* about the client's emotional or cognitive state based on the behavior you witnessed. For example, you might describe your observation of a child by saying, "Natalie was very active in the classroom and did not respond to the teacher's instruction to go to her seat. She appeared more anxious and agitated in the classroom than in the agency office."

Consider cultural factors when you make inferences about the client's behavior with you and in other settings. Communication style, openness in self-disclosure with an authority figure, and other aspects of interpersonal behavior are shaped by cultural norms as well as by prior experiences with medical, mental health, and other professionals.

Mental status exam. A mental status exam is a *semi-structured method of recording your observations* of the client (Wiger, 2012). Performing a mental status exam is standard in psychiatric settings and may be included as part of your assessment in other clinical settings.

A mental status exam describes:

- Behavior—appearance, psychomotor and interpersonal behavior, and speech;
- Emotion—mood and affect; and
- Cognition—memory, attention, judgment, language, thought processes, and thought content.

It is usually reported in narrative form, although some settings use a combination of checklist and narrative.

A mental status exam offers an *overview of the client's functioning at a specific point in time* and can be used to evaluate changes over time. If your training site includes a mental status exam in the assessment, you will probably receive specific training which will include an explanation of some of the psychiatric terms that may be unfamiliar to you.

Questionnaires and Tests

Questionnaires and diagnostic tests may be completed by the client or by others (e.g., teacher, parent, or other professional). These instruments contribute to your assessment because they have statistical reliability and validity and provide standardized information regarding the client's symptoms and psychological functioning in comparison with others. These tests may be administered by you or provided by others.

Self-report questionnaires are available for general screening purposes, for measuring the type and severity of symptoms, and for measuring information relevant to treatment recommendations (Antony & Barlow, 2010; Ey & Hersen, 2004). They are generally easy to administer, score, and interpret. Check with your supervisor about the instruments that are available at your training site and the guidelines for their use. Review the self-report questionnaire before you use it, so you are familiar with its content and the instructions for administration and scoring. Although self-report questionnaires are generally simple and straightforward, you need to be prepared to answer your client's questions and to administer the questionnaire correctly.

Formal diagnostic tests are more comprehensive than self-report questionnaires and require special training and supervision. Unless you are working in a training site that includes formal diagnostic testing experience, your exposure to these tests will probably be through reading assessment reports prepared by others. Child clients often have testing at school, adults are sometimes assessed with formal tests in a residential or day treatment facility, and clients with a complex clinical presentation may have been evaluated at a specialized clinic. I recommend requesting assessment reports from the client and incorporating them in your assessment, as they often contain useful information about diagnosis, the client's cognitive and emotional functioning, and treatment recommendations. Consult with your supervisor if the reports contain terms that are unfamiliar to you.

Information from Other Professionals

Your assessment may also include information from other professionals who are familiar with the client's current and past symptoms, behavior, and history. Your assessment report should identify the people who provided information and should be clear in identifying the source of any information that was not provided by the client.

It is *good clinical practice to request the client's written authorization* for you and the other professional to exchange information or authorization from the parent if the primary client is a child or adolescent under 18. There are exceptions to the requirement to get the client's permission before sharing information, but the therapeutic relationship will be enhanced when you approach this request collaboratively with the client. Be prepared to explain how it will benefit the client's treatment if you are able to speak with the teacher, psychiatrist, prior psychotherapist, case manager, or other professional. See Chapter 12 for information related to client confidentiality and exchange of information between professionals.

Examples of *situations in which you should get information from other professionals* are

- Recent psychiatric hospitalization or residential substance abuse treatment,
- Probation or other court mandated referrals,
- Current or recent psychiatric treatment involving medication,

- Conditions such as developmental disabilities and acute psychosis which limit the client's ability to give an accurate account of current and past life circumstances, and
- Serious medical conditions.

When working with children and adolescents, information from teachers and school counselors should always be included in the assessment. Similarly, when working with adults who are living in residential programs or other structured housing, information from professional and paraprofessional staff is valuable. In other cases not mentioned above, the information from other professionals may enhance your understanding of the client and provide a more complete perspective, so consider requesting the client's authorization whenever she is working with other professionals.

Outcome of the Assessment Process

Assessment Report

The assessment report is a compilation of your interview information, observations, questionnaires, and information you have received from others through conversation or written report. It usually includes a DSM-5 diagnosis, described in Chapter 5, and in some agencies, also includes a clinical case formulation and treatment plan described in Chapters 8 and 9.

Writing a report or completing an assessment form is intimidating at the beginning of training. Some helpful tips are

- Begin the written report after the first session by entering the information you have at that time.
- Complete sections of the report after each session as you get information.
- Ask your supervisor to review a draft to get feedback on your progress and to resolve your questions and concerns.
- Remember the assessment reflects your knowledge and understanding of the client at the time you write the report. Additional information or changes in your understanding can be incorporated into a later treatment summary or update of the original assessment.

Decision Regarding the Unit of Treatment

The decision about who is involved in the treatment is often straightforward, based on the client's presenting problem and reasons for seeking services. When the treatment could be provided through different modalities, you need to consider this decision more carefully. Sometimes the decision about providing individual, couple, or family treatment is determined by the mission and treatment philosophy of the organization or by the requirements of a third-party funder. Other times you will consult with your supervisor about the client's preferences and your assessment information to decide which family members will participate in the treatment and what modality you will use.

Your decision regarding the unit of treatment defines *whether your client is an individual or a family unit*. If the family is your client, your treatment goals and interventions will relate to improving the family's functioning as a whole. Treatment goals and interventions applicable to individuals in the family will generally not be included. For example, in working with a family following the sexual abuse of one child by a family acquaintance, you would choose interventions that strengthen the bonds between family members that were disrupted by the abuse, subsequent investigation, and legal case. If you were working with that child individually, you would choose interventions that promote the child's recovery from the abuse, and you would meet separately with the parents to discuss the child's progress and the effect on the family.

Whether you determine the unit of treatment to be an individual or a family, you may hold both individual and family sessions depending on the treatment goals and the family situation. Sometimes it is helpful to hold family sessions in an individual treatment or to hold individual or couple sessions in a family treatment. For example, a 24-year-old adult with a diagnosis of bipolar disorder who lives with his parents may benefit from family sessions with his parents in response to conflicts that arise in the home. In a case of family treatment, it might be appropriate to see the parent or parents without the children to provide specific parenting support.

Sharing the Assessment Results with the Client

Reasons to Share

Sharing the results of your assessment with the client is important for the same reason that it is important to discuss diagnosis with her (introduced in Chapter 5). Telling the client about your inferences and conclusions *fosters the spirit of collaboration* that contributes to a therapeutic alliance and effective treatment. In addition, the assessment leads to your case formulation, which informs your recommendations for the treatment plan. The client will have a better understanding of your recommendations when you have shared the assessment results first.

Guidelines for Sharing Assessment Results

Follow the guidelines below to prepare for sharing the assessment results with your client in preparation for developing a treatment plan.

- Discuss in supervision the areas that you anticipate being painful or shameful for the client, so you are prepared to approach these areas with sensitivity. Consider doing a role play with your supervisor if you are concerned about the client's response.

- Use language and terminology appropriate for the client's developmental age, education, psychological knowledge, and prior treatment experience.
- Include more detail and specificity with clients who:

  - Request detailed information,
  - Are distrustful of authority,
  - Report symptoms without recognizing the impact or risk of those symptoms, or
  - Are confused or in conflict about the meaning of the symptoms.

- Focus on areas that are most relevant to your recommendations for treatment and any specific questions of concern for the client (e.g., What is wrong with me? Do I have schizophrenia? Why am I so depressed?).
- Share some preliminary impressions after two or more sessions, if your assessment takes longer than that, to help the client feel more engaged in the treatment.
- Be prepared to communicate what you have concluded and what information you are still seeking if the client asks about this before you have completed the assessment.
- Ask for the client's reactions and discuss any strong emotions or disagreements that arise.

Summary

This chapter discussed assessment as part of the therapeutic process, emphasizing the importance of approaching assessment collaboratively. The goals, elements, and outcome of assessment were reviewed, and guidelines for sharing assessment results with the client were provided. Specific areas of professional growth related to assessment are listed below.

1. Using yourself as an instrument of hope, change, and healing:

    a. Examine your conflict about conducting an assessment as a part of treatment.

2. Becoming confident in your authority and professionalism:

    a. Practice aspects of assessment with your supervisor and colleagues.
    b. Use assessment to facilitate effective treatment.
    c. Combine different sources of information into the assessment as needed.

3. Developing interpersonal skills that strengthen the therapeutic relationship:

    a. Integrate assessment with developing a therapeutic relationship.
    b. Share assessment results collaboratively in preparation for developing a treatment plan.

Case Example: Liz's Assessment of Susana

Liz's assessment included the following components:

- Six individual sessions with Susana,
- Administration of the Beck Depression Inventory (BDI-II; Beck et al., 1996) in the third session,
- Administration of the Alcohol Use Disorders Identification Test (AUDIT; Babor et al., 2001) in the third session,
- Consultation with Susana's internist regarding her migraine headaches and any other medical conditions that might contribute to her depression, and
- Consultation with the school counselor meeting with Susana's daughter Maria.

Liz requested Susana's permission to talk with the school counselor after Susana reported in the fourth session that Maria was referred to a counselor by one of her teachers.

Liz gave Dalia two drafts of her report: after the third session and after the sixth when the report was complete. Dalia gave feedback to Liz on the first draft, and they discussed the assessment in subsequent supervision sessions. Dalia approved the final draft after the sixth session, and she and Liz both signed the final copy.

Integration of Assessment and Therapeutic Relationship

Liz integrated the assessment with developing a therapeutic relationship in the following ways:

- She identified areas of Susana's life and history she wanted to explore and discuss in each session.
- She began each session with Susana's present concerns, and then looked for an opening to raise questions related to the assessment.
- She observed Susana's response to her and noted that Susana seemed to become increasingly open and comfortable.

Liz noticed that Susana responded positively to Liz's comments about her tendency to feel guilty and responsible toward others and to Liz's support for noticing and attending to her own emotional needs.

Initial Assessment

Client Name: Susana Rodriguez
Date of Birth: XX/XX/19XX
Date Case Opened: XX/XX/20XX
Clinician Name: Liz Matthews
Funding/Payment: $40 per session, paid by client

Presenting Problems: Client is a 36-year-old Latina, specifically a Salvadoran immigrant, who requested services following an argument with her boyfriend, which resulted in client's 15-year-old daughter calling 9–1–1. Client reported symptoms of depression in the first session as well as conflict with her daughter. She reported ambivalent feelings about the fact that her boyfriend had moved out following the 9–1–1 incident.

Diagnosis:

F33.0 Major Depressive Disorder, Recurrent Episode, Mild

Z62.820 Parent-Child Relational Problem

Z63.8 Disruption of Family by Separation or Divorce

Z65.4 Exposure to Disaster, War or Other Hostilities

Recurring migraine headaches

Symptoms: Client reported depressed mood, diminished pleasure, insomnia, fatigue, and diminished concentration every day for a period of 2 weeks prior to her request for services. These symptoms began when client's boyfriend moved out of their apartment following an argument during which client's daughter called 9–1–1. During the 7 weeks of treatment, client's symptoms have reduced somewhat in severity and frequency, although there was an increase in the last 2 weeks following client's contact with her boyfriend. Client's score on the BDI-II was 18, indicating mild depression. Client reported three prior episodes of depression: the first after one semester of college and the other two after the break-up of her two prior intimate relationships at ages 26 and 31. The first episode was accompanied by a suicide attempt involving an overdose of anxiety medication. Client reports that the two subsequent episodes were similar in severity and frequency to her current symptoms. Client's depression has had a mild impact on her daily functioning. She missed three days of work during the 2 weeks prior to beginning treatment, and she reports spending more time watching television and less time interacting with her children since the onset of her symptoms. Client also reported episodes at the beginning of her intimate relationships in which she felt "high" even though she wasn't using any substances. These episodes were accompanied by a decreased need for sleep, racing thoughts, and taking on new work or volunteer projects. None of these episodes resulted in any impairment in Susana's ability to work or care for her children, and they lasted a few months before her mood and energy level returned to normal.

Mental Status Exam: Client's appearance is neat, and she dresses in a casual professional style. Her activity level is within normal limits. She does not have any abnormal patterns of speech or language. Client is fluent in both English and Spanish, and she speaks English with a slight accent. She participated actively in the assessment, interacting with the clinician in a cooperative, collaborative manner. Client's mood has been mildly depressed, with overall improvement during the first six sessions. Client's affect has been appropriate to the content, and her affective expression was within normal limits. No cognitive deficits in memory, attention, or judgment are apparent, although client's insight regarding the impact of her recent relationship on her children is limited. Her thought processes and content are within normal limits.

Risk Factors: Client does not report any ideation or impulses that present a danger to herself or others. She made one suicide attempt at the age of 18 by taking an overdose of her roommate's anxiety medication. She reports no other history of suicide attempts or ideation. Client reports the presence of frequent verbal conflict in all three of her primary intimate relationships. She has been vague in her descriptions of relationship conflict, so it has not been possible to determine the degree of physical violence that may have been present. Client was born in El Salvador and immigrated with her parents and siblings when she was seven years old. She was exposed to the civil war from the age of 3 until the family's immigration, and several extended family members were killed during the war.

Substance Use: Client received a score of 19 on the AUDIT, endorsing items related to hazardous and harmful use as well as symptoms of dependence. She reports a significant reduction in drinking since her boyfriend left her home, and she does not meet criteria for alcohol use disorder at the present time. Client reports a level of alcohol use over the past year as equal to that during most of her adult life, although she did have one period of abstinence for a year while pregnant and breastfeeding her youngest daughter. Her current use is lower than at any other time since she began drinking at age 15. Client reports no misuse of prescription drugs, with the exception of an overdose of anxiety medication at age 18. She reports occasional use of marijuana from age 17 to 19 as her only use of other substances.

Cultural Influences: Client is a 36-year-old heterosexual female of Salvadoran ethnicity who immigrated to the United States with her parents and siblings at age 7. She became a U.S. citizen at age 13. She is lower middle-class in socioeconomic status and does not report any religious affiliation.

Coping Strategies, Strengths, and Resources: Client's primary coping strategies have been to minimize her emotional pain and to focus on getting through times of discomfort by telling herself that others are in worse circumstances than she is. Client's primary source of self-esteem has been to focus on the happiness of others, especially her intimate partners. This has contributed to her depression when her intimate relationships have ended. Client has maintained a consistent work history and has three children who are making appropriate developmental progress. Since beginning treatment, client has reduced her use of alcohol significantly, reporting that she is aware of a negative impact of her daily alcohol use on her children. Client's primary social support is one close friend with whom she feels able to share the details of her life and concerns. Client's mother and siblings live in Southern California, and she speaks with them by phone weekly. Client describes her family relationships as close, but she seems to feel more ambivalent toward her mother and siblings than she acknowledges directly. Client reports having a close extended family in El Salvador and missing the feeling of community she experienced there. She has no affiliations with religious or cultural groups at the present time.

Treatment Expectations: This is client's first experience with outpatient mental health treatment. She expressed some doubt about the usefulness of talking about her emotions and problems in the first two sessions but has reported feeling some relief since then. She entered treatment at the encouragement of a friend who has been a client at the Community Support Center. Client's goal is to be free of depression sooner than the 6 to 12 months it has taken for previous episodes to abate.

Current Life Circumstances: Client lives with her three children: a 16-year-old son, a 15-year-old daughter, and a 7-year-old daughter. Client's relationship of four years ended about 3 months ago. Client is employed in a clerical position at a small construction business, a job she has held for 6 years. She is a high school graduate and completed one semester of college. Her work and housing have been stable during her adult life, and she reports no significant financial or legal concerns.

History of Mental Health and Substance Use Treatment: Client was hospitalized for a week at the age of 18 following a suicide attempt in which she took an overdose of anxiety medication. She doesn't remember what kind of treatment was provided during this hospitalization, although she believes she was given medication. She discontinued the medication shortly after her release and didn't continue the recommended outpatient follow-up treatment. This is client's first outpatient mental health treatment, and she has no history of treatment for substance use. Client reports three periods of depression prior to the current episode that have lasted between 6 months and one year without intervention from traditional Western medicine or non-traditional healing practices.

Physical Health: Client has migraine headaches which are treated by her internist. This condition has been present since client was about 17 years old. Client reports herself to be in generally good health, which was confirmed by client's internist.

Family and Developmental History: Client moved from El Salvador to Southern California with her parents and two siblings when she was 7 years old. She was exposed to the civil war for 4 years before the move and several family members were killed during the war before and after client's family's immigration. Client's description of her immigration experience is focused on her parents' determination to leave El Salvador for the safety of client's older brother, and she expresses pride that they worked hard to gain U.S. citizenship for the family when client was 13. She and her family made one visit to the extended family in El Salvador approximately 10 years ago, which client reported as being very sad due to the loss of family members and the damage to their village. Despite the loss and disruption in her childhood, client does not report any significant difficulties in her emotional, social, or academic development. However, client does report that she began drinking at age 15, which seems to coincide with her brother's move out of the area. Client left her parents' home at age 18 to begin college but left after one semester, following a suicide attempt and hospitalization. She then married and had a child within the next year. Client's marriage and two subsequent intimate relationships seem to have involved a high degree of conflict and possibly physical violence. It has not been possible to assess the occurrence of physical violence due to client's reluctance to provide specific details. Client's 15-year-old daughter began treatment with a school counselor about 2 months ago, and the school counselor reported significant symptoms of anxiety in the daughter. The school counselor reported that the daughter has been reluctant to talk about the details of the 9–1–1 incident or prior episodes of conflict in the home but that she expresses a desire to continue in counseling to get help with her anxiety. Client reports no mental health symptoms in her other two children and no substance use by any of her children. The school counselor, however, indicated that client's daughter has disclosed some experimentation with alcohol and marijuana on social occasions with friends. Client reports that her father, who died 3 years ago, was alcoholic throughout client's childhood. She describes his pattern of drinking in El Salvador as consistent with cultural norms for men and reports that his pattern of heavy, daily use escalated after the family's immigration. Client's description of her mother suggests that the mother may have had episodes of depression during client's childhood which were undiagnosed and untreated.

Sharing the Results of the Assessment

Before the seventh session, Liz identified several aspects of her assessment that she wanted to discuss with Susana:

- The impact of Susana's exposure to the civil war and possible link with relationship violence,
- The results of the AUDIT indicating that Susana's alcohol use was harmful,
- The potential of genetic predisposition for both alcoholism and depression based on Susana's report of her father's alcoholism and possible depression in her mother, and
- The pattern of episodes of depression following separation from significant relationships.

Liz also wanted to talk with Susana about her conversation with the school counselor who said she could see Maria for 12 individual sessions and recommended a referral to a family therapy program after the 12 individual sessions. The family therapy would be available at no cost to Susana, through grant funding provided to the school.

Liz decided to use this discussion of her assessment to open the subject of relationship violence, which Susana had been reluctant to discuss. She did this in the following way:

Liz: As you know, I've been putting together the things you've shared with me about your life and your past and I wanted to share some thoughts I've had as I reviewed everything we've talked about. The early years of your life were spent in a civil war, with fear and violence a constant presence in your family and your village. Sometimes children cope with the constant threat of violence by pretending it isn't real or seeing the situation as less dangerous than it actually is. Do you think that's a possibility in your case?

Susana: Maybe. I just don't remember much about the war. Mostly I remember playing with my cousins and friends, and sometimes the soldiers would come and take some of the older boys with them to fight. I do remember hearing the fighting sometimes. My mom and my aunts would tell us to hide under the bed and sing songs until the noise stopped.

Liz: Are you aware of ways you were affected by living in the middle of a war? Do you think it has made any difference in how you deal with things in your adult life?

Susana: No, I don't think it has. I'm glad my parents found a way to bring us here and get citizenship. They always said they were glad we weren't there anymore, even though they missed everyone and worried about the people in our family who stayed.

Liz: One thing I wondered about is the difference between you and Maria in how you saw the arguments you had with Carlos. I remember you saying that the arguments weren't that bad, and your anger about Maria calling 9–1–1 was because you thought she was over-reacting. I wonder if your idea that the arguments weren't dangerous or violent might be related to how you needed to see your village as not that dangerous.

Susana: Are you saying Maria was right to call 9–1–1 and I was wrong to be mad at her?

Liz: I'm not thinking of this as right or wrong, but it seems possible that you may not be as aware of danger in your life as someone who didn't grow up in the middle of a war, like Maria.

Susana: I would never do anything that put my kids in danger. That's one thing my parents showed me, how important it is to get your kids out of danger. They found a way to leave when they saw my cousin taken by the soldiers and they thought it might happen to my brother too. Maria needs to understand that we can't have the police coming to the apartment. Carlos could have been deported, and I could have been in trouble. I heard about a mom whose kids were taken away because her husband beat her. When the police come in, bad things happen.

Liz: I can understand how frightened you were when the police came, afraid
        of what could happen to Carlos, to you, and to your kids. It may have
        felt similar to when the soldiers came to your village and took the older
        boys away to fight.

Susana: Maybe. I was really scared but mostly I was mad at Maria for bringing
        the police to the apartment. We still haven't talked about that night even
        though we're getting along with each other again.

Liz: I know you've had some questions about whether it would be a good
        idea for you and Maria to come in together to talk about what hap-
        pened. I spoke with Maria's counselor at school and she told me she can
        see Maria for 12 sessions. After that she recommended a family therapy
        program at the school, which would be available to you at no cost. I
        think it's a good idea for you and me to continue meeting individu-
        ally but it might be useful for you and your children to see a therapist
        together. What do you think about that?

Susana: I like coming here by myself. It's a relief to not be thinking about the
        kids when I'm here, since they take so much of my attention the rest
        of the time. I'm glad Maria has a counselor, but I don't know about family
        therapy. I'm afraid we'd just get mad at each other if we start talking
        about what happened.

Liz: I think Maria still has about six sessions left with her counselor, so you
        don't need to make a decision about that now.

Liz then asked Susana more about how it was to focus on herself and reflected her
experience of putting the needs of others ahead of her own needs. This required
Liz to set aside some of her frustration at Susana's lack of empathy for her children
because she recognized that Susana would be better able to attune to her children's
emotions when she felt understood by Liz.

Later in the session, Liz found an opportunity to share her view that Susana's
episodes of depression had followed separation from significant people in her
life—initially from her parents when she left for college and later from her husband and partner at the end of those relationships. They explored Susana's pattern
of putting a priority on making others happy and blaming herself when things
don't go well. Susana mentioned that her mother had become very sad when
her brother moved back to Los Angeles to work after his high school graduation.
Susana had hoped her mother would be glad that she was going to college close to
home, but her mother continued to be sad and withdrawn. Liz said this sequence
of events seemed to be the first example of Susana's depression following an experience of feeling guilty and responsible for failing to make someone else happy.

Liz decided to defer to the next session her discussion of Susana's harmful
alcohol use and potential genetic predisposition to both alcoholism and depression. She felt the issue of Susana's exposure to the war and possible relationship
violence had challenged her therapeutic relationship with Susana. Because of this,

Liz felt she needed to strengthen Susana's sense of Liz as an ally before bringing up another topic that could raise Susana's feelings of shame and protectiveness regarding her parents, leading to heightened defensiveness.

The Next Step

Chapter 7 will discuss the process of assessment in special situations related to danger to self or others, trauma, serious mental illness and psychosis, substance use and addiction, personality disorders, mandated treatment, and families involved in separation and divorce. The case example of Liz and Susana will continue in Chapter 8 with a description of Liz's clinical case formulation.

References

Antony, M. M., & Barlow, D. H. (Eds.) (2010). *Handbook of assessment and treatment planning for psychological disorders* (2nd ed.). New York, NY: The Guilford Press.

Babor, T. F., Higgins-Biddle, J. C., Saunders, J. B., & Monteiro, M. G. (2001). *AUDIT: The alcohol use disorders identification test* (2nd ed.). Geneva, Switzerland: World Health Organization.

Beck, A. T., Steer, R. A., & Brown, G. K. (1996). *BDI-II: Beck depression inventory* (2nd ed.). San Antonio, TX: The Psychological Corporation.

Ey, S., & Hersen, M. (2004). Pragmatic issues of assessment in clinical practice. In Hersen, M. (Ed.), *Psychological assessment in clinical practice: A pragmatic guide.* New York, NY: Brunner-Routledge.

Hays, P. A. (2008). *Addressing cultural complexities in practice: Assessment, diagnosis, and therapy* (2nd ed.). Washington, DC: American Psychological Association.

Wiger, D. E. (2012). *The psychotherapy documentation primer* (3rd ed.). Hoboken, NJ: John Wiley & Sons, Inc.

7

ASSESSMENT: SPECIAL SITUATIONS

(Note: This chapter will use the male pronoun for supervisor, clinician, and client.)

This chapter describes tools and approaches for complex clinical situations that require specialized assessment. If you are working in a setting that serves a large number of individuals or families with these concerns, your organization may have specialized procedures and tools. However, clients in any setting may present with issues that require specialized assessment, so I provide this information to help you prepare for an accurate assessment of the client's status and needs in those cases. Integrate these areas of assessment into your report as well as your case formulation.

Overview of Special Situations

I will review assessment principles regarding seven clinical presentations that require additional attention and careful consideration in treatment planning.

The first three issues should be included in your assessment of all clients. The discussion in this chapter describes additional steps to take if your client has significant symptoms in any of these areas:

• Danger to self or others,
• Trauma, or
• Substance use and addiction.

The next two areas should be assessed if your client's presentation suggests the presence of either

• Serious mental illness and psychosis or
• Personality disorders.

The last two areas are conditions of treatment that are usually known from the intake and referral information. I describe treatment guidelines for:

- Mandated treatment and
- Families involved in separation and divorce.

Clients who present with one or more of the clinical issues described in this chapter are *particularly challenging for clinicians in training.* The treatment is complex, and the establishment of a therapeutic relationship can be difficult. Be aware that you may need extra supervision and consultation on these cases. Seek out extra support from friends, colleagues, supervisors, and mentors to help you manage the intensity of the client's presentation and your countertransference responses. It is not appropriate to share the details of a specific case with individuals who are not directly involved, but you can discuss the impact on you with those who are close to and supportive of you. A general statement like, "I'm working with someone who suffered severe childhood trauma and it's really hard to hear her stories," is enough to give a context to your feelings of worry and distress without revealing clinical information.

Danger to Self or Others

All of your assessments include *questions about the client's current risk factors, both currently and historically.* Risk factors include suicidal thinking, suicide attempts, thoughts of harming others, and past violence toward others. You will need to go into more depth with clients who have current thoughts and feelings related to self-harm or violence toward others or whose history includes incidents of violence toward self or others. Review the risk assessments of all clients with your supervisor when you begin a new placement and when you begin to work with a client who has current or recent thoughts of harm to self or others. Be aware that your own personal history with self-harm and violence and your personal style in managing overwhelming emotion may lead you to over-estimate or under-estimate your client's risk, so your supervisor's input is an important check.

Suicide Risk

Clinicians in training often worry that asking a client about suicide will precipitate an incident of self-harm or increase the client's risk of acting on suicidal thoughts. However, this is not the case, and it is usually relieving to the client to be able to share thoughts and feelings that may have been hidden from others and reflect his level of distress and pain.

A *strong human connection is the best protective factor* for individuals with suicidal thoughts, feelings, and impulses, and your bond with the client will help him in his painful struggle. Suicidal clients who enter treatment are ambivalent about acting on their suicidality, even if they don't acknowledge their ambivalence overtly. A first step in your therapeutic relationship will be to strengthen the non-suicidal side of the client's conflict.

Initial risk assessment. I recommend *introducing the issue of suicide risk* in a simple, straightforward way, generally with the question: "Have you ever had thoughts of suicide?" or, "Have you ever had thoughts of hurting yourself?" If the client answers "yes" or seems hesitant, follow-up with a more detailed assessment. If the client answers "no" but has severe symptoms, a diagnosis of depression, multiple recent stressors, or a history of hospitalizations, follow-up with a question about a more subtle form of suicidal thinking. For example, you can ask, "Have you ever wished you just wouldn't wake up, or felt like you can't keep going?" and further assess the client's risk based on his answer.

If the client's answers do not lead you to do an in-depth assessment of suicidal risk, it is wise to *indicate your desire to follow-up and to ask the client to let you know if his risk increases.* A sample statement is

> When people are in as much distress as you are, they sometimes have thoughts about harming themselves. I will ask you about this from time to time, but I also want you to let me know if that happens for you. Are you willing to do that?

Detailed risk assessment. If the client indicates he has *current or recent suicidal thinking* based on his answer to your initial question or follow-up, do a suicide risk assessment. Sometimes clients will give you more information spontaneously and other times you will need to ask multiple follow-up questions.

First you can *determine the current level of risk* by asking, "When was the last time you had these thoughts?" followed by additional questions and discussion regarding the factors listed below (Bennett, Bricklin, Harris, Knapp, VandeCreek, & Younggren, 2006).

- Predisposition includes history of psychiatric diagnosis, suicidal attempts and behavior, trauma and family violence, and demographic factors. Males, European Americans, adolescents and young adults, older adults, and unmarried adults are groups at increased risk of dying by suicide. A family history of suicide is also associated with increased risk.
- Precipitants can include recent life events or chronic psychosocial stressors related to work, family, and intimate relationships, criminal justice involvement, health or financial problems, and other situations of loss.
- The severity and nature of symptoms contribute to suicide risk. Depression is the most common disorder associated with suicide, but anxiety, schizophrenia, and substance abuse are also associated with suicidal behavior.
- Hopelessness heightens the client's risk. If other risk factors are present, ask the client directly to rate his hopelessness on a 1-to-10 scale.

- Assess the features of the client's suicidal thinking, including

  - Frequency and intensity of suicidal thoughts,
  - Specificity of plan (e.g., "Have you thought about what you would do if you acted on these thoughts?"),
  - Availability of means (e.g., "Do you have access to _____ to carry out the plan?"), and
  - Intent (e.g., "What would be your purpose in carrying out your plan?") in light of the fact that some clients are seeking to escape pain, communicate their pain to others, or reduce tension rather than wanting to die.

- Previous suicidal behavior includes the number, frequency, and lethality of prior suicide attempts. If the client is at high risk, ask about whether he has made any preparations such as writing a note, giving away possessions, and preventing possible rescue.
- Assess the following indicators of heightened impulsivity:

  - Previous incidents of poor judgment,
  - Acting without thinking about consequences,
  - Quick changes in emotions leading to shifts in behavior,
  - Use of alcohol and other substances that may increase impulsivity, and
  - Level of anger or aggression.

  It is often helpful to ask the client directly about his impulsivity by using a 1-to-10 scale to rate his tendency to act without thinking about consequences or to feel out of control.

- Protective factors that moderate the client's risk are

  - Social support,
  - Problem-solving abilities,
  - Engagement in treatment,
  - Religious belief,
  - Awareness of the negative impact on family and friends, and
  - Other ways the client finds meaning.

The client's risk increases as the number and severity of risk factors increases, moderated by the number and strength of protective factors.

If your client has a high risk of suicidal behavior, *assess the client's ability to work toward decreasing his risk and the likelihood of acting on suicidal impulses.* Start with an attempt to work collaboratively with the client to increase his safety. A sample statement is, "I'm concerned about the risk you may harm yourself. What steps can you take to keep yourself safe until we meet again?" This discussion can lead to *development of a safety plan*, which is a set of steps the client agrees to take if his risk of acting on suicidal impulses increases. If you are working with a child or adolescent or with an adult whose capacity for self-care and judgment is limited, involve the parents or other family members and caregivers in safety planning.

You *may need to take immediate action* to ensure the client's safety if his risk is high and he is unable to collaborate with you on a safety plan. If he is uncertain about his ability to stay safe or if you doubt his ability to follow the safety plan, you will need to consider more immediate action. Consult with a supervisor or colleague if possible, asking the client to wait while you consult with a supervisor. In some settings, it is possible to have a colleague join your session. Actions to consider are

- Evaluate for hospitalization by contacting your local psychiatric emergency service or local law enforcement,
- Contact a family member or friend who can monitor the client's safety and call for assistance if needed, and
- Schedule a follow-up appointment with the client by phone or in person within a few hours or 1 to 2 days.

Self-Harm

Some clients engage in self-harming behavior which may or may not be associated with active suicidal thinking and intent. The term *parasuicidal behavior* is used to describe nonfatal, intentional self-harm (Linehan, 1993) which includes self-mutilation, cutting, and other self-injurious behavior intended to cause bodily harm. Clients who have repeated parasuicidal behavior often have limited ability to regulate emotions and often meet criteria for a diagnosis of borderline personality disorder (Linehan, 1993).

In your assessment of self-harming behavior, inquire about the intent and purpose of the self-harming behavior because it may reflect a desire for communication or tension reduction. Regardless of intent, *develop a safety plan* in collaboration with the client if the client's behavior is potentially lethal, using the guidelines above. Consider a *harm reduction approach* similar to that used with a client engaging in harmful substance use (Denning, Little, & Glickman, 2004). This approach will enable you to collaborate with the client in decreasing the risk of self-harming behavior while he works in treatment to develop different coping strategies.

Danger to Others

If your client makes threats to harm others, *assess the danger of him acting on the threats and take appropriate action* if the danger is high (Bennett et al., 2006). The factors to consider in assessing the client's dangerousness to others are similar to those used in assessing risk of suicide. When the client makes a threat to a third party or indicates a desire to harm someone, you can begin your assessment by asking, "Is this something you are thinking about or something you intend to do?" His response will help both of you distinguish between thoughts and intended actions.

If the client's history includes violence toward others and if there are current stressors and symptoms of impulsivity, *engage the client in safety planning to reduce the risk, or take protective action* if the client's risk remains high. In most settings you will encounter clients who are dangerous to others much less frequently than clients who are dangerous to themselves. However, if you work in a forensic setting or with clients who have a criminal history and/or live in a community characterized by violence, you will need to become familiar with assessment methods and agency procedures for situations that involve danger to others. Consult with your supervisor and other experienced colleagues as you would when working with suicide risk.

Reporting Obligations

The laws in your state may require you to contact law enforcement, warn potential victims, or recommend evaluation for hospitalization when your assessment indicates your client is at high risk of danger to self or others. Be sure you are familiar with the agency procedures for emergency situations. Review these procedures with your supervisor before you meet with a new client whose referral information indicates high risk and before a session with an ongoing client who is in crisis and has an elevated risk.

Trauma

I recommend asking all clients about the presence of past trauma during the assessment process, while allowing the client to determine the pace of specific disclosure. For example, you can say

> I ask all of my clients whether they have experienced trauma in the past. If you have, you can decide when you feel it would be useful to talk about it, but it's useful for me to know whether any past trauma might be related to the issues that are troubling you now.

The client can then respond to you with whatever level of detail is comfortable for him, preserving his sense of control over the degree of disclosure and the accompanying emotions.

Most training settings have a *high proportion of clients who have experienced trauma in the recent and/or distant past.* DSM-5 is the first edition that establishes a specific category of trauma- and stressor-related disorders, which brings together diagnoses that had been in different categories in previous editions. The criteria for two of these diagnoses—posttraumatic stress disorder and acute stress disorder—define a traumatic event as:

> exposure to actual or threatened death, serious injury, or sexual violence by directly experiencing, witnessing the event occurring to others, learning

that the traumatic event occurred to a close family member or close friend, or experiencing repeated or extreme exposure to details of traumatic events in a work context (APsyA, 2013, p. 271).

Lack of control and unpredictability are common to many types of traumatic events, and contribute to the resulting symptoms of intrusive recall, avoidance of reminders, and alterations in cognition, mood, and arousal (Allen, 2001; APsyA, 2013).

Diagnosis

Assessment of the relationship between the client's current symptoms and past traumatic events can be difficult, especially when the trauma occurred in the distant past, and the client may be unclear about the details and/or may not want to discuss them. Survivors of trauma may present symptoms of depression, anxiety, substance use, and/or other disorders in addition to meeting the criteria for a diagnosis related to the trauma.

If the presence and nature of the client's trauma is unclear, begin with another diagnosis and shift to a trauma-related diagnosis if the client reveals more about his life and history that makes it clear the symptoms originate with past trauma. Marking the trauma-related diagnosis as provisional is another way to indicate your preliminary hypothesis to be confirmed later in treatment. Since traumatic events are experienced as uncontrollable and unpredictable, it is important to allow the client to disclose details of these events as he feels ready to do so.

Your agency may have *additional tools for assessing the presence and impact of trauma*, especially if you are using trauma-based treatment models, based on client report and interview (Steenkamp, McLean, Arditte, & Litz, 2010). Be aware that the definition of trauma may vary in different cultural groups and communities, and the impact of community violence may be minimized by some individuals who have experienced multiple traumatic events.

Trauma in Attachment Relationships

Trauma in attachment relationships includes childhood physical and sexual abuse, childhood neglect, domestic violence, and emotional abuse. In these cases, the perpetrator of the trauma is someone on whom the child or adult depended in the past or depends in the present for safety and security, and it is likely that the trauma was repeated multiple times (Allen, 2001). The presence of trauma in attachment relationships increases the severity of the client's symptoms and the negative impact on the client's development and functioning.

I recommend asking all clients in intimate relationships about the level of conflict with their partner and whether there has been any physical contact during an argument (Bennett et al., 2006). Adolescents and adults who have experienced childhood trauma may minimize and be reluctant to disclose the presence of violence in their intimate relationships. You can open this discussion by saying, "All relationships include disagreement and conflict. Could you tell me about how you and your partner express disagreements?" After this general question, ask more detailed questions if the client seems willing to talk about high conflict in the relationship. Examples are, "Have things ever escalated beyond loud voices?" or, "Have you ever felt you or your partner have gone too far in an argument?"

Recent Trauma and Reporting Obligations

State laws and regulations may require you to report instances of abuse and neglect. Familiarize yourself with agency procedures for informing clients of this obligation and for making a report when you are required to do so. Most often, you are required to report instances where a child under 18, an adult over 65, or a dependent or disabled adult has been harmed or is in danger of harm.

Making a report is clinically challenging when the client's treatment is ongoing, so consult with your supervisor to ensure you take steps to keep the client engaged in treatment. Talking with the client before or after making the report about the reasons for your action and the likely result of the report is sometimes clinically indicated. When making a child abuse report, remember that the parent may have experienced childhood abuse and neglect himself. The value of children's safety and protection that you communicate by making a report is relevant to the parent's past trauma as well as his current struggles with his child. You can sometimes address this directly with a statement like

> I know that no one intervened when you were being mistreated as a child, and I know you want a better life for your children. We can work together on different ways to handle the frustration and stress you feel so that your children can feel safer than you did.

Substance Use and Addiction

Ask each client about current and past substance use and the presence of other addictive behaviors. There is a high incidence of co-occurring mental health and substance use disorders for adolescents and adults, and integrated treatment is generally more effective with clients who have symptoms of one or more mental health disorders as well as substance use disorders (Substance Abuse and Mental Health Services Administration, 2009).

Assessment Methods

Your training site may have one or more assessment instruments and methods for substance use and addiction. An approach that includes screening, brief intervention, and referral to treatment (SBIRT) has been developed for use in health care settings and may be used in your training setting (Substance Abuse and Mental Health Services Administration, 2013). The approach involves universal screening of all individuals in order to identify problematic substance use behaviors that may not meet diagnostic criteria but may warrant intervention as a preventive strategy.

Assessment of substance use generally begins with a brief screening to determine whether the client engages in high-risk or problematic use of alcohol or other drugs (Tucker, Murphy, & Kertesz, 2010). If the screening indicates the client's use is problematic, you may continue to a longer interview or questionnaire, depending on the assessment practice in your agency. Be aware that most individuals who engage in problematic substance use or addictive behavior minimize the extent of their use as well as the consequences of their use, due to the presence of denial in addiction (Chamberlain & Jew, 2005). Clients may be more willing and able to be truthful about the extent of their substance use and its associated problems after weeks or months of treatment, at which time they have developed greater trust in the therapeutic relationship.

Introduce the subject of substance use with a general statement like, "At our agency, we ask all clients about their use of alcohol and other drugs since that can be related to physical and emotional well-being." If you believe the client may be reluctant to discuss his use, you can add, "Would it be all right with you if I ask some questions about your use of alcohol and other drugs?" or, "Would you be willing to tell me about your use of alcohol and other drugs?" to reduce the client's feelings of being coerced. This approach is consistent with principles of Motivational Interviewing (Miller & Rollnick, 2002), an approach developed to facilitate a respectful, collaborative treatment relationship with individuals whose use of substances is problematic.

Models of Addiction

The *Stages of Change* model of addiction helps in assessment and treatment planning with clients who use substances in a harmful way (Norcross, Krebs, & Prochaska, 2011). This model conceptualizes five stages that characterize clients' attitudes and movement toward change:

- Precontemplation,
- Contemplation,
- Preparation,
- Action, and
- Maintenance.

Assessment of the client's stage of change will enable you to match your treatment goals and interventions to his needs.

Keep in mind a *biopsychosocial model* of addiction that takes physiological, cognitive, interpersonal, and social factors into account. Intervention can target any of these factors, generally beginning with the area of the greatest motivation for the client. Some areas to consider are medication evaluation, stress management and mindfulness, analysis of cognitive and affective triggers for behavior, insight into family models of addiction and codependence, development of communication skills, and creation of a network of social support that is centered on non-addictive activities.

Serious Mental Illness and Psychosis

During your training, you are likely have experience with clients who have diagnoses of a psychotic disorder or who present with psychotic symptoms but have not been diagnosed by another clinician. The term *serious mental illness* generally refers to the diagnoses in the Schizophrenia Spectrum and Other Psychotic Disorders category in the DSM-5 as well as Bipolar Disorder with Psychotic Features and Depressive Disorder with Psychotic Features. The *features of psychosis* are

- Delusions,
- Hallucinations,
- Disorganized thinking and speech,
- Disorganized or abnormal motor behavior, and
- Decreased emotional expression and self-initiated action, called negative symptoms.

An individual may have symptoms in one or more of these domains of functioning (APsyA, 2013, pp. 87–88). When a client presents with any of the above symptoms, you should do a more complete assessment of psychotic symptoms, and consider a psychotic disorder as the primary diagnosis.

Assessment Methods

You can assess the presence of psychotic symptoms based on:

- Specific assessment measures,
- A diagnosis previously given by a psychiatrist or another clinician, and
- Interview questions.

Check with your supervisor about the availability at your agency of assessment tools for psychosis. If your agency does not have specific measures and your client doesn't have a prior diagnosis, you will need to assess psychotic symptoms by means of interview questions.

I recommend introducing *questions about psychotic symptoms* using language that is non-stigmatizing and that captures the client's subjective experience. Examples are, "Some people find they see or hear things that other people don't. Does that ever happen for you?" or, "Some people find their beliefs are quite different from what other people think, and this can lead to conflict. Has that been true for you?" If a client holds unusual beliefs and pressures you to validate or agree with him, I find it most effective to both express a desire to understand the client and to acknowledge my own perspective is different from his. I would do this by saying

> I can tell that this belief is very important to you, and I'd like to understand it better. I don't see things the same way you do, but I do want to know more about the meaning your belief has for you.

Or I might say

> I don't know whether the police have a conspiracy against you, but I imagine it's pretty frightening for you to have that experience. Maybe we can figure out some ways for you to feel less scared.

Countertransference

Countertransference feelings of fear and confusion are common when assessing a client whose symptoms and behavior are odd and whose ideas and beliefs do not match consensual views of reality. I find my countertransference feelings more manageable when I remember that individuals with psychotic disorders often feel endangered, filled with dread, profoundly isolated, and internally disorganized. A calm, authoritative, straightforward therapeutic style is most effective (McWilliams, 2011; Saks, 2007).

Recovery Model

Since the 1990s, mental health advocates have emphasized the importance of supporting individuals to recover from serious mental illness, manage their symptoms, and live productive lives (Clay, 2012; Copeland, 2002). Assessment of a client's psychotic symptoms should include the impact of his symptoms on school or work, social and family relationships, and independent living so that you can identify steps toward greater recovery and functioning (Pratt & Mueser, 2010). Collaborative treatment planning with clients who have psychotic disorders helps to counteract the disempowerment that often accompanies psychosis. The client will benefit from your active encouragement of his participation in developing a plan for your work together.

Personality Disorders

Personality disorders are usually co-occurring with another diagnosis related to mood, anxiety, or trauma. Accurate assessment is important because a personality disorder diagnosis impacts all aspects of treatment. You can expect that clients with a personality disorder diagnosis will be slower to improve in mood, anxiety, or trauma-related symptoms and that the therapeutic alliance will be more difficult to establish and maintain.

You *may be reluctant to think about your adult clients having a personality disorder diagnosis* due to the stigma attached to the diagnosis or due to anxiety about facing the complexities in treatment that accompany this diagnosis. However, if you fail to consider a personality disorder diagnosis when it is warranted, you are likely to be less effective in helping the client. This situation often leads to both you and the client feeling discouraged and may heighten the client's feelings of distress and failure.

The DSM-5 defines a personality disorder as "an enduring pattern of inner experience and behavior that deviates markedly from the expectations of the individual's culture, is pervasive and inflexible … is stable over time, and leads to distress or impairment" (APsyA, 2013, pp. 646–647). The diagnosis is usually applied only to adults over 18. Maladaptive personality traits may be apparent in children and adolescents, but personality continues to be malleable during the developmental process of adolescence.

Assessment Methods

Consider a personality disorder diagnosis when your client presents with:

- Repetitive interpersonal problems and conflicts,
- Continued use of coping strategies that are maladaptive and ineffective, and/or
- An intense positive or negative response to you.

Your supervisor's experience and perspective will contribute to your assessment, since it is difficult early in your training to recognize the signs of a personality disorder.

A personality disorder diagnosis is *based on the individual's deviation from cultural standards*, so become familiar with the relevant norms before making a diagnosis. Cultural variables are especially relevant when assessing dependence and suspiciousness, since these factors are highly affected by cultural norms and by experiences of discrimination (Hays 2008). Norms for emotional expressiveness and development of self-identity are also highly variable among different cultural groups.

There are a number of *empirical measures that can be used for assessment*, including structured and semistructured interviews as well as questionnaires (Widiger & Lowe, 2010). Most clinicians diagnose personality disorders through an unstructured clinical interview and the ongoing therapeutic relationship. The diagnostic system in the Psychodynamic Diagnostic Manual (PDM Task Force,

2006) contains a more complex diagnostic system for diagnosing personality disorders and is a valuable clinical tool.

Countertransference

Your *countertransference is often informative* regarding the presence of a personality disorder diagnosis. Because a personality disorder involves a pattern of thoughts, feelings, and interpersonal behaviors that occur across different situations, you will experience aspects of the client's pattern directly and repeatedly. For example, you may feel intimidated or confused, you may have trouble remembering what the client said or what happened in the session, you may find yourself talking much more or much less than usual, or you may even feel bored and sleepy. Other common countertransference responses are feeling intensely affected by the client in either a positive or negative direction, responding to the client in ways that feel unfamiliar and uncharacteristic of you, or experiencing rapidly shifting emotional responses throughout the session or between sessions.

Early in training, most clinicians have difficulty connecting these unfamiliar and troubling responses to the client. You may explain these responses to yourself by saying or thinking such things as

- I don't know enough to help this person,
- I have a test tomorrow and I was preoccupied,
- The client really needed my advice, or
- I didn't get enough sleep last night.

Over time and with your supervisor's help, you will learn to evaluate the degree to which your responses are related to the client's presentation and diagnosis. This will contribute to your assessment of the client's personality pattern and a possible diagnosis of personality disorder.

Mandated Treatment

Some examples of situations involving mandated treatment are probation requiring treatment, diversion programs for drug or alcohol offenses, alternative sentencing programs, or plans for a parent to retain or regain custody of his children after a child abuse report. When treatment is mandated or required by another authority, you will face *challenges in obtaining an accurate assessment of the client's symptoms and functioning*. The client will usually be reluctant to disclose information if he knows or believes you will report it to the mandating authority. He may also be motivated to be compliant with your expectations and to withhold information from you in order to receive a positive evaluation from you.

Communication with Mandating Authorities

When you begin treatment with a mandated client, check with your supervisor about the *agency procedures for communicating with mandating authorities*. It may be possible to limit your reports to general information such as dates of attendance, diagnosis, treatment goals, and a general description of progress.

Once you are clear about your required communication, inform the client as to what information you will report to the mandating authority, and acknowledge the clinical dilemma created by the situation. An example of how you might communicate this to the client is

> I will need to tell your probation officer when you attend and what goals we are working on, but I won't give him the details of what we talk about. Even so, I imagine it's hard for you to feel comfortable talking to me since coming here wasn't your choice. You might also be worried about how the information I give your probation officer will affect you.

The client may be reluctant to acknowledge any difficulty with the situation, but your recognition of his dilemma will contribute to the therapeutic relationship.

Give the client a copy of all written reports you send, and tell him about all phone conversations you have with the authority. This will also *help the client to build trust in the therapeutic relationship* over time. Keep in mind that the client may hear a different version of your conversation from the mandating authority, so invite him to let you know if he has any questions about your communication. Continue to raise the dilemma about mandated treatment as examples arise in the treatment. The client may be able to disclose more as he experiences your openness about your communication with the authority.

You can address the clinical dilemma of mandated treatment in a different way *when the client tells you about something positive*. For example, he may tell you about staying clean and sober, attending required classes, or managing interpersonal conflict in a nonviolent way. A statement that acknowledges his accomplishment and invites discussion of the dilemma is

> I'm glad to hear that you were able to meet one of your goals, but I also wonder if you'd be able to tell me if you weren't. Do you have any thoughts about how you might handle that situation if it happened?

Professional Boundaries in Mandated Treatment

In mandated treatment, you may feel pulled at times to shift from the role of clinician to that of advocate. The client may give you information that suggests he has been treated wrongfully or that the mandating authority is unreasonably demanding. You will do the client a disservice if you assume an advocacy role, and doing so is a violation of professional boundaries. As the treating clinician, your job is to support and assist the client to manage his requirements and legal situation with as much emotional strength and stability as possible. Any action you take outside of that role detracts from your ability to be therapeutic and to foster your client's coping skills. Your supervisor should approve all written reports, information you give to anyone connected with your client's case, and decisions you make about contacting authorities or community resources.

Families Involved in Separation and Divorce

(Note: This section will use both male and female pronouns when referring to parents, in order to be clear that the issues described apply equally to mothers and fathers.)

In most training settings, you will serve a number of children and parents who are affected by separation and divorce, whether they identify those circumstances as a precipitating factor to their entering treatment. There are a number of issues you need to address in these cases, and it works best to do this at the beginning of treatment, during the period of assessment and treatment planning, rather than later when the issue may become more complicated.

Unless otherwise noted, these issues apply to individual treatment with a parent, individual child treatment with collateral parent sessions, family treatment with the participation of one or both parents, and couple treatment of parents who make a decision to separate. The legal issues for parents who were never married may be different from those of parents who were married and subsequently divorce. Check with your supervisor and become familiar with your agency policies to ensure that you have addressed all relevant issues, especially when you are working with children whose parents are separated or divorced.

Common Clinical Presentation

A common clinical presentation involving divorce is that a parent requests treatment for him or herself and/or a child. The parent requesting treatment often describes the other parent as abusive and uncaring and says he or she needs support for the difficult and costly court battle in which he or she is at a disadvantage because the other parent has more money or power with the court. In such cases, the parent often presents for treatment with a desperate request for support for him or herself and for the child. He or she reports that the child returns from visits with the other parent highly anxious and distressed but that the court has ordered the child to continue visits based on joint custody.

When you hear this presentation, you are *likely to feel a sense of urgency to intervene* and make things better for the parent and child. It will require a lot of effort for you to remain objective in the face of the parent's emotionally compelling presentation, but you will only be able to serve the family appropriately if you do. Often the other parent has an equally charged but divergent version of the situation. The child's symptoms are more likely related to the high degree of conflict between the parents than to the child's experience during visits with the non-custodial parent. High parental conflict is the primary factor affecting children's well-being during and after divorce (Kelly & Emery, 2003).

The sample presentation above highlights several issues that commonly arise for the clinician treating families involved in separation and divorce, specifically

- Parents' desire for advocacy in legal custody cases,
- Decisions about parental consent and involvement in child treatment,
- Pressure to fill multiple roles for the family, and
- Holding different perspectives of two parents.

I discuss each of these issues below and offer guidelines for maintaining professional boundaries, objectivity, and care for the child's emotional well-being.

Parents' Desire for Advocacy in Legal Custody Cases

There are many factors involved in the request for treatment by divorcing parents, especially if they are in high conflict. The request for treatment for themselves or their children is likely due to a number of undisclosed and possibly unconscious factors, including desires to strengthen their position in a custody case and to create an advocacy relationship with the clinician against the other parent. Usual assumptions you make about a parent coming to treatment voluntarily, presenting accurate information, and having a goal of enhancing the child's well-being may be unfounded in these cases (Bennett et al., 2006).

It is imperative to inform a separated or divorced parent at the beginning of treatment that *you will not provide any testimony or records to support his or her position in any legal matter related to the divorce or custody*. Your agency may include this information as part of the standard informed consent process, and if not, I suggest working with your supervisor to create a written statement that you give to the parent and keep in the file. If you receive any communication or request from an attorney or court official or if your client requests that you talk with his or her attorney, consult with your supervisor before you respond.

Decisions about Parental Consent and Involvement in Child Treatment

It is best clinical practice to request consent from both parents when treating a child, either individually or with one parent. An exception can be made when one parent has sole legal custody and produces a supporting court document. State law may not require consent of both parents if they are married, living together, or are divorced with joint custody; however, you will avoid many difficult clinical situations if you request consent from both parents and document your efforts to do so. In a high-conflict divorce, consider requiring consent from both parents before beginning the child's treatment. Check with your supervisor about this issue when a new case is assigned to you, so that you can be clear with the requesting parent in your initial phone conversation.

Best clinical practice when doing individual child treatment is to *meet collaterally with both parents in separate sessions at the same frequency*. Often one parent is highly anxious and desires contact on a weekly basis or more often, and the other parent is reluctant to participate. Talk with your supervisor about how to set appropriate limits with the anxious parent and to engage the reluctant parent.

Pressure to Fill Multiple Roles for the Family

Support in custody cases. The most common request from divorcing parents is for you to provide support for their position in a custody case. This request is often accompanied with a statement like, "You know me so well and you know how hard I've worked to be a good parent to my kids." If you are the parent's individual therapist and are unfamiliar with common dynamics in divorcing families, you may understand the parent's position, feel convinced that your client is the better parent, and want to support him or her in court. If you are the child's therapist and have not included the other parent in treatment, you may also believe it is in the child's interest for you to support the parent's request.

Taking sides in this way is a mistake, and it is a *violation of the ethical principle regarding dual roles* (AAMFT, 2001; APA, 2002; NASW, 2008). Expressing an opinion about an individual's fitness as a parent is part of the role of an evaluator and is different from the role of a therapist. As a therapist, your role is to understand and support your client and his or her perspective. An evaluator's role in a custody case is to be objective in looking at the strengths and weaknesses of both parents in relation to the child's needs. Meeting a parent's request for your support in a custody case creates a dual role relationship and is an ethical violation.

Different therapeutic roles. You may get requests from divorcing families to fill different therapeutic roles. These families often have multiple needs, especially in cases of high-conflict divorce, and the parents may request multiple services from you. This request is often accompanied with a statement like, "I don't want to start over with another person. Since you already know my child and my situation, I'd like to see you myself to talk about how stressful this is." Examples of different therapeutic needs and roles are (a) individual parent treatment, (b) individual child treatment, (c) family treatment for the child and one parent, and (d) family treatment for the siblings.

When working with any configuration of family members during or after divorce, *establish a clear role for yourself* at the beginning of treatment and limit your involvement to the activities that are consistent with that role. Treating the individual parent, the child with collateral parent sessions, or the family entail different types of therapeutic relationships and should not be mixed. Your supervisor can be helpful in defining your role and setting limits with the parent when necessary.

Therapeutic and other legally defined roles. Parents of your child clients may also request that you meet with them together to make decisions about the divorce, mediate conflicts about parenting issues, or develop plans for co-parenting. You may see the need for the parents to be more cooperative with each other and want to help create a better environment for your child client. However, the roles of mediator, co-parenting counselor, and parent coordinator are incompatible with the role of therapist. Meeting the parents' request *creates a dual role relationship and is an ethical violation* as described above (AAMFT, 2001; APA, 2002; NASW, 2008).

In addition to the dual role relationship, mediation, co-parenting counseling, and parent coordination are *legally defined specialty areas*. They require specialized training and should not be attempted unless you have ongoing training and supervision from someone with that expertise. It may seem as though your training in couple therapy would prepare you to work with parents in these ways, but working with divorcing parents does not involve the same goals as couple therapy. Many ethical dilemmas can arise when working with families who are involved with the court system (Greenberg, Gould-Saltman, & Gottlieb, 2008).

Holding Different Perspectives of Two Parents

Divorcing parents often have widely differing opinions, feelings, and beliefs about themselves, the other parent, and their children. It is important to keep these differences in mind when you are seeing an individual parent going through divorce, but they will enter the treatment directly when the child is your client, often creating confusion and discomfort in you. You are likely to feel that only one parent can be right, you may wonder if one parent is lying, you may be tempted to reduce the frequency of collateral sessions with one or both parents to reduce your discomfort, and you will almost certainly feel protective of the child. Countertransference feelings often include discouragement, hopelessness, and anger.

Remember that your child client is exposed regularly to these widely disparate experiences and perspectives of the two parents and that one of the ways you can be helpful is to *find ways to hold the feelings of all the parties involved*. It is very difficult to do this, but if you can succeed it will be invaluable to the child. Holding these disparate feelings also gives you an experiential basis for talking with the parents about the importance of reducing their conflict with each other in order to help their child. The child is best served when he or she is able to have a relationship with each parent based on that parent's strengths and caring for the child.

Summary

This chapter reviewed seven areas of clinical presentation that require specialized assessment and require some specific interventions to establish a strong therapeutic relationship: (a) danger to self or others, (b) trauma, (c) substance use and addiction, (d) serious mental illness and psychosis, (e) personality disorders, (f) mandated treatment, and (g) families involved in separation and divorce. Specific areas of professional growth related to these areas are listed below.

1. Using yourself as an instrument of hope, change, and healing:

    a. Seek extra supervision, consultation, and support when working with these complex cases.
    b. Reflect on countertransference responses when working with psychosis and personality disorders.

2. Becoming confident in your authority and professionalism:

    a. Learn procedures for assessment of danger to self or others and for safety planning.
    b. Become familiar with reporting obligations.
    c. Learn to use assessment tools and techniques for trauma, addiction, psychosis, and personality disorders.

3. Developing interpersonal skills that strengthen the therapeutic relationship:

    a. Practice skills applicable to different populations:
        i. Allow clients to set the pace of disclosure about past trauma.
        ii. Use principles of Motivational Interviewing, Stages of Change model, and biopsychosocial model with harmful or problematic substance use and addiction.
        iii. Acknowledge the clinical dilemma present in mandated treatment.
        iv. Maintain professional boundaries, objectivity, and care for the child's emotional well-being with families involved in separation and divorce.

References

Allen, J. G. (2001). *Traumatic relationships and serious mental disorders*. Chichester, West Sussex, England: John Wiley & Sons.

American Association for Marriage and Family Therapy. (2001). *Code of ethics*. Alexandria, VA: Author.

American Psychiatric Association. (2013). *Diagnostic and statistical manual of mental disorders* (5th ed.). Arlington, VA: Author.

American Psychological Association. (2002). Ethical principles of psychologists and code of conduct. *American Psychologist, 57,* 1060–1073.

Bennett, B. E., Bricklin, P. M., Harris, E., Knapp, S., VandeCreek, L., & Younggren, J. N. (2006). *Assessing and managing risk in psychological practice: An individualized approach.* Rockville, MD: The Trust.

Chamberlain, L. L., & Jew, C. L. (2005). Assessment and diagnosis. In Stevens, P. & Smith, R. L. (Eds.). *Substance abuse counseling: Theory and practice* (3rd ed.). Upper Saddle River, NJ: Pearson Prentice Hall.

Clay, R. A. (2012). Yes, recovery is possible. *Monitor on Psychology, 43,* 53–55.

Copeland, M.E. (2002). *Wellness recovery action plan®* (Rev. ed.). West Dummerston, VT: Peach Press.

Denning, P., Little, J., & Glickman, A. (2004). *Over the influence: The harm reduction guide for managing drugs and alcohol.* New York, NY: The Guilford Press.

Greenberg, L. R., Gould-Saltman, D. J., & Gottlieb, M. C. (2008). Playing in their sandbox: Professional obligations of mental health professionals in custody cases. *Journal of Child Custody, 5,* 192–216.

Hays, P. A. (2008). *Addressing cultural complexities in practice: Assessment, diagnosis, and therapy* (2nd ed.). Washington, DC: American Psychological Association.

Kelly, J. B., & Emery, R. E. (2003). Children's adjustment following divorce: Risk and resilience perspectives. *Family Relations, 52,* 352–362.

Linehan, M. M. (1993). *Cognitive-behavioral treatment of borderline personality disorder.* New York, NY: The Guilford Press.

McWilliams, N. (2011). *Psychoanalytic diagnosis: Understanding personality structure in the clinical process* (2nd ed.). New York, NY: The Guilford Press.

Miller, W. R. & Rollnick, S. (2002). *Motivational interviewing: Preparing people for change* (2nd ed.). New York, NY: The Guilford Press.

National Association of Social Workers. (2008). *Code of ethics.* Washington, DC: Author. Retrieved May 4, 2012, from http://www.naswdc.org/pubs/code/code.asp.

Norcross, J. C., Krebs, P. M., & Prochaska, J. O. (2011). Stages of change. In Norcross, J. C. (Ed.). *Psychotherapy relationships that work: Evidence-based responsiveness* (2nd ed.). New York, NY: Oxford University Press.

PDM Task Force. (2006). *Psychodynamic diagnostic manual.* Silver Spring, MD: Alliance of Psychoanalytic Organizations.

Pratt, S. & Mueser, K. T. (2010). Schizophrenia. In Antony, M. M., & Barlow, D. H. (Eds.). *Handbook of assessment and treatment planning for psychological disorders* (2nd ed.). New York, NY: The Guilford Press.

Saks, E. R. (2007). *The center cannot hold: My journey through madness.* New York, NY: Hyperion.

Steenkamp, M., McLean, C. P., Arditte, K. A., & Litz, B. T. (2010). Exposure to trauma in adults. In Antony, M. M., & Barlow, D. H. (Eds.). *Handbook of assessment and treatment planning for psychological disorders* (2nd ed.). New York, NY: The Guilford Press.

Substance Abuse and Mental Health Services Administration. (2009). *Integrated treatment for co-occurring disorders evidence-based practices (EBP) KIT: The evidence.* Retrieved January 18, 2016, from http://store.samhsa.gov/shin/content//SMA08-4367/TheEvidence-ITC.pdf.

Substance Abuse and Mental Health Services Administration. (2013). *Systems-level implementation of screening, brief intervention, and referral to treatment.* Technical Assistance Publication (TAP) Series 33. Retrieved March 3, 2014, from http://www.integration.samhsa.gov/sbirt/TAP33.pdf.

Tucker, J. A., Murphy, J. G., & Kertesz, S. G. (2010). Substance use disorders. In Antony, M. M. & Barlow, D. H. (Eds.). *Handbook of assessment and treatment planning for psychological disorders* (2nd ed.). New York, NY: The Guilford Press.

Widiger, T. A. & Lowe, J. R. (2010). Personality disorders. In Antony, M. M., & Barlow, D. H. (Eds.). *Handbook of assessment and treatment planning for psychological disorders* (2nd ed.). New York, NY: The Guilford Press.

8

CASE FORMULATION

(Note: This chapter will use the female pronoun for supervisor, clinician, and client.)

This chapter discusses the process of clinical case formulation, which emerges from your assessment and guides your thinking about a treatment plan that will be helpful to your client. The case formulation consists of your ideas about how and why the client developed her current symptoms, what factors contribute to her distress and maladaptive behavior, and what strengths and resources she has available to help her manage and overcome her symptoms. In this chapter, you will learn about the purpose of a case formulation, how to connect the client's past history and presenting symptoms in a formulation, and the importance of including strengths in your formulation. I will introduce a model for writing case formulations from any theoretical perspective.

Purpose of Case Formulation

A clinical case formulation is a necessary step in an effective treatment. It is an opportunity to reflect on the information you have gained from the client and other sources during your assessment. Its purpose is *to develop a cohesive explanation for the client's symptoms and presenting problem* that leads to goals and interventions that are likely to help the client. You will describe the factors that maintain the client's symptoms, as they are key to making therapeutic interventions that will lead to an improvement in those symptoms. For example, a client who is depressed following a break-up with an abusive partner may need assistance with recognizing and avoiding patterns of control and exploitation by others in order to increase her self-efficacy. In contrast, a client whose depression is associated with a longstanding pattern of social isolation may benefit from an exploration of her fears about being in close relationships.

Also essential to the case formulation is a *description of the client's strengths and coping strategies,* as they will influence your choices for treatment goals and interventions. For example, a client who has coped with early loss by becoming independent and self-reliant may benefit from interventions that support her engaging in activities on her own. You might consider encouraging her to research options for dealing with her particular symptoms and to discuss what she finds in session with you. By contrast, a client who coped with early loss by becoming a caregiver may need support for finding activities in which she can feel connected and useful to others.

The case formulation also provides *an orientation and guide during treatment* as circumstances and crises change. It can be helpful to review your case formulation at different points in your work or any time you feel confused or bewildered. The case formulation is a bird's eye view that can stabilize your thinking when you become lost in the details of the moment. You may need to revise aspects of your case formulation as you work with the client over time and gain more knowledge of her relational patterns and obstacles to full functioning. However, the main core of the formulation should remain stable if it is founded on a comprehensive assessment and a sound theoretical base. It is useful to hold the formulation in mind as the treatment unfolds.

Connecting Past History and Presenting Symptoms

Regardless of the theoretical perspective you choose, your formulation should describe the *link between the client's past experiences and her current symptoms,* using the explanatory framework of your chosen theory. Your assessment will identify the coping strategies your client developed to manage early adverse and painful experiences. While these strategies were the best adaptation she could make in childhood, they usually have long-term consequences that interfere with leading a satisfying and productive life.

Over time you will learn that clients who have experienced similar childhood events have different symptoms that bring them to treatment. For example, one young woman who was sexually abused during childhood might leave home at 17 and cut off contact with her family while another might remain with her family and begin using substances at age 17. Both might enter treatment at age 25, with the first woman showing symptoms of isolation and depression while the second describes anxiety and dependence on others. Therefore, your formulation should provide an explanation of *how this particular client interpreted, coped with, and was shaped by her early experiences* in ways that led to her current difficulties.

A clinical case formulation is *grounded in a theoretical orientation* that addresses psychological development, psychopathology, and therapeutic change. Based on that theoretical orientation, you prepare an explanation for your client's current symptoms, in view of her early life circumstances and coping strategies. Depending on your clinical setting, you may be expected to write a formulation from one specific theoretical orientation or you may be able to choose among several orientations. It is generally helpful to write a formulation from one orientation rather than trying to combine aspects of different orientations. While the client's presentation may be complex, it is helpful to develop a case formulation that is clear and concise. The more clarity you can bring to your understanding of the client, the more focused you will be in using treatment interventions that are consistent and effective. If you have difficulty addressing an aspect of the client's presentation using a particular orientation, it may be helpful to consult with your supervisor or another colleague for suggestions. For example, if you are developing a psychodynamic formulation and want to bring in family systems issues, you can talk about internalized relationship patterns and unconscious identifications. With a cognitive-behavioral formulation, you can include family systems issues by focusing on the impact of early learning and role models as well as cognitions that lead to repetition of earlier relationship experiences.

Generally, a *cognitive-behavioral* case formulation will emphasize cognitive schemas as well as biological and social factors that contribute to and maintain a particular emotional or behavioral state (Eells, 2007). A *psychodynamic* case formulation will emphasize particular affective states, defenses, and representations of self and others (McWilliams, 1999) that are related to the development of the client's psychological symptoms. A *family systems* formulation will describe factors in the family context, structure, and relationship patterns that play a part in the problematic symptoms of individuals in the family and dysfunctional dynamics in the family as a whole (Catherall, 1998; Gladding, 2002). There are specific methods of case formulation within each of these theoretical orientations as well as in other theories of psychotherapy (Carr, 2000; Eells, 2007). You may also have been exposed to integrative approaches to case formulation that combine aspects of different theoretical perspectives (Horowitz, 1997; Teyber & McClure, 2011).

If your client is a child, couple, or family, your case formulation will include a description of both individual and family variables that have contributed to the development of the current symptoms and that maintain the presenting issues. A case formulation for *child treatment* needs to include your understanding of the family context and the role of the parents in maintaining the child's problematic behavior and in fostering change, along with your understanding of how the child's cognitive and affective development is related to the presenting problem (Carr, 2000). A case formulation for *couple or family treatment* generally has a primary focus on the relationship dynamics and structure, but needs to include a description of how each individual contributes to the difficulties in the couple or family system. Your formulation may be rooted in a particular model of couple or family therapy that defines the variables central to the model for therapeutic intervention (Carr, 2000).

Since there is evidence for biological vulnerability or predisposition as a factor in many diagnoses (Wood, Allen, & Pantelis, 2009), you may be uncertain how to develop a psychologically oriented case formulation when working with a client whose symptoms have a strong physiological component. The solution generally lies in identifying the past and current factors that affect the specific expression of the client's diagnosis, events that have precipitated increases in symptoms, and the impact of the symptoms on the client's view of herself and relationships with others. For example, in working with a client who has a diagnosis of schizophrenia and symptoms of auditory hallucinations that are self-blaming and critical, your clinical assessment might include information about a history of bullying and teasing by peers, interpersonal rejection precipitating psychotic episodes, and the client's self-description as a loser with no chance of success at an independent adult life. These psychological and interpersonal factors could be combined in a case formulation that would identify underlying contributions to the course of the client's illness, and goals for treatment to decrease the number and severity of psychotic episodes.

Inclusion of Strengths

Successful treatment depends on the client mobilizing her personal strengths and outside support. Therefore, it is important to include a description of these strengths and resources in your case formulation. It is easy to overlook these abilities and see only the challenges your client is facing in her life. At the beginning of treatment, you may be focused on the client's symptoms and impairments because the tasks of diagnosis and assessment emphasize those aspects of her life. Some clients also enter treatment in a way that emphasizes their difficulties rather than their capacities. However, *the client's strengths play an important part in the selection of treatment goals and interventions,* and your recognition of these strengths will help her to maximize her capacity for change.

As you begin your case formulation, I recommend reflecting on *the client's coping strategies and the internal and external resources* she has used to manage life events of trauma and loss in the past. I am often struck by how well a client is functioning in light of early trauma and psychosocial stressors once I know more about her history and daily life. Acknowledgment of your client's strengths is an important counterpoint to an assessment of impairments in her ability to work, care for her children, and establish mutually satisfying relationships. The determination and courage needed to survive overwhelming and chaotic circumstances are evident in the lives of many clients who present for treatment, and these qualities represent an impressive achievement.

Model for a Case Formulation

The model I present below helps you write a clinical case formulation relatively quickly and easily. In clinical training, you may have a case load of 10 to 15 clients, and it is difficult to stay current on all of the clinical documentation requirements for a large case load. This model will enable you to write *a concise formulation leading to a treatment plan.* You can review and update the formulation when you revise your treatment plan, which is usually required every 3 to 12 months.

Like many beginning clinicians, you may find the process of developing a clinical case formulation somewhat daunting. After compiling information about the client across different areas of functioning in the past and present, it can be difficult to organize these details into a conceptual, explanatory overview that is concise and appropriate for the client's clinical record. The model below takes you through the steps of identifying clinically relevant information in order to make inferences about the client's difficulties. It will help you move from the details of the client's life and your interactions with her to a conceptual explanation that will guide your decisions about treatment.

Once you master the basic steps in this chapter, you may wish to consult other resources that are more complex and comprehensive. The references in this chapter include helpful resources that outline specific steps toward formulation from a specific theoretical orientation or using an integrative approach. Your clinical setting may also use a framework for case formulation that outlines the factors that are considered important to include.

I recommend discussing your case formulation with your supervisor while you organize your thoughts. You might start with the question, "How do I understand the reason for this client's symptoms?" to clarify your understanding. Then talk with peers individually or in group supervision, and review the formulation with your supervisor. Many training settings require that you review a draft of your formulation with your supervisor and incorporate her comments before finalizing it. With practice you will become comfortable with the shift from absorbing the detailed information in your assessment and treatment sessions to writing a conceptual overview of the client's symptoms.

In general, a simple outline for a case formulation should address five areas:

- The client's symptoms or problematic behaviors,
- Developmental history and recent events that are relevant to the symptoms,
- Factors that contribute to the symptoms, both internal and external,
- Cultural issues, and
- Strengths and resources that are available for alleviating or lessening the symptoms.

Generally, it is sufficient for a case formulation to include a short paragraph of three to five sentences about each of these areas. You may need a longer paragraph to describe the factors that contribute to the symptoms, but the case formulation will be more useful to your treatment if it is focused and concise. Remember that a clinical case formulation is not simply a case summary. The case formulation does more than describe the presenting problem and its history. It explains how and why the client's symptoms developed and are maintained and what resources are available to improve the client's condition.

The first area of the formulation is a *short description of the client's symptoms or problematic behaviors* that are the focus of treatment. You do not need to repeat the full diagnosis or list every issue that may be problematic in the client's life. Rather, you should list only the symptoms or behaviors that are most relevant to the current treatment.

Second, describe the *developmental factors and historical events that are related to the client's symptoms*. These might include (a) childhood trauma or loss, (b) significant mental health and substance use issues in the client's family of origin, (c) other disruptions in the client's development, (d) disabilities, and (e) events that precipitated the onset or recurrence of symptoms.

The third part of a case formulation describes the *factors that you believe contribute to the client's symptoms, based on your chosen theoretical orientation*. These factors include internal mechanisms such as schemas or core beliefs, affective states, unconscious defenses, and internalized relationship patterns as well as external factors such as family dynamics and structure, current psychosocial stressors, trauma, and the use of substances or prescribed medication.

Fourth, discuss *cultural issues*, which may include cultural identities, explanations of symptoms, cultural factors related to stressors and functioning, and cross-cultural issues in treatment. It is usually best to include these issues in a separate paragraph, although an alternative approach is to integrate them into the other sections.

Last, describe the *client's strengths and external supports* that can assist in decreasing her symptoms or problems. Being explicit regarding these positive factors will ensure that you incorporate them into your treatment planning.

Summary

This chapter described the purpose and nature of a case formulation and presented a model for writing a concise, focused formulation leading to a treatment plan. The formulation provides an explanation for the client's current symptoms using concepts from your chosen theoretical orientation. Specific areas of professional growth related to case formulation are listed below.

1. Using yourself as an instrument of hope, change, and healing:

    a. Expand your awareness of the balance between the client's difficulties and strengths.

2. Becoming confident in your authority and professionalism:

    a. Use case formulation to guide decisions about treatment planning and interventions.
    b. Apply a theoretical orientation to link client's developmental history with presenting problem.
    c. Practice writing concise case formulations.

3. Developing interpersonal skills that strengthen the therapeutic relationship:

    a. Reflect and validate the client's inner resources.

Case Example: Liz's Clinical Case Formulation

The case example below contains Liz's case formulation. It contains alternative formulations from three different orientations: cognitive-behavioral, psychodynamic, and family systems. These three formulations give you a sense of how the same clinical material would be organized differently based on the explanation of development, psychopathology, and change inherent in each theory. Using the model outlined above, four of the five sections of the formulation are the same across the three theoretical orientations. Only the section describing the factors contributing to the symptoms varies for the three orientations. These variations illustrate how case formulations derived from different theoretical orientations can lead to the same treatment approach and goals. Although an actual case formulation would not include headings for the different components, they are included in this case example for clarity.

Symptoms and Problematic Behavior

Client presented with symptoms of depression, harmful use of alcohol, and some symptoms of alcohol dependence. She also described anger and conflict with her 15-year-old daughter in her initial contact with the agency, which she reported had improved by the time of the first session.

Developmental Factors and Historical Events

Client experienced the trauma of civil war from ages 3 to 7, followed by the family's immigration to the United States. The disruption of the immigration was likely exacerbated by the physical separation from extended family and the death of several family members during the remainder of the war. Client reports that her father was alcoholic, and her description of her mother suggests episodes of untreated depression. Client has a history of depressive episodes following separations from important relationships and began using alcohol after her brother moved from the area. Her adult intimate relationships are described as highly conflictual and may have included physical violence.

Factors Contributing To Symptoms

Cognitive-behavioral formulation. Following the family's immigration, client seems to have developed a schema of others as absent or preoccupied and a schema of herself as unimportant unless she was attending to the needs of others. These schemas led to client's core beliefs regarding a lack of self-worth and being responsible for her relationship partners' satisfaction. These core beliefs contribute to a cycle of self-critical thoughts and accompanying depressive feelings when experiencing separation from an important relationship. Client's choices in adult relationships have reinforced her core beliefs and schemas, leading to depressive episodes. Using alcohol as a coping strategy was modeled by client's father and has been adopted by client.

Psychodynamic formulation. Client's early trauma, disruption, and loss led to a vulnerability to experiences of separation in her adolescence and adult life. She adapted to her parents' psychological absence by minimizing her pain, neglecting her emotional needs, and tending to the needs and demands of those on whom she depends. She seeks validation of her self-worth from her partner and blames herself when her intimate relationships end. Her lack of early experiences of comfort and soothing has led to multiple depressive episodes following separation from relationships and reliance on alcohol to numb her painful feelings. Her symptoms of depression and alcohol abuse also represent unconscious identifications with her parents.

Family systems formulation. Client's early family life was characterized by the trauma of war, which overwhelmed the family's ability to cope adequately with their subsequent immigration and the ongoing loss of family members. Client's parents became emotionally inaccessible, and client took a parental caretaking role. As an adult, client has continued in the role of caretaker in her intimate relationships with partners, repeating her insecure attachment pattern. Client's depression and alcohol abuse reflect her identification with the family's inability to integrate and mourn their experiences of trauma and loss. Client may also be more vulnerable to the re-emergence of depression at this time because her youngest child is 7—client's age when the family immigrated—and her older daughter is 15, which was client's age when she began using alcohol.

Cultural Factors

Client identifies as American and seems not to place a positive value on her Salvadoran heritage. Her identification with the majority culture may be reflected in the fact that she has not expressed any culturally related explanations of her symptoms or ideas about treatment. This identification may also be reflected in her choice to see a non-Latina therapist. Client's life includes several areas of stress related to cultural factors, including her physical and emotional distance from her mother and siblings, which is outside cultural norms; loss of the extended family in El Salvador, which seemed to have provided a protective function during the war; identification with traditional cultural gender roles, which value males over females; and relationship conflict related to her partners' immigration status. It is significant that the treatment is being conducted in English, client's second language, which may present barriers to emotional expression. In addition, client's need for additional social support and the role of culturally prescribed gender roles in her depression will be important factors in the treatment.

Strengths and Supports

Client has engaged readily in treatment and has responded positively to therapeutic intervention, resulting in a reduction in her depressive symptoms. Client has also significantly reduced her use of alcohol to the lowest level since she began drinking at age 15. Historically, client has maintained a consistent work history despite her depressive episodes and has successfully parented her three children. Client's primary social support is limited to one close friend, but she reports being able to share openly with this friend.

The Next Step

Chapter 9 will discuss treatment planning, which involves decisions about treatment frame and structure, goals, and intervention methods. The case example will illustrate how to involve the client in developing a treatment plan.

References

Carr, A. (2000). *Family therapy: Concepts, process and practice.* Chichester, England: John Wiley & Sons Ltd.

Catherall, D. R. (1998). Treating traumatized families. In Figley, C. R. (Ed.). *Burnout in families: The systemic costs of caring.* Boca Raton, FL: CRC Press.

Eells, T. D. (Ed.). (2007). *Handbook of psychotherapy case formulation* (2nd ed.). New York, NY: The Guilford Press.

Gladding, S. T. (2002). *Family therapy: History, theory, and practice* (3rd ed.). Upper Saddle River, NJ: Merrill Prentice Hall.

Horowitz, M. J. (1997). *Formulation as a basis for planning psychotherapy treatment.* Washington, DC: American Psychiatric Press, Inc.

McWilliams, N. (1999). *Psychoanalytic case formulation.* New York, NY: The Guilford Press.

Teyber, E. & McClure, F. H. (2011). *Interpersonal process in therapy: An integrative model* (6th ed.). Belmont, CA: Brooks/Cole.

Wood, S. J., Allen, N. B., & Pantelis, C. (2009). *The neuropsychology of mental illness.* New York, NY: Cambridge University Press.

9
TREATMENT PLANNING

(Note: This chapter will use the male pronoun for supervisor, clinician, and client.)

This chapter describes the process and decisions involved in treatment planning, which means reaching agreement with the client about the specific focus of your work together and the way you will work toward the desired goals. I begin with defining the term *treatment planning*, and then review the components and ways to reach decisions about each component. The chapter closes with a discussion of the client's involvement in the development of a treatment plan.

Definition of Treatment Planning

Your assessment and case formulation lead to a focus on the issues you address in treatment and how you help the client make progress on those issues. Your client has told you his reasons for seeking treatment and you may have identified other issues that you feel are necessary to address in order to achieve the outcome he wants. Your discussions with him about his priorities and interests and your recommendations for what and how you will work together constitute treatment planning. *The agreement you reach with the client about these goals and interventions is referred to as the treatment plan* (Wiger, 2012).

Often the treatment plan is formalized in a written document that you review with the client, although in some settings you may have an informal discussion and reach agreement without a written document. Your *treatment plan completes the treatment contract you established with the client in the first session,* when you discussed other more general aspects of the scope and limitations of your work together (reviewed in Chapter 3). As with the initial assessment, you may be required to develop a treatment plan within a specific time frame, usually 30 to 60 days after the first session. This means completing your assessment and case formulation before the deadline for your treatment plan, since the assessment information and conceptual framework of the case formulation contribute to developing the treatment plan.

Your treatment plan contains decisions about three aspects of treatment:

- Frame and structure,
- Goals, and
- Interventions.

Decisions Regarding Treatment Frame and Structure

Your clinical training setting or the treatment funder may determine some aspects of the treatment frame and structure; however, I recommend explicitly considering each of the following decisions to ensure that you are providing the most appropriate care to meet the client's needs within organizational and funding policies:

- Unit of treatment,
- Intensity and length of treatment, and
- Additional services required or recommended.

Unit of Treatment

One of the most important issues regarding the frame and structure of treatment is the decision regarding the unit of treatment. As mentioned in Chapter 6, your assessment of the client leads you to determine whether an individual or a family unit is your client. This decision guides your recommendation about who will participate in treatment. It is especially important to be clear about the question of whether you consider the individual or the family to be your client because your *goals, interventions, and practices regarding sharing of information among family members are based on this decision.*

If you view an *individual as the unit of treatment*, your primary focus will be to facilitate the individual client's progress in the areas of concern to him.

- Goals are oriented toward the individual's needs and improved functioning.
- Interventions are targeted to address the individual's symptoms and behavior.
- Sharing information with family members requires authorization for adult clients; use clinical judgment to decide what information to share with family members of child and adolescent clients.

  - With an *individual child client*, you will hold most of your sessions with the child alone and have less frequent sessions with the parents, with or without the child. You will talk with the child about how you will share information with his parents, as appropriate for the child's age and developmental level. Clinical issues and family dynamics will also determine your decisions about sharing information with parents.

- With an *individual adult client*, you must have the client's written permission to share information with family members, except in emergency circumstances. It can be useful to speak with family members by telephone or in person, since they have a perspective on the client's symptoms and progress, and their support of the client's progress is often vital to the success of the treatment. Meeting with family members in person gives you an opportunity to assess the degree and type of family support available to the client and to encourage and facilitate family interactions that are consistent with the client's goals. I generally recommend including the client in sessions with family members, in order to maintain clarity about your primary role, but in some cases it may be clinically appropriate to meet with the family members alone. Your supervisor's guidance is critical in any case involving adults and family members.

If you view a *family as the unit of treatment*, you will focus on improving the overall functioning of the family and facilitating more adaptive communication and roles within the family.

- Goals are oriented toward the family's needs and improved functioning.
- Interventions are targeted to address the family's communication and relationships.
- Sharing information with family members is part of family treatment. I recommend setting a clear guideline at the beginning of family treatment about how you will handle information disclosed by one family member when others are not present. This issue is discussed in more detail in Chapter 3.

Intensity and Length of Treatment

In many clinical settings, you will be able to make decisions about the intensity of treatment within limits prescribed by the organization and funders. Psychotherapy is traditionally offered in weekly sessions of 45 to 60 minutes; however, some clients may need and benefit from more or less frequent sessions (twice a week or every other week) or shorter or longer duration (30 minutes or 90 minutes). Case management and other behavioral health services are usually scheduled more flexibly to meet the needs of the client, based on his symptoms and circumstances. You might see him several times a week during a crisis and every two to four weeks when he is stable. Your sessions might be as short as 15 minutes or as long as several hours.

Length of treatment can range from a few weeks to over a year, is often influenced by requirements of third-party funders, and may require periodic documentation of the client's status and progress. However, you and the client may have some degree of discretion within those requirements especially related to the frequency of sessions. If the length of treatment is limited, it is often helpful to lessen the frequency in the weeks leading up to the end of treatment. For example, you might begin with weekly sessions, and then meet every other week for 6 weeks and once a month for 2 months before ending.

The expected *intensity and length of the treatment will affect your decisions about the treatment goals.* If you are meeting with the client for a 2-hour session once a month, you will develop more limited treatment goals than if you are meeting for a 1-hour session weekly. Similarly, the goals you set for treatment extending for eight sessions over 3 months will be different from the goals you set if treatment is for 26 sessions over a year.

You may work in a clinical setting that has an organizational standard regarding the intensity and the length of treatment. These standards are often based on the mission and theoretical approach of the organization as well as the level of demand for service that affects the size of caseload for each clinician. If you are assigned to work with a large number of clients, you will need to reduce the intensity or length of your treatment and adjust your treatment goals accordingly.

Additional Services Required or Recommended

Many of your clients will have complex difficulties related to their symptoms and life circumstances. For this reason, some clients may be receiving other services when you begin working with them, and some may have needs that become apparent during your assessment but are outside the scope of your treatment. *The effectiveness of your treatment may depend on the client's use of other resources* that address his symptoms in a different way or complement the focus of your treatment. In these cases, your treatment plan will include goals related to services such as medication management, support to locate stable housing and employment, or participation in a group related to the client's presenting issues. In these cases, part of your treatment responsibility will involve case management and coordination of the client's care. This aspect of treatment is discussed in more detail in Chapter 12.

Decisions Regarding Treatment Goals

A treatment plan generally lists specific goals, sometimes called objectives, for your work with the client. I recommend writing treatment goals in terms of *what the client wishes to change* or, in the case of young children, what the child's parents and other adults want to be changed. The treatment goals describe what will change in the life and experience of the client; treatment interventions describe what you will do to help the client achieve his goals. Treatment planning is a collaborative process, as you and the client each contribute to achieving the goals. Having a clear understanding and agreement with your client about the purpose of your work from the beginning is essential to a successful outcome.

The task of developing treatment goals with a client can be difficult and overwhelming for beginning clinicians. Many of the clients you see have multiple, longstanding psychological symptoms and disorders along with past and current psychosocial stressors, and this multiplicity of issues can be emotionally challenging for the clinician as well as the client. Depending on how you deal with such challenges, you may find yourself at a loss as to how to begin to develop treatment goals, and you may doubt that you can help mitigate the seriousness of the client's circumstances. Alternatively, you may attempt to address too many of the client's issues in your treatment plan in an attempt to gain a sense of some mastery over the situation.

It is natural in the training process to develop treatment goals that describe what you will do rather than what will change in the client's behavior or experience. You may focus on the question of what you will do to be helpful, i.e., your interventions, rather than the question of what aspects of the client's life he wants to change. Whether your treatment plan is in the form of a written document, it is helpful to *think and talk with the client first about the desired changes in his experience and behavior*, which will define the treatment goals. Having done this, you can better identify the interventions that will assist and support the client in making the desired changes.

Writing Achievable Treatment Goals

Following these guidelines will help ensure that your treatment goals are achievable:

* Be realistic about what can be accomplished during the expected length of treatment.
* Focus on what the client can control.
* Stay within your scope of practice.

Being realistic about the change that can happen during the time you will work with the client will take practice and input from your supervisor. I have found that it is easy for beginning clinicians to agree with a client who has very broad goals that involve major changes in longstanding patterns. Your supervisor can help you break down these large goals into smaller ones. For example, if you have six months to work with a woman who has a history of childhood sexual trauma, it is unlikely that she will be free of her posttraumatic symptoms by the end of treatment. However, you can probably help her learn to use strategies to reduce the intensity and frequency of her symptoms.

Working with realistic treatment goals makes it more likely that the client will feel a sense of success and achievement by the end of treatment, rather than feeling defeated and disappointed in himself and you. It also gives you a chance to talk early in treatment about the significance of the client's difficulties and to address fantasies or expectations the client may have about the nature and possibility of change. Often, part of the treatment process is coming to terms with the things that cannot be changed (McWilliams, 1999) while addressing those things that can.

Maintaining a *focus on aspects of the client's life that are within his control* can also be challenging. Many of the stressors in clients' lives are caused by poverty and other societal forces or by the actions of other people. An unemployed client may enter treatment with a desire for his partner to be less demanding or to find a job at a specific salary. He may feel worried about being blamed or feel a high degree of shame and guilt. As you express understanding and empathy, he is likely to become more open to identifying what he wants to change within himself. Appropriate treatment goals with an unemployed client would be that he use strategies to manage his anxiety about the job search or that he communicate clearly with his partner about their finances and his contribution to them. You would not include a treatment goal related to finding a job with a specific salary or to reducing his marital conflict about money, since those goals are not within his direct control. Helping the client focus on what he can influence is a step toward empowerment and reduced feelings of helplessness.

Since some of the client's needs may fall outside the areas of your training and the mission of your organization, be sure to *stay within your scope of practice*. The treatment goals need to fit your skills and qualifications as well as the resources that are available to you. As I indicated above, with an unemployed client, you would usually not provide direct assistance in his job search unless that type of case management is part of your role; rather, the treatment goals would reflect your role of addressing the psychological obstacles and providing support for the client's progress.

Setting Priorities

Most of the clients you will see during your clinical training have multiple symptoms and life problems, so you need to *prioritize the issues that will be the focus of your work* together. Generally, it is wise to have no more than three goals in a treatment plan so you and the client will need to determine the areas of greatest need and priority. You may be required to review and revise the treatment plan on a regular basis, and the frequency of the review could range from every 60 days to once a year. Regardless of the requirements of your organization, I recommend reviewing the treatment plan with the client and updating the treatment goals at least twice a year. This review gives you an opportunity to reflect on the progress the client has made and to revise or add goals to reflect his current concerns.

The first priority in developing initial treatment goals with the client is to *identify any areas of high risk or safety concerns*. Examples are suicidal ideation or impulses, imminent loss of housing or other basic needs, or a serious health condition requiring medical attention. You should address these safety issues in an initial goal because work on other goals won't be productive until the client's safety has been ensured. This may require some collaborative discussion with your client if he is minimizing his level of danger. Treatment goals for risk and safety concerns are usually related to additional resources and psychological support the client needs. Examples of such goals are "Client will use DBT distress tolerance skills when feeling suicidal," "Client will contact the emergency housing office," or "Client will schedule a visit with the community medical clinic." When the goal is related to the client accessing other resources, you will identify treatment interventions that will help the client deal with the emotional obstacles, such as depression or anxiety, which interfere with accessing those resources.

After you have identified issues of risk and safety, *focus on the areas that are most important to the client and that he has the greatest motivation to address*, in order to prioritize the remaining goals for the initial treatment plan. The client's priorities may be different from yours, but it is the client's treatment and your role is to support him in achieving his goals. Therefore, the client's priorities should form the basis of the treatment plan. For example, the client's anxiety may interfere with his ability to search for a job and you consider addressing his anxiety to be a high priority because the client is unemployed and in financial hardship. However, if he is highly motivated to address his pattern of sabotaging intimate relationships, that goal would take priority in his treatment plan. This approach to setting goals communicates your belief in the client's ability to set a direction for his life and establishes a collaborative relationship in which you provide the help and support he requests rather than the help you believe he needs.

A discrepancy in treatment priorities between you and the client is especially common when you are working with *clients who have a substance use disorder*, whose use of alcohol and/or other substances interferes with their stability and progress. In these instances, your sense of priority regarding the client's substance use may conflict with his, and you will need to resolve this conflict. One way to resolve the conflict, which is often implemented in residential addiction treatment settings, is to require that the client agree to remain abstinent from substances. In contrast, most outpatient mental health settings and some outpatient addiction treatment centers use a harm reduction model that supports the client in reducing the harm that results from his substance use (Denning et al., 2004). In settings using harm reduction models of treatment, abstinence may be seen as desirable for many clients, but it is not a requirement for receiving treatment.

Motivational interviewing is an intervention, often used as part of a harm reduction model, which is useful in identifying the client's priorities and motivation regarding substance use and in developing treatment goals based on the client's interests (Miller & Rollnick, 2002; Tomlin & Richardson, 2004). This approach enhances the client's motivation to change by aligning with his interests and concerns while exploring and helping him resolve his ambivalence regarding substance use and life goals.

A final issue to consider in prioritizing the treatment goals is the *presence of opportunities and constraints* in your organization or in the client's life that facilitate or interfere with the client addressing certain issues of concern. For example, if your client is the mother of a 2-year-old and you work in an organization that provides support for families with young children, you could offer the client the opportunity to address some of her goals related to parenting. On the other hand, if your organization is a small outpatient clinic serving individual adults, you may work with the mother on her depression and developing ways to cope with stress. An example of a constraint in the client's life is a depressed young man working to improve his ability to develop friendships who then receives a serious medical diagnosis. In this instance, your focus would shift to supporting the client's emotional well-being during his medical treatment until he is stable and again able to focus again on his interpersonal relationships.

Translating Goals into Behaviorally Specific Terms

Often you will be required to state the treatment goal in behavioral terms. Even if it is not a requirement, *talk with the client about his expected outcomes to be clear about the target you are working toward.* It will help you translate your goals from abstract to behaviorally specific terms if you ask the question, "How will we know that the treatment is helping?" Even if you are not using a theoretical perspective that focuses directly on behavioral change, you and your client have expectations about what will change in the client's life if your work together is successful, and this question can help you identify those expectations and align yours with his.

As an example, the client may identify a desire to feel better about himself, which you would understand as an improvement in his self-esteem. An increase in self-esteem could be reflected in a number of ways, such as a decrease in his self-critical statements, an improved ability to notice the triggers for self-evaluation, or identification of a supportive person or group. Ask the client how he knows he doesn't feel good about himself and how he would know if he were feeling better, and by his response you'll be better able to identify the treatment goal you are targeting.

Look at sample treatment plans to develop a language for describing the desired outcomes of treatment. You may have access to treatment plans used by other clinicians in your agency or a treatment planning reference book that lists sample goals for different disorders and behavior problems (Jongsma, Jr., & Peterson, 2006; Taubman, 2005). It is a common misconception that working toward behavioral treatment goals requires using a behavioral treatment intervention. While behavioral perspectives lend themselves more easily to behavioral goals, all clinical perspectives were developed to result in symptom relief and improved abilities to cope with painful feelings and interpersonal conflict. With practice, you will learn how to develop behavioral treatment goals that are consistent with the use of treatment interventions from your specific theoretical approach.

Some clinical training settings require the *behavioral change in the treatment goal to be defined in terms that are observable and measurable.* One way to write treatment goals that are behaviorally specific, observable, and measurable is to use the phrase, "Client will (general description of behavior change) as evidenced by (the observable result of the behavior change)." Examples are, "Client will experience reduced anxiety as evidenced by a reduction in self-report of anxiety symptoms from a baseline level of 8/10 to 5/10," or "Client will increase his support network as evidenced by reporting two positive interactions with a friend per week." Including observable, measurable goals in your treatment plan requires introducing a method for measuring and tracking change, which may be unfamiliar if you are not using behavioral interventions. However, it is possible to incorporate a weekly check-in about the client's behavioral goal into a treatment approach that uses interventions from other theoretical perspectives.

Short-Term, Medium-Term, and Long-Term Goals

Most of the issues that are the focus of clinical treatment are complex, and change happens in small steps. Be sure to *match the client's treatment goals to the period of time you anticipate working with him.* The treatment plan for a 60-day treatment should include only short-term goals that can be achieved in that period of time. If you have up to 6 months, you can include both short-term and medium-term goals keeping in mind that it is best to limit your treatment plan to three goals. If you anticipate working with the client for a year or more, it is wise to include some short-term goals that can be achieved in a few weeks or months, in addition to longer term goals, in order to focus your interventions and to enhance the client's sense of progress and success. Each treatment plan and update should include at least one goal that extends through the effective term of the plan so that you are clear about the focus of the treatment.

While some clients present with immediate needs that are easily translated into short-term goals, more often the client's initial desire for change is diffuse and long-term (e.g., "I want to get over my depression" or "I want to stop getting into bad relationships"). Your assessment and case formulation will help you to identify some of the steps the client will need to take to reach his larger goals. You can then present your suggestions for short-term and medium-term goals that will lead to the change the client wants. Treatment planning guides are also useful in breaking down larger goals into smaller steps (Jongsma, Jr., & Peterson, 2006; Taubman, 2005).

Symptom Relief and Strengthening Capacities for Maintaining Change

One additional issue regarding treatment goals is related to the relevance of both immediate symptom relief and strengthening the client's capacities to maintain the positive changes achieved during treatment. While symptom relief is often the initial goal of treatment, it is important to help the client identify changes he can make that will maintain his improved psychological state. The issue of maintaining positive changes is viewed as important from a number of treatment perspectives. In addiction treatment, the focus on the client's capacity to maintain change is called relapse prevention (Tomlin & Richardson, 2004). The peer support movement in the mental health field emphasizes concepts of wellness and recovery, and there are resources to assist clients with serious mental illness to maintain wellness and minimize the impact of a recurrence of symptoms (Copeland, 2002). In psychodynamic psychotherapy, there is explicit emphasis on supporting the client in developing internal capacities that lead to greater enjoyment and meaning in life (Shedler, 2010).

Embedded in the views referenced above is the idea that someone who has psychological symptoms, which may include addiction, is vulnerable to a recurrence of those symptoms. Therefore, a comprehensive treatment plan includes goals and interventions related to *both a diminishment of the specific symptoms that led the client to seek treatment and an increase in the client's psychological capacities and skills* that will enable him to maintain the growth and change achieved during treatment. If your work is focused on crisis management and stabilization in a limited time frame, you may not be able to work directly with the client to strengthen his capacities and develop new skills. However, you can talk with him about strategies and resources to prevent another crisis.

Decisions Regarding Intervention Methods

The treatment goals describe the client's desired behavioral changes, and the *treatment interventions describe what you will do to help him achieve his goals.* These interventions may be specific to your treatment approach, such as teaching DBT distress tolerance skills, or they may be more general, such as supporting the client's growth through interpretation of underlying dynamics. The interventions may or may not be included in the written treatment plan format used at your clinical setting but in either case, give careful consideration to the particular interventions that are likely to be helpful to the client. Ideas for effective interventions can come from your prior experience; your supervisor, peers, and colleagues; and clinical training. You will be most effective in helping the client make progress toward his goals if you begin with a clear idea about the types of interventions you plan to use. If you find that your original choice of interventions isn't effective, you can revise your plan, but treatment will be easier if you begin with clear ideas about what you believe will be helpful.

As mentioned above, clinicians sometimes believe that identifying treatment goals in behavioral terms requires the use of behavioral interventions. However, *interventions from a variety of perspectives can be used to help the client reach goals that are defined in behavioral terms.* For example, a treatment goal of increasing a client's support network by having two positive interactions with a friend each week could be facilitated by interventions involving social skills training, analysis of thoughts and feelings associated with social interactions, examination of parental models and messages related to interpersonal relationships, and discussion of the client's experience of interactions with you in treatment. Your choice of treatment interventions is influenced by the client's preference, the theoretical perspective used by your organization and your supervisor, the clinical style that best fits your personality, and the effectiveness of the intervention for the client's treatment goal.

As with all aspects of treatment, your choice of interventions needs to be made in *the context of the client's cultural identities*. Interventions are culturally responsive and more effective when you

- Consider the support available through traditional healing and religious practices;
- Define "family" to include extended family members and non-related individuals who are important in the client's life, including the partners of gay, lesbian, bisexual, and transgender individuals;
- Adapt interventions to the client's cultural context when appropriate; and
- Recognize the client's cultural expectations and beliefs about medication as well as other aspects of treatment (Hays, 2008).

Client's Involvement in Treatment Planning

The treatment plan completes the contract between you and the client that was begun in the first session. Therefore, *the treatment goals need to reflect the client's priorities and the issues he is ready to change*. He must be involved in developing the treatment goals and agree with the treatment approach and interventions that you plan to use. The treatment plan is useful only to the extent that it comes out of a collaborative discussion between you and the client, rather than being a plan you develop on your own or solely in compliance with funder requirements or administrative regulations.

You will probably find that *some clients express little interest in participating in a discussion about the purpose and goals of your work together*. This lack of interest may be related to prior experiences of having their wishes, opinions, and needs ignored or criticized by others. It may also be related to either (a) a pattern of repetitive emotional crisis or anxiety that interferes with being reflective and thoughtful, or (b) the client's fear of failure and rejection if he doesn't meet your expectations. If you find your client reluctant to engage in developing the treatment plan, it may be helpful to offer him some explanation of the reasons for the discussion. For example, you might say

> I realize you have a lot of important issues on your mind today, but I'd like to take some time to talk about what is most important to you in our work together. I want to support you in reaching your goals and I think I can be more effective if I know what you would like to change. Would you be willing to take some time for that today or next time we meet?

You may be required to document the client's agreement with the treatment plan in your progress note for the session or by getting the client's signature on a written document. In all cases, it is important to have a discussion about the goals of the treatment and how both of you will know if the treatment is successful. This helps to establish a collaborative working relationship and may be the client's first experience of being seen as a valued partner in improving his health and well-being. Ideally, the treatment plan should contain contributions from both of you, reflecting your discussions about what changes the client wants to make and what help you feel able to offer. These discussions should cover the different interventions that you might use to help the client reach his goals, in addition to the goals themselves, so that the client is able to express his preferences about the way you will work together.

The treatment plan gives you the direction and focus of the treatment, and is therefore something to keep actively in mind in each session. Often your client may begin a session with a concern that seems unrelated to the goals for treatment. Rather than simply following this new concern, it is useful to ask yourself how this issue could be related to one of the client's goals and to bring focus to the discussion. For example, a client who has a goal of increasing his use of social support may begin a session by describing a crisis with one of his children, which has required multiple conversations with school personnel. After getting a sense of the situation and your client's way of handling it, you might say, "It sounds like it's hard to focus on your own goals, like getting more support for yourself, when you have a crisis like this on your hands," or, "I wonder if there's a way you could use the focus and determination you showed in dealing with the school problem to work on increasing the support in your life." These kinds of observations can help the client maintain the focus on his treatment goals without neglecting the events that may need his attention.

Summary

This chapter discussed the definition of treatment planning and the decisions that are made as part of developing a treatment plan: the frame and structure, the treatment goals, and the intervention methods. I included a number of suggestions for collaborating with the client in developing the treatment plan. Specific areas of professional growth related to treatment planning are listed below.

1. Using yourself as an instrument of hope, change, and healing:

    a. Be aware of your response to the challenge of developing treatment goals.
    b. Notice discrepancies between your priorities and the client's.

2. Becoming confident in your authority and professionalism:

    a. Consider different options for treatment structure to provide the best care.
    b. Practice writing achievable treatment goals and effective interventions.
    c. Be familiar with requirements for documentation of treatment planning.

3. Developing interpersonal skills that strengthen the therapeutic relationship:

    a. Engage in collaborative discussions with clients about their interests, priorities, and motivation.
    b. Address immediate concerns and developing capacities to maintain change.

Case Example: Susana's Treatment Plan

After Liz completes her assessment and clinical case formulation, she develops a preliminary treatment plan that fits Susana's reasons for seeking treatment and her understanding of the factors that contribute to Susana's symptoms.

Treatment Frame and Structure

Based on her assessment and discussion of the case in supervision, Liz has decided on individual therapy with Susana as her *unit of treatment*. She plans to continue to coordinate with the school counselor meeting with Susana's daughter but feels that Susana can benefit from individual therapy which focuses on her needs and will help her develop greater self-understanding.

Regarding the *intensity and length of treatment*, Liz meets with Susana once a week for 50-minute sessions, which is the standard at her agency, and Liz feels these parameters are appropriate for Susana's level of symptoms. Susana is paying for treatment herself so there are no third-party funding limitations on the length of treatment, and the Community Support Clinic does not have a specific limit on the number of sessions that clients may attend. Agency policy is that clinicians review treatment plans every 6 months, evaluate the client's progress, and discuss the client's desire to continue or end treatment. Liz talked about this agency practice with Susana in their fourth session when Susana asked how long Liz thought she would need to come to therapy in order to feel less depressed. Liz plans to bring this question up again in their review of the treatment plan, so she and Susana are clear about how they will evaluate their work.

Liz has talked with Susana about the *additional services* that her daughter Maria is receiving at school. Liz has recommended that Susana consider family therapy when Maria reaches the limit of 12 individual sessions available at her school. In their initial discussion of this possibility, Susana was hesitant about family therapy, so Liz plans to talk with her more about her concerns as her daughter's therapy ends.

Review of Preliminary Treatment Plan in Supervision

Liz develops *three preliminary treatment goals* related to Susana's depression, feelings of grief and loss related to the family's immigration during the war in El Salvador, and beginning family therapy. She brings this to Dalia who notes that Liz has not included a treatment goal related to Susana's use of alcohol. Liz says that Susana's use of alcohol is no longer problematic, but Dalia reminds Liz that Susana's use and the accuracy of her self-report of use are likely to remain a therapeutic issue for the coming months. They discuss the wording of a treatment goal that Liz feels comfortable bringing up with Susana. Dalia also questions Susana's readiness to address her feelings related to the family's immigration, and she suggests that Liz wait to bring up this issue until Susana's symptoms are more stable and she has developed stronger coping strategies. Liz agrees to defer that goal until the next review. Dalia also reminds Liz that the agency requires that clients sign the treatment plan listing the goals and interventions.

Preliminary Treatment Plan

After her supervision session, Liz revises her treatment goals and brings the preliminary written plan to her eighth session with Susana, along with a blank form to complete if Susana wishes to make changes. The plan consists of the following goals and interventions:

Treatment Goal 1: Client will experience a reduction in symptoms of depression, as evidenced by a score of 13 or less on the Beck Depression Inventory.

Interventions: Clinician will provide psychoeducation regarding the impact of early trauma and loss. Clinician will identify and support client in examining thoughts and feelings of guilt and responsibility toward her intimate partners.

Treatment Goal 2: Client will reduce her use of alcohol, as evidenced by a score of less than 8 on the Alcohol Use Disorders Identification Test.

Interventions: Clinician will explore client's ambivalence about her current use of alcohol and support client's motivation to reduce her use.

Treatment Goal 3: Client will evaluate the option of beginning family therapy, as evidenced by identifying at least two potential benefits.

Interventions: Clinician will assist client in identifying her feelings about family therapy and will provide psychoeducation about potential benefits.

Discussion of Treatment Plan

Liz begins the eighth session in the following way:

Liz: I'd like to talk with you today about the goals we have for our work together. I have written down some suggestions, and I brought them with me today for us to discuss. But first I'm interested in what is on your mind today and whether you had any thoughts about our session last week. We talked about some things that were pretty difficult for you and I wanted to check in about that.

Susana: I don't remember much of what we talked about last week. I think you said something about how growing up in the war means I'm used to danger and that's different from my kids.

Liz: I was wondering if growing up in the war led you to see situations as less dangerous than others might see them, including your kids. Have you thought more about that?

Susana: Not really. This week I got a call from Amelia's teacher saying that she hasn't been bringing in her homework so I had to figure out why she wasn't turning it in. I know she does it, because I look at it every night after dinner or in the morning before she goes to school. That took up most of the week.

Liz talked with Susana about the situation with Amelia's homework and how she handled it. She noted that Susana initially reacted with irritation but was responsive to Amelia saying she wanted to spend more time with Susana in the evening. She commented on Susana's ability to encourage Amelia's expression of need and to respond positively. After discussion of this situation and a general review of the week, Liz asked Susana if she was ready to talk about the goals of their work together and Susana agreed.

Liz: This is the form we use here for our Treatment Plan. I've written some goals based on what you've told me you want to work on and change, but I'm interested in how this looks to you and fits with your current ideas about your treatment.

Susana: The first one looks fine. I'm already less depressed. Do you want me to take that test again now?

Liz: No. As I mentioned to you before, our agency asks us to review treatment plans with clients every 6 months, so I'll ask you to answer those questions again at that time. We can compare your score on the two tests then to see how things have changed. I'm glad you're already feeling some improvement in your depression.

Susana: I don't know about the second one, though. I'm not drinking in front of the kids, like I told you, but I don't want to take that test again. It was really upsetting to answer all of those questions.

Liz: It sounds like you do want to reduce your use of alcohol, and you already have. What is your goal for cutting back on your drinking?

Susana: I'm only drinking on the weekends, Friday and Saturday night, and I don't have more than two drinks. Sometimes I only have one, and sometimes I have two.

Liz: Would you be comfortable if the goal was, "Client will reduce her use of alcohol to one or two drinks on Friday and Saturday only"?

Susana: Yes, I'm okay with that.

Liz: What about the third goal?

Susana: I thought about what you said about Maria's counselor sending us to family therapy, and I don't want to do that. I'm afraid she'll want to talk about that night and about Carlos. I'm not as mad at Maria as I was then, but it was really bad for her to call the police. I'm afraid we'll get into another fight if we talk about Carlos. The kids don't understand that I have needs too, and I get lonely. They just think about themselves and what I can do for them. If all three of them are there, they'll talk about how bad Carlos was, and the therapist will probably agree with them.

Liz: It sounds like you're afraid the kids will agree with each other and the therapist won't be able to see your point of view. I understand that the topic of Carlos still feels like too much to talk about. I also have a sense that you want to feel closer to your kids, and you're sad they're getting older. Jorge and Maria are spending more time with their friends, and Amelia is less cuddly than she used to be. Even though you know that's normal for their ages, you miss some of the fun times you had when they were younger.

Susana: You're right about missing them, even though a lot of the time I just want them to leave me alone. I did promise Amelia I'd try to pay more attention to her in the evening after dinner, and she was really happy about that. Maybe that will help, and I won't need to do that family therapy.

Liz: I can hear that you're worried about being judged on how well you're doing as a mom. Maybe a better way to describe your goal is that we'll talk about how your family is working and whether you want to make any changes. Would that be helpful?

Susana: Yes, that sounds better. But maybe that's not enough of a goal. I know you work with lots of people, and maybe I can't change as fast as some of them. Or maybe your supervisor will tell you to stop seeing me if I don't get better.

Liz: I'm really glad you let me know you're worried about that. I can understand how writing down these goals might make it seem like you're being evaluated by me or by my supervisor. I want to reassure you that your treatment here isn't dependent on a certain amount of change and that the goals are yours, not mine or anyone else's. Would it be helpful to take some time to talk about your relationship with your kids, how you feel about that, and how things are working?

Susana: I know I want them to understand that I have needs too. You're probably thinking about something different though.

Liz: I'd like to hear more about what you want in your family. I know from what you've told me that you want things to be different with your kids from how they were for you with your parents. Sometimes it's hard to know what we want when we haven't experienced it before. It's also important to think about what's going well, along with things you'd like to be different.

Susana: Sometimes it doesn't seem like anything is going well. I don't need a therapist to tell me that.

Liz: I can tell you sometimes feel discouraged and hopeless about your relationship with your kids, and you're afraid I'll be critical of you. It seems like you're pretty critical of yourself, and I guess it's hard to imagine I wouldn't be too. I really would like to support you to think about what you want for your family. If I put that in the language we use here, it would say, "Client will develop goals for her family, as evidenced by identifying one thing that is working well and one thing she would like to change." How does that sound?

Susana: I guess I could do that. Maybe there is something I'm doing right. So often I get mad at them or feel too tired to do what they want, but then when Jorge and Maria are out with their friends or spending time on the computer I miss them. When I was growing up, I didn't do much with my parents after we moved to San Francisco. My dad was usually drinking, and my mom went to bed right after dinner. I guess I don't know what to do with my kids or what they want from me.

Liz: It's really important to realize how your experience with your parents affects you as a mom. Do you remember what you wanted from your parents during that time?

Susana: I don't have any idea what I wanted. I never thought about it. I just figured I was supposed to manage on my own and not make trouble.

Liz and Susana continue their exploration of Susana's feelings during her adolescence and those feelings might be affecting her relationship with her children, especially her two teenagers. At the end of the session, Liz asks Susana to sign the revised treatment plan she has prepared based on the changes they have discussed.

Revised Treatment Plan

Treatment Goal 1:   Client will experience a reduction in symptoms of depression, as evidenced by a score of 13 or less on the Beck Depression Inventory.

Interventions: Clinician will provide psychoeducation regarding the impact of early trauma and loss. Clinician will identify and support client in examining thoughts and feelings of guilt and responsibility toward her intimate partners.

Treatment Goal 2:   Client will reduce her use of alcohol to one or two drinks on Friday and Saturday only.

Interventions: Clinician will explore client's ambivalence about her current use of alcohol and support client's motivation to reduce her use.

Treatment Goal 3:   Client will develop goals for her family, as evidenced by identifying one thing that is working well and one thing she would like to change.

Interventions: Clinician will support client to examine her feelings and needs in her relationships with her children. Clinician will provide psychoeducation about developmental stages and the factors that contribute to children's developmental progress.

The Next Step

Chapter 10 will discuss clinical documentation including access to behavioral health treatment records and requirements for different types of clinical documents. The case example includes sample progress notes for a session and for a telephone contact.

References

Copeland, M.E. (2002). *Wellness recovery action plan®* (Rev. ed.). West Dummerston, VT: Peach Press.

Denning, P., Little, J., & Glickman, A. (2004). *Over the influence: The harm reduction guide for managing drugs and alcohol.* New York, NY: The Guilford Press.

Hays, P. A. (2008). *Addressing cultural complexities in practice: Assessment, diagnosis, and therapy* (2nd ed.). Washington, DC: American Psychological Association.

Jongsma, Jr., A. E., & Peterson, L. M. (2006). *The complete adult psychotherapy treatment planner* (4th ed.). Hoboken, NJ: John Wiley & Sons, Inc.

McWilliams, N. (1999). *Psychoanalytic case formulation.* New York, NY: The Guilford Press.

Miller, W. R. & Rollnick, S. (2002). *Motivational interviewing: Preparing people for change* (2nd ed.). New York, NY: The Guilford Press.

Shedler, J. (2010). The efficacy of psychodynamic psychotherapy. *American Psychologist, 65,* 98–109.

Taubman, S. (2005). *The BTA treatment plan documentation guide.* Berkeley, CA: Berkeley Training Associates.

Tomlin, K. M. & Richardson, H. (2004). *Motivational interviewing and stages of change.* Center City, MN: Hazelden.

Wiger, D. E. (2012). *The psychotherapy documentation primer* (3rd ed.). Hoboken, NJ: John Wiley & Sons, Inc.

10
CLINICAL DOCUMENTATION

(Note: This chapter will use the female pronoun for supervisor, clinician, and client.)

This chapter discusses issues related to clinical documentation or recordkeeping. I first review professional standards and access to client records, then discuss requirements related to assessments and treatment plans, progress notes and psychotherapy notes, other client contacts, and special clinical situations. You will become familiar with legal and ethical requirements and suggested ways to meet those requirements in your recordkeeping.

Standard of Care

Clinicians are required to meet a professional standard of care in all aspects of treatment, which means providing care that is consistent with generally accepted standards in the behavioral health field. One of these standards is the requirement to maintain a written record of the client's treatment in compliance with the requirements of third-party funders, legal regulations, and professional codes of ethics (APA, 1993; Wiger, 2012).

Once you establish a treatment contract, as described in Chapter 3, you must *document the services you provide, the goals of treatment, and the basis for your treatment decisions.* At a minimum, the client record should contain an assessment conducted at the beginning of treatment, a treatment plan, and progress notes for each session or contact with the client. These three components of the record should be consistent so that the treatment plan follows logically from the assessment, and the progress notes reflect the steps taken to achieve the goals in the treatment plan.

The *primary reason to document treatment is for the client's welfare* (APA, 1993; Bennett, et al., 2006). The client's record contains valuable information for other clinicians who are working with the client concurrently. For example, maintaining a clear, complete, and timely record of your clinical work enables your supervisor or colleague to help your clients when you are on vacation or called away for an emergency. Also, clients may resume treatment at the same setting or a different one, and your treatment record provides valuable information about diagnosis, history, and treatment progress that will enhance subsequent treatment experiences.

A client record also *documents your treatment decisions and interventions*. This documentation helps you and your supervisor review your work, it is required by third-party funders, and it is necessary in the event of a client complaint or legal action. Documenting your treatment decisions and interventions means that you describe the treatment progress so that by reading the record, someone other than you can understand what you did and why and how the client responded.

For the purpose of quality assurance and improvement, many organizations have regular chart reviews in which records are reviewed and evaluated by a supervisor who gives feedback to improve documentation. Check with your supervisor about your organization's standards for documentation, and ask for review and feedback when you begin working in a new setting so you are clear about the expectations of your organization. The professional associations publish guidelines that provide general standards for clinicians (AAMFT, 2001; APA, 1993; NASW 2008), but each clinical setting has unique requirements based on funding, population served, and services provided.

The clinical documentation you create is part of a treatment record that *may be viewed by the client and other third parties who are not clinicians*. The language and approach you use in creating the client's treatment record should be different from the way you talk about your clients or clinical work in supervision or in discussions with colleagues. The following are recommendations for creating professional clinical documents.

- Use objective descriptions.
- Omit unnecessary details.
- Write legibly and clearly.

Use objective descriptions of your client's symptoms and behavior rather than making subjective judgments. For example, "Client spoke in a loud, agitated voice and reported being angry" is a more objective description than "Client was intimidating and aggressive." When you need to make inferences or draw conclusions about the client's behavior, you should describe the data you used to draw the conclusion, such as "Client's abrupt shift in tone and topic when asked about her childhood suggests she is not ready to discuss the traumatic events of her past." If you are describing the client's life as she reports it, you should make it clear that you do not have firsthand information by saying, "Client reports her husband is verbally abusive," or "Client reports frequent demeaning and blaming statements made by her husband." A professional record should be free of conjecture, emotionally charged reactions, or unsubstantiated judgments.

Omit unnecessary details related to the client's history and life outside of treatment. You are creating a record of the client's diagnosis, symptoms, and treatment progress, so it is unnecessary to include details about specific interactions or events. Keep in mind that many details shared by the client are emotionally sensitive and could bring psychological harm or shame to the client if they were revealed to a third party. General statements like, "Client reported extensive sexual abuse by male relatives in childhood and by two male acquaintances in adolescence" or "Client described a conflict with a female co-worker" are preferable to a more detailed description. It is wise to avoid using names of anyone who is not part of the treatment. Use relationship terms like wife, partner, or son or use first initials if necessary for clarity (e.g., client's friends K and B). This preserves the confidentiality of individuals who are not under your care. Details that are clinically relevant can be kept in psychotherapy notes, *described below.*

Write legibly and clearly so that others can read and understand the record. If you work in a setting that does not have an electronic health record and your handwriting is difficult to read, check with your supervisor about how to create a legible record. If you create documentation on your own computer or other electronic device, follow your agency's guidelines for protection of the client's identity. Avoid using professional terms, jargon, or abbreviations that may be unfamiliar to professionals outside your agency or to non-clinicians.

One helpful strategy to ensure the professionalism of your clinical writing is to create your own psychotherapy notes (described below) when you begin working with a new client, when the client reveals a complicated piece of history or current experience, or when you have a session that is emotionally charged. You can capture important clinical details and your emotional responses in a psychotherapy note, while keeping them separate from the treatment record. Another strategy to use when you feel emotionally stimulated by a particular client or session is to ask your supervisor to review your assessment and progress notes to ensure that they are objective and professional.

Access to Client Record

The Health Insurance Portability and Accountability Act (HIPAA) was passed in 1996 and applies across the United States. It includes a number of regulations that standardize practices regarding disclosure of protected health information including records of mental health treatment (U.S. Department of Health and Human Services, 2003). *HIPAA requires that treatment providers allow clients to access their record except in rare circumstances,* so keep in mind that your client may read what you have written about her treatment. If you are doing psychotherapy, HIPAA allows you to keep psychotherapy notes in a file separate from the client chart which contains the progress notes. Psychotherapy notes are not part of the client's treatment record (Wiger, 2012). Additional guidelines about progress notes and psychotherapy notes follow later in this chapter.

The requirements of HIPAA and other legal and ethical requirements apply equally to paper and electronic records. Many clinical settings use electronic health records as a supplement to or substitute for paper records, and you may be asked to communicate client information by electronic means. Be aware that storage and communication of client treatment information electronically is subject to additional security requirements under the HIPAA Security Rule (Bennett, et al., 2006). Check with your supervisor about agency policy regarding electronic storage and communication of client information.

With a few exceptions for provider operations, situations of crisis or danger, and coordination of care, *information about the client's treatment can be disclosed only with the client's written authorization.* This requirement applies to disclosure of the written record as well as communication between you and a third party by phone, fax, or email.

It is good clinical practice to request the client's authorization, even in situations covered by the exceptions mentioned above, unless there is an immediate risk to safety. For example, communicating with your client's psychiatrist is permitted under HIPAA as part of coordination of care. However, your client will feel more empowered if you talk collaboratively with her, explaining the benefit to her treatment of your contacting the psychiatrist, and asking for her authorization before doing so. If she learns about your contact with the psychiatrist after the fact, she may feel betrayed or devalued. As mentioned in Chapter 3, it is also important to review the limits of confidentiality with the client in the first session so she knows the conditions under which you are required to disclose information to others.

HIPAA contains a provision that regulates release of information, called the *minimum necessary* requirement. When the client authorizes you to communicate with another person about her treatment or to disclose her treatment record to a third party, you are obligated to release the minimum amount of information necessary for the purpose of the communication or disclosure. For example, if a client gives you permission to speak with her child's teacher in order to help the client understand and manage the child's behavior, you would talk with the teacher about issues related to parenting, family relationships, and the child's behavior. You would not discuss the client's diagnosis or personal history.

In addition, when the client authorizes you to disclose information to a third party, you are required to *communicate only with the individual identified in the authorization* or the person who is authorized to receive the information. If you are sending hard copy information by mail, it should be addressed to a specific person or department (e.g., medical records). If you are unsure whether you are leaving a phone message on a private voice mail, it is safer to leave your name and contact information without the client's name, noting that you are calling to discuss a client at the client's request. When you consider sending information by fax, ask about the location and privacy protection of that information if you have any concern that the fax machine may not be secure.

Email is a common form of communication between providers, but it is imperative to remember that *email is not a secure, private means of communication.* Information you share with another provider about a client's treatment, including the fact that the client is receiving mental health services from you, cannot be sent by email unless it is encrypted or is sent without any information that would identify the client. You should send only client initials without name, date of birth, or other identifying information if the email communication is not encrypted. Check with your supervisor about agency policies for electronic communication and the availability of an encryption program.

Your obligation to maintain the confidentiality of your clients' protected health information means that *taking client charts or identifiable clinical documentation outside your workplace should be done only under strict protection.* If you are required to have hard copies of clinical documentation with you outside your workplace, check with your supervisor about how to protect that information, for example by keeping it in a locked file box. If you use an electronic health record or have access to client information on a personal computer or other electronic device, your device should be password protected. Never leave a computer or other device unattended when you are working on client documentation. Your agency may have other specific requirements for accessing client information remotely on personal electronic devices.

Assessment and Treatment Plan

Chapters 5, 6, and 9 discussed the clinical reasons for developing a diagnosis, conducting a thorough assessment, and developing a treatment plan. These documents are part of the client's treatment record and may be viewed by others, and they serve specific functions for third-party funders and other professionals or organizations.

Third-party funders generally pay for treatment only when it meets *requirements for medical necessity* (Wiger, 2012) which include three components:

- The client's symptoms are consistent with a diagnosis that is approved and covered by the third party,
- The client's ability to function is impaired by the symptoms, and
- The treatment provided has been shown to be effective in alleviating the symptoms or can be expected to be effective.

You demonstrate that your client's treatment is medically necessary when your *assessment and treatment plan provide evidence for these requirements.* This means documenting the nature of the client's symptoms, the diagnosis fitting those symptoms, the functional impairments resulting from the symptoms, and the goals and interventions that form the basis of treatment. If you are doing couple or family therapy, keep in mind that the third-party funding is tied to an individual so that the assessment and treatment plan need to show how the couple or family therapy serve the purpose of reducing the individual's symptoms.

Other medical practitioners, social service organizations, or government agencies may request a copy of your assessment and treatment plan when your client requests services or benefits. Eligibility for financial assistance and other benefits is often based on a mental health diagnosis and functional impairment. If this information is requested while the client is in treatment, talk with your client as well as the other party before deciding what information is most relevant. Requests may come to your organization after treatment has ended and you are no longer working there, so all of your assessment and treatment planning documents should reflect the client's symptoms and resulting impairments.

Progress Notes and Psychotherapy Notes

HIPAA makes a distinction between progress notes, which are part of the client record, and psychotherapy notes, which are the property of the clinician (Gehart, 2010; Wiger, 2012). This section describes the differences between these two types of notes and guides you in deciding how to record different aspects of the treatment.

Psychotherapy Notes

Psychotherapy notes contain details of the client's history or aspects of the treatment that are *clinically relevant to you* but do not fall within the guidelines for documentation in a progress note, as discussed below. Your psychotherapy notes may also include *impressions and hypotheses* that are important to your analysis of the psychotherapy, including comments from supervisors or consultants. If you keep psychotherapy notes, they must be in a *separate file* and I recommend that you use client initials or a number so the notes cannot be identified as protected health information.

Psychotherapy notes are *not intended for release to the client or any other party* (Wiger, 2012). Check with your supervisor about how you should store and dispose of psychotherapy notes when they are no longer needed. If you are providing case management or other supportive services in a mental health or substance use setting, check with your supervisor about whether and how to keep notes about the client and treatment that are not appropriate for the progress notes and other clinical documents.

Progress Notes

Progress notes generally follow a format specified by your agency. They are *part of the client's record* and usually include the following information (Gehart, 2010; Wiger, 2012):

- Context of the session such as the date, time, and length of the session;
- Who attended;
- Location of the session; and
- Your hand or electronic signature including your degree and licensure status or title, and date. (In some cases, your supervisor's signature may be required.)

The body of each progress note is a *report on the status of the client's symptoms and functioning and the progress in treatment.* The progress notes form the ongoing record of the client's treatment and should describe both what is changing in the client's life outside of treatment and what is happening in your interaction in the sessions. A progress note should include:

- The client's report and your observations of symptoms and current functioning,
- A description of your interventions and the client's response,
- Assessment of areas of crisis or danger and any action taken based on that assessment,
- Progress toward the treatment goals, and
- Your plan for continued treatment or changes in the treatment plan.

You can include *general information about the content or topics you talked about* without the details of the client's interactions with others. Statements like, "Client discussed conflict with her partner about financial issues," or "Client reported having contact with her mother, which brought up painful feelings of rejection" provide a context for understanding the session while preserving the privacy of the client and others.

A guide for the *appropriate level of detail* is that a progress note for a session lasting 45 to 60 minutes should be one-half to a full page. An exception is when the client is in crisis or at risk, in which case your assessment and plan for safety may require one to two pages.

Timeliness of progress notes is another important aspect of documentation. Your agency will probably require that you enter a progress note in the client's chart within 24 to 72 hours. I recommend writing the note on the same day as the session while it is fresh in your memory, which means scheduling time for writing notes on the days you hold client sessions. If you don't enter the note on the same day, take handwritten notes with enough detail to write a full progress note within the time required and definitely before the next session occurs. It will serve you well to develop a routine for writing progress notes in a timely and efficient way during your training, as you will then be able to carry the habit into independent clinical practice.

Contacts Outside of Scheduled Sessions

It is good clinical practice to *document contacts that occur outside of your scheduled sessions*. This includes communication with the client, family members, and other professionals as well as attendance at meetings for case coordination.

Documenting *communication with the client about scheduling* is usually not required; however, important clinical information is often contained in the timing and content of the client's requests to change an appointment. Talk with your supervisor about the value of recording the sequence of calls or emails related to scheduling in your psychotherapy notes or in a progress note that summarizes a series of communications. For example, after having a series of phone calls and messages you might write a short note saying:

> Client left a message at 11 p.m. asking to change her appointment for the next day. Several messages were exchanged with client over the next 2 days before she agreed to come at 6 p.m. on Friday. Client didn't come to her appointment and called at 8 p.m. saying she was sorry she forgot the appointment.

A progress note documenting *telephone contact with the client* should include the reason for having telephone contact and the content of the conversation. If the client is in crisis, your note should document your risk assessment, decision-making process, and plan. Since face-to-face contact is generally considered preferable to telephone contact, it is wise to include the clinical purpose of contact with a client by telephone if it is frequent or the primary method of communication. For example, you may be unable to schedule an in-person interview with the parent of an adolescent and conduct the initial parent interview by telephone in order to begin treatment promptly. In some settings, telephone communication may also be used as a method of outreach and risk assessment to engage clients who are reluctant to participate in treatment.

A progress note documenting *telephone contact with a family member or other professional or attendance at a meeting* should include the name of the individual or individuals with whom you had contact, their relationship with the client, the purpose of the communication or meeting, a description of the contact, and any decisions or recommendations that result. There are some situations in which you may have more contact with family members and other professionals for a period of time than you have with the client. Examples are treatment with adults who are unwilling or unable to participate actively in treatment due to the severity of their symptoms and children who are very young or whose behavior requires coordinated planning by a treatment team. Information about coordination of care is contained in Chapter 12.

If you have *email communication with or about a client*, I recommend that the emails be included in the client's record, either in hard copy or electronic form, or summarized in a note. As mentioned above, email communication should be sent in encrypted form or should omit information that would identify the client.

Special Documentation Situations

Some of the complex client situations discussed in Chapter 7 that require specialized assessment also require careful attention to documentation. My recommendations for the following situations are described below:

- Danger to self or others,
- Trauma,
- Substance use and addiction,
- Mandated treatment, and
- Other legal involvement.

You should consult with your supervisor when you are faced with any of these issues so she can guide you in making clinical decisions and documenting those decisions.

Danger to Self or Others

When a client is at risk of harming herself or someone else, you need to *document your assessment and safety plan*. This means your progress notes for these sessions need to be more detailed than your progress notes for sessions that do not involve risk.

Examples of high risk situations are

- Suicidal ideation or impulses,
- Threats or recent incidents of violence toward others,
- Domestic violence, and
- Self-harm or parasuicidal behaviors.

If your client reports any high risk symptoms or involvement in a high risk situation, you should document the following:

- Assessment of risk factors and protective factors,
- Analysis of the client's level of risk,
- Actions you considered and what you did to respond to the client's risk,

- The safety plan you developed with the client, and
- Follow-up measures you will take.

It is important to indicate what steps you decided not to take and why, in addition to your response, plan, and follow-up (Bennett et al., 2006). A sample summary of your analysis, response, and plan follows:

> Client was assessed at a moderate risk of suicidality but did not meet the criteria for involuntary hospitalization. Client refused voluntary hospitalization but agreed to ask a friend to stay with her overnight. Safety plan is that client will call the 24-hour crisis line if suicidal impulses increase and will attend an additional session with clinician in three days. Client agreed to adhere to this safety plan.

This statement documents your analysis of the client's risk, consideration of hospitalization, steps you took to ensure client's safety, and the safety plan. In addition to the progress note, your organization may require clinicians to complete an administrative report for the purpose of tracking high-risk incidents, so check with your supervisor about the guidelines and requirements in your work setting.

Trauma

As mentioned in Chapter 7, some incidents of recent or past trauma require *reports to law enforcement or social services*. All states have laws related to mandated reporting of child abuse, and some states require reporting of abuse of elders and dependent adults as well (Bennett et al., 2006). Your graduate courses probably introduced you to the reporting laws in your state, but be sure to *check with your supervisor about documentation of abuse reporting* when you begin a new training site. Guidelines and practices vary in different settings regarding the level of detail to include in the progress note compared with the abuse report, whether abuse reports are included in the client record, whether abuse reports are released with the rest of the record to the client or a third party, and how to document communication with law enforcement or social service workers during the investigation.

Substance Use and Addiction

If you work in a clinical setting that provides alcohol or drug abuse diagnosis, treatment, or referral for treatment, be aware that your clinical records may be covered by a federal law, 42CFR, Part 2, which protects *the confidentiality of records for clients with substance use disorders* (Substance Abuse and Mental Health Services Administration, 2011). 42CFR, Part 2, has different requirements for release of records and other information about substance abuse treatment from those of HIPAA, which covers medical records, including those for mental health treatment. Check with your supervisor about the policies and consent forms that apply to your documentation of substance abuse diagnosis and treatment.

Mandated Treatment

When the client's treatment is mandated by a third party, ask the client to bring in the written order or get the client's permission to speak with the mandating authority at the beginning of treatment so you can *be clear about the expectations and requirements for reporting.* Once you are certain of these requirements, talk with your supervisor about how you will keep written documentation and how you will communicate with the authority. You can then let the client know what information will be in her record, what you will write in a separate report, and who will have access to the record or other information about her treatment.

You *may be able to limit the information you report to mandating authorities,* disclosing only the client's record of attendance, the areas that are the focus of treatment, treatment goals, and a general statement about progress. If you are required to report the client's attendance, document your conversations about scheduling so you have a complete record of the timing and reasons for cancellations or missed appointments.

Some mandated treatment programs have an *interdisciplinary treatment team approach.* If you are part of a team working with clients who are in mandated treatment, there may be a requirement that clients give permission for team members to share clinical information and progress updates with each other and the mandating authority.

Other Legal Involvement

Examples of treatment with clients who are involved in an active legal case are divorce and child custody cases, civil suits in which the client alleges physical and psychological injury, immigration cases, and criminal cases against the client. In these cases, you may receive a request from the client or an attorney for treatment records or testimony, so pay close attention to your documentation.

If you learn that your client is involved in a legal case, consult with your supervisor. As discussed in Chapter 7, you need to *clarify that your role is to provide treatment* rather than advocacy in your client's legal case. Legal consultation is often helpful and is usually available from your professional association or through your agency. It is wise to communicate to the client the scope and limits of your role regarding her legal involvement clearly and preferably in writing. You may also need to clarify your role with the client's attorney as well. Always document any communication with the client and her attorney in a progress note.

Your records may be requested as evidence in the client's case even if you have informed the client that you cannot provide any evaluative opinion or advocacy. Therefore, all of your *documentation should be objective and focused on the treatment goals* without taking a position on the client's legal issues. There may be some situations in which it is appropriate to provide factual information to the client for use by her attorney, but always consult with your supervisor before providing any information to the client for use in a legal matter.

Summary

This chapter discussed professional standards related to clinical documentation and access to client records and information about treatment. Guidelines were provided relevant to assessments and treatment plans, progress notes and psychotherapy notes, other contacts, and special situations requiring attention to documentation. Specific areas of professional growth related to clinical documentation are listed below.

1. Using yourself as an instrument of hope, change, and healing:

    a. Notice when you are emotionally triggered by a client or a session, get support, and ask someone to review your documentation in that client's record.

2. Becoming confident in your authority and professionalism:

    a. Educate yourself about the requirements and standards for recordkeeping.
    b. Ask for feedback on your clinical documentation from your supervisor when you begin to work in a new clinical setting.
    c. Develop a routine for writing progress notes in a timely and efficient way.
    d. Pay close attention to documentation in complex clinical situations.

3. Developing interpersonal skills that strengthen the therapeutic relationship:

    a. Develop comfort in talking with clients about exchanging information with family members and other providers.
    b. Practice responding to client requests for records or questions about the content of the record.

Case Example: Liz's Documentation of Susana's Treatment

Assessment and Treatment Plan

Liz's agency, Community Support Center, requires completion of an assessment and treatment plan that document the medical necessity of the treatment for all clients regardless of funding source. Liz received training in how to complete these documents so that the client symptoms, degree of functional impairment, and purpose of interventions was clear. After Liz completed the assessment and treatment plan, her supervisor reviewed them to ensure that they met agency standards.

Progress Note

The following is the progress note written by Liz for her second session with Susana, described in Chapter 4.

Progress Note
Client Name: Susana Rodriguez
Date of Birth: XX/XX/19XX
Date of Session: XX/XX/20XX, 5 p.m., 50 minutes
Clinician Name: Liz Matthews

Client reported no change in her depressive symptoms since the first session, although she appeared somewhat more animated and less guarded. Therapist inquired about client's cultural background, and client described herself as an American citizen. She reported immigrating from El Salvador at age 7 with her parents and siblings, due to the danger posed by the war. She described the impact of the war on her extended family and the sadness and loss she felt on a family visit to their village about 10 years ago. Additional information about client's children and client's history of depression was obtained.

Therapist commented on client's pattern of feeling responsible for the happiness of her intimate partners as a factor contributing to her depression. Therapist also made a link between the trauma and loss related to the war and client's pattern of depression. Client accepted therapist's statements but didn't elaborate on them or express further insight.

Due to client's history of a suicide attempt in college, therapist assessed client's current risk. Client denied any current suicidal ideation or impulses and reported the attempt in college as the only time she has felt suicidal. Client agreed to meet weekly, which she had been reluctant to do at the time of the first session, indicating increased confidence and engagement in treatment.

Therapist will continue to assess client's current psychosocial functioning and history and will develop treatment goals with client within the next month. Initial treatment interventions will be to (1) strengthen and support client's insight into the emotional and relational factors contributing to her depression, and (2) identify strategies to lessen depressive symptoms.

Psychotherapy Note

The following is a psychotherapy note written by Liz for her second session with Susana, described in Chapter 4. She keeps this note along with psychotherapy notes from other client sessions in a folder separate from her client charts. She uses her psychotherapy notes to identify issues for supervision and to review issues to bring up with her clients in future sessions.

Client SR, session XX/XX/20XX

Likes herself when she's with a man and he's happy. Being partnered makes her vulnerable since her self-esteem is dependent on her partner. Feel like I want to support her finding self-esteem in other ways. Is that my agenda or hers?

Partners have been undocumented—C and husband A, difference in legal status was a source of conflict in relationships. S's anger toward M is greater because C was in danger of deportation if police were involved.

She seemed defensive when I asked about cultural background, maybe related to conflict with partners about legal status? Or sensitive to my judgment of her due to our ethnic differences? Should I ask more about her experiences of other people assuming she is undocumented? Is there an ambivalent attachment to El Salvador leading to her strong identification as American? Could I have brought it up in a more sensitive way? I need to watch for her sensitivity to feeling disrespected or judged.

Socioeconomic implications of move—was there a change in the family's status in coming to the U.S?

Father's alcoholism—ask about this in a future session, impact of the move to U.S. on father's drinking patterns.

Looking at photos from visit 10 yrs ago, follow up next session.

Progress Note for Telephone Contact

The following is a progress note for Liz's telephone conversation with Maria's school counselor, which occurred after Liz's fourth session with Susana.

Progress Note

Client Name: Susana Rodriguez

Date of Birth: XX/XX/19XX

Date of Session: XX/XX/20XX 2 p.m., 15 minutes

Clinician Name: Liz Matthews

Therapist contacted Anna Jones, the school counselor who is treating client's 15-year-old daughter Maria at Northside High School. The counselor reported that Maria was referred by her teacher about 6 weeks ago due to a change in Maria's attention in class. The counselor has observed significant symptoms of anxiety. She reports that Maria has been reluctant to talk about the details of her life at home but has expressed a desire for help with her anxiety. Maria has also disclosed some experimentation with alcohol and marijuana on social occasions with friends but denies any problems resulting from her use. Therapist shared the family history of alcoholism with the counselor, indicating that Maria is at increased risk of addiction.

The counselor's plan is to meet with Maria for a total of 12 sessions, which is the maximum provided by the school counseling program, and to refer the family to a school-based family therapy program, which is provided at no cost to families through a grant-funded community collaboration. Therapist and counselor agreed to encourage and support both mother and daughter to participate in family therapy, acknowledging the reluctance of both of them to do so.

Review of Liz's Documentation

Liz's progress note for the second session contains less detail than the assessment report, reflecting the difference in the purpose of these two parts of the record. Progress notes primarily document the course of treatment. The assessment report is an overview of the client's history and current functioning, and therefore contains more detailed information. Neither the assessment report nor the progress note discuss Susana's partners' undocumented status, since this is sensitive information that is both unnecessary and potentially damaging if released to a third party. Liz's psychotherapy note contains her clinically relevant observations, including the fact that two of Susana's partners were undocumented, as well as her questions and inferences. Her progress note for her contact with the school counselor outlines the information shared between the two providers and their plan for continued treatment. The note illustrates the usefulness of collaborating with other providers to ensure coordination of care.

The Next Step

Chapter 11 will discuss the unfolding of the therapeutic relationship and strategies for managing the challenges and obstacles that can emerge during treatment. The case example illustrates some of these difficulties.

References

American Association for Marriage and Family Therapy. (2001). *Code of ethics.* Alexandria, VA: Author.

American Psychological Association. (1993). Record keeping guidelines. *American Psychologist, 48,* 984–986.

Bennett, B. E., Bricklin, P. M., Harris, E., Knapp, S., VandeCreek, L., & Younggren, J. N. (2006). *Assessing and managing risk in psychological practice: An individualized approach.* Rockville, MD: The Trust.

Gehart, D. (2010). *Mastering competencies in family therapy: A practical approach to theories and clinical case documentation* (1st ed.). Belmont, CA: Brooks/Cole, Cengage Learning.

National Association of Social Workers. (2008). *Code of ethics.* Washington, DC: Author. Retrieved May 4, 2012, from http://www.naswdc.org/pubs/code/code.asp.

Substance Abuse and Mental Health Services Administration. (2011). *SAMHSA's confidentiality law and regulations (42 CFR) FAQ.* Retrieved January 18, 2016, from http://www.integration.samhsa.gov/financing/SAMHSA_42CFRPART2FAQII_-1-,_pdf.pdf.

U.S. Department of Health & Human Services. (2003). *Summary of the HIPAA privacy rule.* Retrieved April 3, 2013, from http://www.hhs.gov/ocr/hipaa.

Wiger, D. E. (2012). *The psychotherapy documentation primer* (3rd ed.). Hoboken, NJ: John Wiley & Sons, Inc.

11

UNFOLDING OF THE THERAPEUTIC RELATIONSHIP

(Note: This chapter will use the male pronoun for supervisor, clinician, and client.)

This chapter reviews aspects of the ongoing therapeutic relationship that develops between you and the client. I begin by discussing the contribution of the clinician's interpersonal style to the relationship. I follow by offering suggestions on maintaining the treatment alliance, responding to changes in the client's symptoms and disclosure of new information, managing obstacles that arise, and maintaining professional boundaries. Managing these issues well will enable you to provide more effective treatment.

Contribution of the Clinician's Interpersonal Style

Your relationship with the client begins to unfold from your first contact and develops over time as you learn more about him and become accustomed to his way of relating to you. You usually find a *unique rhythm or pattern in your work with each client* within the first 6 to 8 weeks of regular contact, largely determined by the client's accustomed ways of relating to others.

Your initial clinical task is to *find a way to interact therapeutically with the client within his familiar relational style*. This task will be easier or more challenging, depending on the match between you and the client in your interpersonal styles. If you work in a treatment team with other clinicians, you will probably notice that you and your colleagues have different responses to the same client, based on your interpersonal styles and preferences. Remember that it is your responsibility to respond to the client's interpersonal presentation in a therapeutic way, to be flexible interpersonally within professional boundaries, and to make adaptations to enable the client to feel as safe as possible in treatment.

You will become more skilled at developing therapeutic relationships with your clients when you *reflect on your own interpersonal style, your assumptions about yourself and others, and what leads you to feel safer or more fearful with others.* When you are clear about your contribution to the therapeutic relationship, you will be able to identify aspects of the client's interpersonal style that are similar or complementary to yours and those that are different from or in conflict with yours. For example, if you like and need to feel some degree of control in relationships, you will enjoy and feel safe with clients who are somewhat deferential and compliant. Conversely, if you value honest expression of disagreement, you will feel safer with clients who openly question your suggestions and conclusions.

When a client's style matches or is complementary to yours, *watch for blind spots in your assessment* of his interpersonal style. Your client may need to expand his repertoire of responses to different interpersonal situations. A client who is pleasantly compliant in treatment may need your encouragement to develop more assertiveness, and a client who questions authority appropriately in treatment may benefit from being selective in challenging authority figures in work situations.

Your primary task with most clients is to identify the interpersonal stance that will facilitate your client's engagement in treatment. However, at times you may face *situations that present a potential risk to your safety.* If you work with clients who have a history of violence and are emotionally volatile or hostile, ensuring your safety as well as the safety of your clients should be your top priority. Seek assistance and support from your supervisor and follow agency procedures for safety. The physical and emotional safety of both clinician and client are essential to a productive treatment relationship, and treatment cannot proceed until safety is established. This might require scheduling appointments when your supervisor or other experienced clinicians are present, having access to an emergency alert system, and/or arranging the seating in the room so you can exit the room rapidly if necessary. You may also need to set limits on the client's behavior in the session, as in the following statement:

> I understand that you're very upset about things that have happened in your life, and I want to help you with the issues we have discussed. It's hard for me to pay attention to what you're saying when you're yelling at me, though, so I need to ask you to speak in a lower voice.

Developing and Maintaining a Treatment Alliance

As noted in Chapter 3, a therapeutic alliance is characterized by a sense of collaboration between you and the client with a shared feeling of working together toward the same goal (Teyber & McClure, 2011). The quality of the therapeutic alliance is a strong predictor of treatment effectiveness (Norcross, 2010; Shedler, 2010).

Empathy is one of the primary factors in your ability to develop and maintain a therapeutic alliance with your client (Elliott et al., 2011). You will need to express empathy with your client's emotional experience, to understand his ways of coping with painful events and feelings, and to support his hope for being able to live a life that is more rewarding.

Often you maintain an alliance with the client by being aware of feelings, desires, and beliefs he holds outside of awareness as well as those that are consciously accessible. Therefore, your empathy is broader than attunement with his emotional state from moment to moment. Clients often have protected themselves from experiencing anger, fear, hope, or a desire for connection, because these feelings have been painful or dangerous in the past. Having empathy for these unacknowledged states and helping the client become aware of a broader range of his experience may be essential in helping him reach his goals.

The following are some aspects of the client's interpersonal presentation that affect the ease with which a therapeutic alliance can be developed initially and maintained throughout treatment:

- Client's attitude of cooperativeness or hostility toward treatment,
- Rigidity of the client's interpersonal style, and
- The degree of reactivity or sensitivity in the client's interpersonal interactions.

Client's Attitude of Cooperativeness or Hostility Toward Treatment

The client's attitude of cooperativeness or hostility toward treatment is a primary factor in establishing a therapeutic alliance. You will find it more difficult to achieve a therapeutic alliance with clients who begin treatment with a degree of hostility, whether that hostility is due to treatment being mandated or because of prior negative experiences with treatment providers. Reflect on your own reactions and assumptions regarding your clients' hostility in order to develop flexibility in your approach with those clients who do not enter treatment with a cooperative and positive attitude. Remember that interpersonal hostility is often based in fear and may have developed as a way to cope with traumatic experience. Examine your assumptions and come to understand the purpose of your client's attitude toward you in order to be empathic if he seems uninterested in your help.

At the other extreme, a client who presents as highly cooperative may have an overly deferential and passive interpersonal style that will interfere with treatment progress. This coping style is more socially acceptable than a hostile attitude, and you may not recognize for several months the obstacle it can present to the therapeutic alliance. Often an initial clue that your client may fit this pattern is that you feel overly protective of him, believe he is incapable of making changes, and find yourself putting forth more effort in the treatment than you do with other clients.

Rigidity of the Client's Interpersonal Style

The therapeutic alliance is more difficult to establish and maintain with clients who have limited coping strategies and are inflexible in their responses to interpersonal situations (Teyber & McClure, 2011). You can *identify the client's familiar and preferred interpersonal style in his pattern of past and current relationships.* His report may reflect consistent experiences of others as inferior, untrustworthy, exploitive, or exerting power, and of himself as superior, victimized, or dependent. Interpreting the client's report as reflecting his interpersonal style doesn't mean you should doubt the truth of his report, but it means you should focus your attention on his interpretation of his experiences and his adaptation to them.

The client's interpersonal style will also be evident in his interaction with you (Gelso & Bhatia, 2012). You may feel put off by the client or critical of him if his preferred style is unfamiliar to you or triggers associations to unpleasant experiences in your personal life. Use self-reflection and intentional cultivation of empathy in order to develop an alliance in these cases. Clients whose interpersonal style is familiar and comfortable to you will be easier to work with initially. However, take note of the degree of rigidity or flexibility in the client's relational style in all cases, since it may become an obstacle later in treatment even if it does not interfere with your initial alliance with him. See the section on "Representation of the Client's Life Obstacles" in this chapter for further discussion of this challenge.

The Degree of Reactivity or Sensitivity in the Client's Interpersonal Interactions

It is challenging to develop and maintain a therapeutic alliance with clients who are highly reactive or sensitive to interpersonal interactions. These sensitivities often manifest in strong emotional responses to the clinician, which may feel like demands for you to behave in specific ways in order to gain the client's trust. Your response to interpersonal reactivity may be that you work hard to comply with the client's requests or that you withdraw out of resentment and frustration.

Clients who present with high emotional reactivity often meet the DSM-5 criteria for *borderline personality disorder* and specific skills and knowledge may be required to provide effective treatment to them (Linehan, 1993a; McWilliams, 2011). As you develop these skills, follow the general principle that attending to the limits and boundaries of the therapeutic relationship is a primary, recurring theme. The client needs to experience both firm, clear limits and nonjudgmental support from the clinician. This way of responding to the client creates a treatment relationship that is different from the client's interpersonal relationships which have been unsatisfying and sometimes traumatic.

Variability in Alliance during Treatment

The degree of alliance you feel with the client often varies throughout treatment. This variability may be related to the content of the sessions, the client's feelings of vulnerability, changes in how you view and react to the client, your experiences with other clients, or events in your personal life. When working with *couples and families*, you have an alliance with the individual family members as well as with the family unit, making your task especially complex. If you feel more allied or empathic toward some family members than toward others, notice these changes and work to restore balance in your alliance with the couple or family.

Changes in Symptoms and Presenting Issues

We develop a treatment plan with the *expectation that the client's symptoms will be alleviated or that there will be gradual improvement*. Often the course of treatment is uneven, with periods of improvement alternating with periods of deterioration in functioning or escalation in symptoms. The concept of relapse as part of recovery, initially developed in conjunction with a harm reduction approach to substance use disorders (Denning, et al., 2004), can be applied to symptoms of mental health disorders as well. Applying this concept means acknowledging that symptoms may recur and that progress rarely follows a consistent, linear pattern.

As you discuss the client's progress and symptoms in each session, help him *identify the external events and internal coping responses that are associated with changes in symptoms*. Doing this fosters insight and self-efficacy, as the client is able to identify factors that trigger his symptoms or contribute to improvement. With these insights, he can become more proactive in managing his life.

Lack of Improvement in Symptoms

If the client's symptoms remain at the same level or increase in severity despite your adherence to the treatment plan, examine your diagnosis and assessment and discuss the client's lack of progress with your supervisor. Timing and expectations for improvement often vary, and symptoms and disorders that are more severe and longstanding may require more time for improvement. However, if there is no improvement within 3 months of developing your treatment plan, talk with your supervisor about seeking consultation from another supervisor or expert clinician who can provide a different perspective.

The following are steps to take in evaluating the reasons for a lack of improvement.

- Reevaluate the primary diagnosis.
- Consider a secondary personality disorder diagnosis.
- Inquire about substance use which may have been unacknowledged at the time of your original assessment.
- Ask the client about his use of psychotropic medication and evaluate whether it is being used as prescribed.
- Reflect on cultural variables that affect the client's response to treatment interventions and adapt your goals and interventions if necessary.
- Assess family dynamics, which may interfere with change.
- Consider whether there is secondary gain from continued illness or disability.

- Encourage the client to acknowledge any ambivalence about his participation in treatment.
- Explore the client's ideas about his symptoms and what may be contributing to the lack of progress.

Going through these steps, reviewing your diagnosis and assessment, and seeking consultation may lead you to *revise the treatment plan*. You and the client may decide to change the focus of the treatment goals, revise the goals to be more specific or to reflect smaller steps toward a larger goal, or shift the treatment modality or intervention.

Change in Presenting Issues or Life Circumstances

Sometimes the client's life circumstances change and the client's attention shifts to a crisis or a new event that wasn't present when you developed the treatment plan. For example, the client may lose his job, begin a new intimate relationship, or be contacted by an estranged sibling. When these kinds of events happen, evaluate whether the existing treatment goals are relevant or require revision, remembering that your progress notes should document the client's progress toward the goals in the treatment plan.

Before assuming that the goals need to be revised, *consider whether the existing goals apply to the new situation*. For example, the goal of reducing symptoms would remain relevant if the client is facing a potential crisis, although progress may be somewhat slower and the client may need your help in focusing on managing the crisis in a way that does not exacerbate his symptoms. Similarly, goals related to interpersonal functioning can be applied to a variety of the client's relationships.

When the client seems to be changing the focus of treatment, the apparent change may reflect a *pattern of difficulty prioritizing and maintaining consistency in working toward his needs and goals*. The best approach may be to bring the client's attention back to the goals he set for treatment and question what it would mean to return to those issues. If you and the client discuss the situation thoroughly and determine that a new or revised goal is warranted, document the change in your progress notes and check with your supervisor about doing a formal revision of the treatment plan.

Disclosure of New Information

You will continue to learn more about your client as you work together and he talks about aspects of his life that he didn't disclose during your assessment. New clinicians sometimes wonder if receiving new information means that their initial assessment was inadequate. It is natural to feel surprised, critical, or annoyed when your client tells you something significant after weeks or months of working together. It may seem like an intentional manipulation that invalidates your assessment, case formulation, and treatment plan. However, the disclosure of new information is *often a phenomenon that accompanies significant progress in the treatment relationship.*

Most clients feel emotionally vulnerable when entering treatment, and they may present themselves in a way that is self-protective or reflects their assumptions about what the clinician wants to hear. Usually the client is not intentionally misleading the clinician, but is acting out of familiar, ingrained patterns of relating to others. When there is conscious deception, it usually stems from the client having felt betrayed in the past when he was open and vulnerable. As *the client experiences the treatment relationship as different from past relationships,* he will feel more confident in expressing to you more of his thoughts, feelings, and experiences.

At other times, a client may reveal new information that was previously outside of awareness. Painful experiences of the past are often kept out of awareness due to feelings of shame or guilt. *When the client develops a sense of safety in treatment,* he may access memories of these past experiences due to reduced shame and fear of rejection (Weiss, 1993). Often the new historical information provides a detail that shifts the meaning of the past event, and you may help the client connect the past experience with a distressing feeling. For example, a client may recall having a disagreement with his father on the day of the father's sudden death, and this recollection helps explain his avoidance of conflict in relationships.

Client disclosures of new information should be *incorporated and documented in the treatment in several ways.* Your progress notes and periodic assessment updates should include additional details of history and current functioning that are clinically important. You may also revise and expand your clinical case formulation by incorporating your understanding of the client's feelings of shame and his strategies for managing interpersonal rejection that were operating to keep that material outside of the treatment relationship. If you learn more about the client's current functioning, consider whether any change in the treatment goals is appropriate. Examples of new information that might result in new or different treatment goals are (a) difficulties in parenting, (b) disclosure of substance use after initial denials of use, and (c) additional symptoms that were not reported in the beginning of treatment.

Representation of Client's Life Obstacles in Treatment

As you and the client work to resolve issues of concern and distress, a primary focus of your attention is outside the treatment relationship. For example, you may focus on symptoms, life circumstances, and relationship difficulties. If you work in a short-term treatment model, you may find that this outside focus persists throughout your treatment relationship. However, in some short-term treatment relationships and in nearly all longer term treatment relationships, *the client's symptoms, life circumstances, and relationship difficulties are reflected in the treatment relationship itself.*

When the client's life obstacles enter the treatment relationship, this may be accompanied by *a shift in your attitude toward him*. You may find yourself judging him to be unmotivated, resistant, manipulative, or untreatable. You may feel discouraged, impatient, and frustrated at the client's lack of progress or lack of engagement. You may talk with a colleague or supervisor about transferring the client to another treatment setting or professional, or you may research different treatment methods or protocols looking for more powerful interventions.

Changes in your treatment plan or structure are sometimes necessary, but more often the appearance of these obstacles presents an *opportunity to understand and impact the client's difficulties directly*. Though you may be surprised and disheartened when obstacles emerge in the treatment relationship, it is a predictable development and brings the client's authentic experience into the therapeutic alliance. When treatment progress seems stalled, be sure to ask your supervisor for guidance before making any changes in the treatment goals or structure.

When you notice a shift in your attitude or other indications that the client's life obstacles have entered the treatment relationship, *reflect on your recent interactions with the client and notice your thoughts and feelings without acting on them*. Doing this gives you the opportunity to learn about yourself and the client. The ability to reflect and examine your responses is essential to developing a professional therapeutic style that is different from your interpersonal style in personal relationships. Remember that your professional obligation is to maintain your focus on facilitating the client's treatment and to engage in self-examination when you are tempted to blame or reject the client. Supervision, consultation, and personal support are vital in this process.

Clients' life obstacles may enter the treatment relationship in any of the following ways:

- Emergence of symptoms during sessions,
- Repetition of client's maladaptive interpersonal style,
- Sensitivity to issues of control and autonomy, and
- Negative or critical responses by family members.

Emergence of Symptoms during Sessions

The client's difficulties may enter the treatment relationship through the emergence of symptoms that are the focus of treatment. A depressed client may respond to your suggestions with hopelessness, a psychotic client may be preoccupied with hallucinations during a session, an anxious child may be fearful about coming into the treatment room, and a traumatized family may have difficulty organizing themselves to come to sessions as scheduled. At times, outside resources, such as medication evaluation and assistance from a case manager, are helpful in reducing or managing these symptoms so that the client can benefit from your treatment. Other times you may need to modify the structure by meeting in the client's home or another familiar setting or by including a trusted family member or another professional in the session.

Remember that the emergence of symptoms directly in treatment *is a way for the client to communicate to you about the nature and severity of his problems.* This communication is not usually intentional or conscious, but it is effective in conveying the depth of his despair, fear, and overwhelming feelings. It is valuable to express your empathy and understanding in addition to looking for ways to reduce the impact of the symptoms. You might say

> When you told me last week about your depression I wasn't able to understand it as fully as I can today, when you're showing me how hopeless you feel about being able to do anything that will make it better.

Repetition of Client's Maladaptive Interpersonal Style

At some point in treatment, your client is likely to repeat his familiar but problematic interpersonal style in the treatment relationship (Teyber & McClure, 2011). This behavior is most prominent with clients who have a personality disorder diagnosis, but this type of repetition also occurs with clients who do not meet the full criteria for a personality disorder. The client's maladaptive interpersonal style is reflected in (a) distortions in his perceptions of himself and others, and (b) strongly held beliefs and relational patterns, primarily outside of awareness, that influence his ways of relating to you and others.

When your client has an inflexible, maladaptive interpersonal style, your treatment may be challenged by the client's

- Emotional volatility,
- Strong reactions to you,
- Interpersonal struggles for dominance or compliance in sessions,
- Suspicion and distrust of your purpose and motives, and
- Argumentativeness or helplessness in response to your suggestions.

The treatment will also be *challenged by the intense emotions that are stimulated in you* by the client's interpersonal style. Examples of such emotions are grandiose feelings of responsibility, feelings of specialness and personal gratification, intense despair or fear, and overwhelming anger or revulsion. You may also experience some triggering of your own past traumas, if such experiences are part of your history.

The following *strategies will help you maintain a therapeutic relationship* with a client who presents some of these challenges.

- Notice and use your emotional responses to the client to increase your understanding of his relationships outside treatment.
- Identify a way of relating to the client that will provide an interpersonal experience different from his familiar patterns.
- Implement therapeutic techniques specific to treatment of individuals with personality disorders (Linehan, 1993a, and McWilliams, 2011).

- Get extra support from supervision, consultation, and your peer relationships to manage your intense countertransference emotions.

Sensitivity to Issues of Control and Autonomy

Challenges also occur in treatment due to the client's issues regarding control and autonomy, reflected in a sensitivity and reactivity to feeling dominated by others or a reluctance to take initiative due to a fear of blame or rejection. Clients who have difficulty feeling a sense of self-efficacy or agency often are conflicted about using treatment to make improvements in their lives. It is difficult for both you and the client to manage the *paradox of accepting the client while advocating for change* (Linehan, 1993b).

The following are some *common conflicts* that clients may experience related to control and autonomy.

- Asking for help leads to fears about being controlled.
- Expressing a desire for change heightens fears about being judged or rejected for taking initiative or exerting autonomy.
- Changing one's behavior may trigger feelings of shame because change is experienced as confirmation of inadequacy.

These conflicts become apparent when the client asks for advice or suggestions but fails to follow the advice or when he shows improvement but doesn't maintain therapeutic gains. *Countertransference responses* to these conflicts include frustration, feelings of helplessness, and feeling the need to become more active and directive. You may begin to view the client as sabotaging the efforts you and he are making and consider ending treatment.

Instead of ending treatment or becoming more directive, use self-reflection and the support of supervision to return to a therapeutic stance of empathy for the client's conflict. You can then *acknowledge the treatment dilemma directly* and engage the client in collaborative problem solving. Following are examples of ways to talk with the client.

- I notice you haven't followed through on the steps we have discussed and I wonder if it feels as though I'm taking control of our work together.
- You seem to be reluctant to try different ways to manage the problem we're working on, and I wonder if you're worried about being blamed or judged if it doesn't work out as well as you'd like.
- Last week you had made some changes and were feeling better, but this week things seem to be worse again. Is there something about making changes that feels scary or unpleasant?

Negative or Critical Responses by Family Members

Your treatment relationship may be challenged when the client's family responds to change in a negative or critical way. Family systems theorists have described the tendency of all living systems, including families, to maintain stability through implicit homeostatic mechanisms (Teyber & McClure, 2011). While family members usually express a desire for the client to change, there is often an *unacknowledged benefit to the family system to maintain the existing symptoms and relationships*.

The following interventions can help to address the ambivalence of family members to the changes that occur during treatment.

- When your client is a *child, couple, or family*:

  - In your initial session, ask about the function of the presenting problem and symptoms;
  - During assessment and treatment planning, identify the desired and undesired consequences of change on the family system;
  - During treatment, comment on the responses you see in family members when they are faced with actual or potential change; and
  - Throughout treatment, schedule regular sessions with the parents of a child client to assess and manage their challenges when change begins to occur.

- When your client is an *individual adult*:

  - Inquire about the role of family members in the client's decision to initiate treatment,
  - Assess the client's family relationships and the likely impact of therapeutic change on those relationships,
  - Continue to discuss family members' responses to changes in the client's symptoms and behavior during treatment, and
  - Refer for couple or family therapy when the client feels undermined or when the client's improvement highlights another issue or problem in the relationship system.

Maintaining Professional Boundaries

As mentioned in Chapter 1, the concept of professional boundaries refers to the structure and limits that are placed on your relationship with the client in order to ensure that your focus is on the client's needs and welfare. Maintaining this focus means managing the intense feelings that arise in clinical work in a different way than you manage them in your personal life. Initially, you will probably respond to clients in ways that are consistent with your personal relational style. You will find that your personal style of relating is helpful with some clients but is distracting or even damaging to your therapeutic relationship with others or with the same client at different times. Learn to develop *a professional role that you can return to* when you are drawn into a familiar relational pattern.

Some situations which may lead to concerns and conflicts about professional boundaries are

- Finding yourself wanting to take a caretaking or rescuing role,
- Experiencing critical and judgmental attitudes toward a client,
- Dealing with agency requirements that affect treatment decisions, or
- Feeling pulled to make exceptions to professional boundaries.

Caretaking or Rescuing Roles

You are probably familiar and comfortable with caretaking and rescuing others in distress or need, since this provides some of the motivation for many of us who enter the behavioral health field. Our role as professionals does involve some caretaking and in extreme situations may even involve rescuing. However, a primary aspect of all treatment relationships is to *facilitate and support the client's sense of agency and self-efficacy.* When you adopt a caretaking role, you inadvertently communicate a belief that the client is unable to care for himself, and this undermines his self-worth.

Most often we take a caretaking role to meet our own needs even though we believe we are serving the client. *Examine your need to feel important and effective,* and use your supervisor's guidance about appropriate boundaries in your professional role. If caretaking is a familiar and comfortable role for you, you will need to shift your focus to be sure you think clearly about the clients' needs in the full context of their lives and goals. You will also need to focus on identifying ways to support both attachment and autonomy. Since you will provide time-limited treatment during your clinical training, it is a disservice to encourage your clients to view you as the source of answers rather than as a support for them in developing their own strengths.

Two clinical settings that contain especially strong pulls toward caretaking are working with children and providing case management to children and adults. In both of these settings, be mindful of ways to foster the client's self-efficacy while being responsive to his developmental readiness for independence and initiative. Remember to support the client to do what he is able to do for himself and only take tasks on yourself that are clearly outside his developmental capacities. In child cases, you should make choices based on both the developmental stage of the child and the capacities of the parents, while keeping in mind that the child's attachment to the parents is his primary attachment.

Critical and Judgmental Attitudes

Critical and judgmental attitudes can present a challenge to professional boundaries when they lead to actions that are punitive rather than serving to support the client's therapeutic goals. You may become aware of these attitudes at times when you feel frustrated, angry, or blaming of the client, or when you use clinical terms like *borderline, acting out, non-compliant,* and *testing the limits* to characterize the client's behavior.

You will facilitate the therapeutic process if you *view critical or judgmental attitudes as countertransference* and work to understand them in the context of the client's difficulties and goals. Take care to wait until you have reached an empathic understanding and have returned to your professional role before you make and implement decisions about the client's treatment. Doing this will ensure that you are not enacting a punitive relational pattern that may be familiar to both you and the client.

Agency Requirements Affecting Treatment Decisions

During clinical training, you will work in agency settings that have requirements regarding attendance, payment, and compliance with treatment recommendations. These are part of the initial treatment contract and therapeutic frame you establish in the first session. When the client has difficulty meeting these or other requirements, your professional role requires that you talk about the issues and their impact on the client's ability to participate appropriately in his treatment.

You are likely to face situations in which you appreciate the structure and support of agency requirements for treatment and others in which you disagree or resent them. There may be times when you want to discontinue services but are prevented from doing so, and other times when you want to continue services with a client but are required to end because he has failed to attend regularly or make payment. The pull toward adopting a caretaking role or assuming a judgmental attitude can be strong at these times.

When you find yourself in conflict with agency requirements, consider the concept of *parallel process,* described in Chapter 2. Your feelings about your supervisor or agency administration may parallel the client's feelings or conflict with authority figures including you. Talk thoroughly about the situation and your countertransference with your supervisor when you disagree with an agency requirement. If you are required to either continue or discontinue services when you want a different outcome, use your supervisor's support to carry out the required action in a professional manner.

When you discontinue services with a client who has not complied with agency requirements, *keep your professional composure and relate to the client in a calm manner while holding firm limits.* You may need to work hard to counter the pull away from your professional role, but a therapeutic outcome is possible when you relate to the client in a situation of conflict without blame and judgment. This is easier to do when you have established clear professional boundaries at the beginning of treatment and harder when you have been inconsistent or lax with the treatment frame.

Pulls to Make Exceptions to Professional Boundaries

There will be times when you feel unduly constrained by the limitations of your professional role as a clinician. When you form a strong connection with a client, it is natural to want to respond as you would with a friend or family member. You might want to give your client a gift, see him outside of the professional setting of treatment, or give a hug to comfort his distress. When you have these thoughts about breaking professional boundaries, talk with your supervisor to understand the pull you are feeling.

Moments when you feel pulled to break professional boundaries are *opportunities for personal and professional growth*, and you need support to work through your feelings and make a professional decision. Consider talking with your therapist as well as your supervisor to identify the relevance of the clinical situation to your personal history. It will take time to have confidence in the value and power of a therapeutic relationship that is different from a personal relationship. It is part of the professional growth process to develop appreciation, understanding, and value for the professional boundaries and role of a clinician. However, this growth can only take place only when you stay within these boundaries.

We are most tempted to cross professional boundaries when we are faced with an intense and unpleasant feeling, and we want to avoid or deflect our discomfort by stepping outside the professional role. It is often difficult to know whether we are acting in the client's interest in these situations because we are preoccupied by our own feelings. By managing your feelings and sharing the client's discomfort, you communicate your commitment and care to the therapeutic relationship as well as your belief in his strength to manage his pain.

An example of a clinical situation that might prompt you to consider crossing professional boundaries follows:

> Your 24-year-old male client describes the death of his father due to a drug overdose when the client was 4 years old. He wonders whether to visit the gravesite for the first time, having recently learned that his father was buried in the town where the client now lives. You may feel pulled to offer to go with the client to visit his father's grave in order to provide support in this emotionally difficult time. However, your offer to go to the gravesite closes off the opportunity to explore your client's feelings about his father and the meaning of visiting his grave. Staying in your professional clinical role allows the client to experience your support as he grieves, discovers the variety of complex thoughts and feelings associated with visiting his father's grave, and comes to a decision about the best course of action, including who he wants to go with him if he makes the visit. This process will provide therapeutic benefit and is different from the responses of family members or friends who are motivated by their own needs and feelings.

Summary

This chapter discussed different aspects of the therapeutic relationship as it develops over the time of treatment. I offered suggestions related to the clinician's interpersonal style, therapeutic alliance, changes in symptoms, disclosure of new information, representations of the client's life obstacles, and professional boundaries. Specific areas of professional growth related to the unfolding of the therapeutic relationship are listed below.

1. Using yourself as an instrument of hope, change, and healing:

    a. Reflect on the similarities and differences in the familiar interpersonal styles of you and the client.
    b. Welcome new information as a sign of therapeutic progress.
    c. Be aware of changes in your attitude toward the client as indications of obstacles entering the treatment relationship.

2. Becoming confident in your authority and professionalism:

    a. Reevaluate your diagnosis and assessment when there is little or no improvement.
    b. Assess the impact of the client's change on the family system.
    c. Understand the importance of professional boundaries and develop confidence in your professional clinical role.

3. Developing interpersonal skills that strengthen the therapeutic relationship:

    a. Become skilled in managing client hostility, rigidity, and reactivity in the therapeutic relationship.
    b. Learn to respond therapeutically to issues that present obstacles to the treatment relationship: emergence of symptoms, maladaptive interpersonal styles, and issues of control and autonomy.

Case Example: Therapeutic Relationship of Liz and Susana

Overview of Sessions 1 through 16

Liz and Susana met for 16 sessions in 5 months. Susana missed one session without notice in the second month and two additional sessions with 24 hours' notice in the third and fourth months. They also missed one session due to Liz's scheduled vacation.

Liz evaluated their *therapeutic alliance* as positive and cooperative, after Susana's initial reserve and caution lessened. Liz was alert to Susana's tendency to view Liz as an authority and to be compliant with her recommendations. In light of this tendency, Liz was careful to frame her suggestions in the form of questions and to be explicit in asking for Susana's opinion and feedback. She was pleased when

Susana was able to disagree with her because Liz is comfortable with open conflict due to her family's cultural norms and the interpersonal style she has developed in her personal adult relationships. She felt wary of Susana's level of compliance and received guidance from Dalia that led her to modify her expectations of the therapeutic alliance. Dalia helped Liz see her comfort with open disagreement as a personal preference and a culturally based expectation rather than as a measure of the quality of her alliance with Susana.

In the last month, Liz has felt more *concerned about the quality of her therapeutic alliance* with Susana, following two missed sessions and her sense of Susana being more guarded. Liz has begun to feel discouraged at the lack of progress and momentum in the treatment. Dalia has helped Liz examine her expectations in light of the significant amount of loss and trauma in Susana's past. They have also discussed the possibility that Susana may be under-reporting her use of alcohol, since it would be difficult for most clients to maintain such a significant reduction in drinking. Susana has not reported any increase in her alcohol use, but the stall in treatment progress raises a question about Susana's use and the accuracy of her self-report to Liz.

Dalia suggests that Liz seek *consultation from another agency supervisor* who specializes in substance abuse treatment. This supervisor provides Liz with suggestions for creating an open atmosphere for discussion of Susana's drinking, using Motivational Interviewing techniques (Miller & Rollnick, 2002). She also normalizes the slow and uneven progress involved in changing patterns of addiction, and she comments on the fact that Susana has relied on alcohol to cope with painful feelings for more than half of her life. Liz feels relieved after the consultation and recognizes that she developed unrealistic goals for her work with Susana. She also feels confident about having additional tools to address Susana's drinking.

Session 17: Lack of Progress and Disclosure of New Information

Session 17 begins in the following way:

Liz: Where would you like to start today?

Susana: I've been wondering if I should stop coming here because I seem to be getting worse instead of better. It's hard for me to pay for this and to get here every week, especially now that I'm going to the other therapist with the kids. Maybe it's time for me to take a break and try something different.

Liz: Have you thought of what you might try instead of coming here?

Susana: Not really. It just doesn't seem like anything is getting better. I'm having a lot of trouble getting up in the morning, although I haven't missed any work. The kids are fixing their own breakfast because I don't get up early enough to do that. And I feel really lousy like I did when I first came in here.

Liz: I can understand how discouraging that is, and I've been a little puzzled too about why your depression seems to be worse again after you felt better for a few months. Would it be okay with you if we review the different symptoms you had then and what's happening now?

Susana: Sure. As I told you, I have a hard time getting up in the morning, and I just feel bad most of the time.

Liz: How is your sleep and appetite?

Susana: I have a hard time falling asleep. Usually I watch TV after the kids go to bed and sometimes that helps me fall asleep. My appetite is all right.

Liz: You mentioned having trouble concentrating when you first came in. Is that happening again?

Susana: Yes, I find myself drifting off at work, and sometimes my boss has to tell me something two or three times before I get what he's saying. The same thing happens with the kids. The other night I asked Maria about her homework, and she said I had asked her already, but I didn't remember what she told me.

Liz: So it does sound like your symptoms of depression are about the same as when you came in, is that right?

Susana: Yes, about the same or maybe a little bit worse.

Liz: Another thing we talked about when you first came in was your drinking. Before Carlos left, you had been drinking daily with him, then you had reduced to only drinking on the weekends. What has been happening lately with that?

Susana: I'm still not drinking in front of the kids, like I told you.

Liz: So sometimes you have a drink after they've gone to bed?

Susana: Sometimes. It helps me fall asleep and just feel relaxed. You know, I work hard all day, and then I fix dinner and help Amelia with her homework, check on the older kids' homework, and send them all to bed. I'm tired but I can't go to sleep right away. So I watch TV with a drink or two and that helps me get to sleep. Sometimes I wake up at 2 or 3 in the morning and realize I fell asleep on the couch.

Liz: How often are you finding you need a drink or two after the kids go to bed?

Susana: Not that often, maybe a couple nights a week. I don't drink in front of them though, at least most of the time.

Liz: Most of the time?

Susana: Well, on the weekends I go out when Amelia is with her dad and Jorge and Maria are with their friends. During the week I sometimes have a glass of wine with dinner, but that's not really drinking. It's not like my dad who started drinking when he got home from work and didn't stop until after I was asleep.

Liz: I remember you telling me how upset you felt about your dad drinking every night and getting angry with you over small things or sometimes

<table>
<tr><td></td><td>not paying attention to you. You said you wanted things to be different for your kids, but it sounds like it's been hard to maintain the change you wanted to make.</td></tr>
</table>

Susana: I'm not as bad as him, and I wouldn't drink so much if I could fall asleep and if I felt better.

Liz: Am I right in remembering that you were only drinking one or two drinks on Friday and Saturday for a period of time after we started working together?

Susana: Yes, after that 9–1–1 call, I got scared about the police, and I didn't drink at all at home. That lasted a few months, but then I decided I had over-reacted and the police weren't going to come search my apartment.

Liz: It seems to me that the period of time when you were drinking only on the weekend was the same period of time you were less depressed and that your depression has gotten worse as you returned to drinking during the week. Since alcohol operates in the body as a depressant, it can have the effect of making depression worse. Do you think those things could be related?

Susana: When I feel bad, I want to drink more. Are you saying the drinking makes the depression worse and that I might feel better if I stopped drinking during the week again? How would I get to sleep?

Liz: How did you manage getting to sleep in those months when you didn't have alcohol in the house?

Susana: I don't remember. I stayed up worrying about the police for a few weeks, but then I was just able to go to sleep after the kids were in bed.

Liz: Do you feel ready to do something different with your drinking this week and see if it makes a difference in your depression?

Susana: I guess so. I could try not drinking until I go out with Judy on Friday.

Liz then talked with Susana about what might help her relax in the evening without alcohol, and they generated a few alternative strategies that Susana felt comfortable using. Liz and Susana also talked about the family therapy, which Liz knew was difficult for Susana. Liz supported Susana attending regularly with her children as a reflection of her commitment to the well-being of her family, and she asked if Susana would be willing to sign an authorization for Liz to speak with the therapist. Susana signed the authorization and gave Liz the therapist's name, Jan Davis, and agency, Northside Family Services.

Liz then made connections between Susana's adolescent feelings of loneliness with her feelings of being alone as a parent. Liz suggested that Susana might sometimes resent her children's needs of her when she feels depressed and depleted. Liz brought up the impact of Susana's early experiences of loss and trauma before and after her immigration, and she linked those experiences with her present feelings of loneliness.

Review of Session 17

Liz worked slowly and gently in getting information about Susana's drinking. Before raising the question of alcohol use, she reviewed Susana's other symptoms in response to Susana's report of feeling as bad as when she began treatment. Liz was intentional about creating an atmosphere of openness and acceptance to facilitate Susana being truthful, and she was pleased that Susana disclosed her increased use. She was careful to get information from Susana about her symptoms before using psychoeducation regarding the relationship between increased depression and increased alcohol. In order to lower Susana's resistance, Liz asked about her readiness to make a change in her drinking rather than suggesting a change.

During the session, Liz noted that Susana seemed to minimize her alcohol use and was evasive at times. She inferred that Susana was still under-reporting her drinking, since some aspects of her sleep and concentration difficulties could be alcohol related. However, she felt good about the progress they made in discussing the topic more openly and in developing strategies to support Susana's desire to reduce her use.

Summary of Sessions 18 to 24

Over the next 2 months, Susana made slow progress in reducing her alcohol use, and her depression lifted as it had at the beginning of treatment. The therapeutic alliance seemed stronger to Liz, since Susana was more forthcoming in talking about her alcohol use. Liz consulted with the family therapist and learned that Susana was attending regularly, although it seemed challenging for Susana to respond to her children's feelings.

In the eighth month of treatment after 24 sessions, Susana again missed a session without notice the week before Liz had a scheduled vacation. Liz left a message for Susana after the missed appointment, reminding her of the vacation week and confirming their regular appointment the following week.

Session 25: Representation of Life Obstacles

Session 25 began with Susana asking Liz if she had had a good vacation. Liz responded that she had enjoyed her time away and was glad to be back. Susana reported doing well in terms of her depression and alcohol use. She also said things were better at home, and she felt the family therapy was helping her children communicate more openly with her. They discussed these issues in more detail throughout the first 30 minutes of the session.

Liz noted that Susana didn't include payment for the missed session when she paid at the beginning of the session. She waited to see if Susana would comment on having missed the session before Liz's vacation. When Susana didn't bring it up, Liz did so in the following way:

Liz: I'm glad to hear that you've continued to do well since we met last. I remember we didn't meet the week before I was gone and I wonder if you felt less need to come in since things have improved so much.

Susana: Oh, that's right. I know I need to pay for that session because I forgot it. I don't know why it slipped my mind. I got mixed up about what day it was and didn't realize until you called that I was 1 day behind. All day I thought it was Monday instead of Tuesday.

Liz: Some people find they're more likely to forget an appointment before or after a week I'm away. They may have feelings about me being away, or the disruption of our regular schedule may make it harder to remember our appointments.

Susana: Oh, no. I was just mixed up that week. I'm glad you took time off. You work hard, and you deserve to have a nice vacation. I'm sorry I didn't include payment in the check I gave you at the beginning. I have my checkbook so I can write another one now. Here it is.

Liz: Thanks.

Susana: I was wondering what we would talk about today, since everything is going well. I haven't been feeling depressed, I'm sticking with my plan to only drink on the weekends, and the kids seem to like the family therapy. I think it's good for them to be able to tell me what they feel and what they want from me. Jan seems like a good therapist and they like her.

Liz: How is it for you? You have told me it's sometimes hard for you to hear what the kids have to say.

Susana: I've started just focusing on being a good mom with them. I know they need that, and I want to be there for them even though my parents weren't there for me. I decided what happened to me isn't my kids' fault, so I shouldn't be mad at them. I guess it helps that I have my own thing going on now too.

Liz: Your own thing?

Susana: Didn't I tell you that Carlos and I are seeing each other? Maybe that happened while you were gone or even a little before. He called me and said he wanted to start dating, nothing more for now. I was so happy to hear from him. I'm not ready to jump back into a relationship with him, but I'm tired of being lonely. In fact just a few days before he called, I had been thinking about the good times we had together and missing him. Then he called, so it seemed like it was meant to be.

Liz: How has it been for you to be with him again?

Susana: It's been great. It's like when we first met. He's really interested in me and he appreciates everything I do, like when I offered to pay for our dinners after the first time we went out since he's not working right now. He tells me over and over how nice I am and says he'll pay me back as soon as he finds work.

At this point in the session, Liz felt surprised and irritated about Susana resuming her relationship with Carlos. Because she knew she could not make any interpretive or challenging remarks without expressing judgment and frustration, she continued the session by making comments reflecting Susana's feelings and asking clarifying questions. She then confirmed their session for the following week, hoping she had contained her emotions sufficiently to not damage her alliance with Susana. She was glad to have a week to understand her reactions and to make a plan for her next session with Susana.

Supervision after Session 25

In supervision, Liz told Dalia that Susana was dating Carlos again. Dalia encouraged Liz to describe the countertransference feelings that came up in the session. Liz said she felt some distance between her and Susana at the beginning of the session but attributed it to the fact they hadn't met for 2 weeks. When Susana revealed that she had begun seeing Carlos again, Liz was shocked and angry.

As Dalia helped Liz examine her countertransference, Liz realized she felt betrayed and excluded by Susana in her decision to begin dating Carlos. She also felt critical of Susana as she seemed to be minimizing the impact of her decision on her children. Dalia was accepting and empathic as Liz identified her countertransference feelings, and then helped Liz to understand how Susana's loneliness made her vulnerable to returning to this relationship.

Dalia also suggested they look at the timing of Susana's decision to return to her relationship with Carlos in light of Liz's vacation and Susana's interpersonal patterns. She and Liz developed an understanding that Susana probably felt abandoned or neglected by Liz's planned vacation but was unable to acknowledge these feelings to herself or Liz. The heightened feelings of neglect would make Susana more likely to return to her familiar pattern of being a caretaker in an intimate relationship and to distance herself from Liz's support.

After they developed this understanding of Susana's decision, Liz asked Dalia what she should do in the next session, saying she didn't know how to help Susana any more. Dalia questioned Liz's lack of confidence and helped her view this recent incident as a reflection of Susana's attachment to Liz rather than a weakness in their alliance. Liz said she felt guilty about having taken a vacation and wondered if Susana would have made a different choice about being with Carlos if Liz hadn't been away. Dalia reminded Liz that therapists need to have time away and that Susana's vulnerability to returning to her familiar role with Carlos may have been heightened but wasn't created by Liz's vacation.

Liz and Dalia then returned to the question of the next session. Dalia encouraged Liz to identify how she could relate to Susana differently than the way Susana expects from her prior experience. Liz was aware that her feelings of anger and betrayal made her feel distant from Susana and that she wanted to shift to a more empathic and therapeutic stance. Dalia helped Liz think about Susana's relational experiences as either feeling abandoned and neglected or feeling connected by focusing on the needs of the other person. Liz then identified that her goal was to communicate a sense of connection to Susana with a focus on Susana's feelings. This would be a different relational experience for Susana and consistent with the relationship they had developed over their 8 months together. Liz thanked Dalia for helping her sort through her intense countertransference feelings and regain confidence in her ability to help Susana.

Session 26

The next session began in the following way:

Susana: I'm still doing really well, so it seems like I might be ready to stop coming here.

Liz: I can understand you might be thinking about that. Can you tell me more about this week?

Susana: Nothing much has changed since last week. I'm not really depressed anymore and I'm getting along with the kids better than ever.

Liz: I'm happy to hear that. You've made a lot of changes since we started working together.

Susana: As I walked in the building today, I remembered how bad I felt when I first came in to see you. It's sure different now.

Liz: Maybe it would be helpful to talk about the things you've done that made the difference.

Susana: You've helped me a lot, talking to me about how the war and my dad's drinking affected me and how I got depressed like my mom. You're a good therapist, so I guess I got lucky.

Liz: Thank you, but it seems to me you're downplaying your part in our work together. I think we've made a good team.

Susana: I guess so. Do you think it's time for me to stop coming in?

Liz: I'm not sure. Some people find it helpful to meet for awhile after things improve, to get a better understanding of what has made a difference and to talk about what will help maintain the changes they've made.

Susana: I guess I could do that if you think it's a good idea. I haven't done this before, you know, so I don't know how it's supposed to work. There are probably other people you could see instead of me who need it more.

Liz: I want to continue seeing you until we decide it's a good time to end. What would you like to focus on today?

Susana: I guess I should tell you more about Carlos. I could tell you were surprised last week when I told you I was seeing him again.

Liz: Yes, I was surprised. How was that for you?

Susana: I was worried you'd be upset with me. Jan thinks it's a bad idea for me to date him again, even though we're just dating. Maria was really upset when she overheard me talking to him on the phone. She figured out it was him, and she started yelling at me. Then she went and told Jan I was seeing Carlos again even though I told her not to say anything.

Liz: You didn't want Jan to know about Carlos?

Susana: No, because the kids have told her how much they didn't like him, and she's more interested in how they feel than what I want.

Liz: It must be hard to think you have to choose between what your kids want and what you want and to feel like Jan doesn't care about your needs.

Susana: It's not that she doesn't care about me, it's just that the kids are her priority.

Liz: It occurs to me that you often feel it isn't possible for everyone's needs to be met in a relationship. We've talked about how you tend to focus on your partner's happiness and how you sometimes resent your kids, because it already seems like they have so much more from you than you had from your parents.

Susana: It sounds like you think I shouldn't date Carlos if it upsets them.

Liz: I'm not making a judgment about what you should do; that's your decision. But I was noticing the way you see the decision as a choice between what you want and what your kids want. It reminded me of how hard it's been for you to feel supported by people who say they care about you.

Susana: I think Judy's mad at me too. I haven't seen her since I started dating Carlos, because I go out with him on the weekend instead of her. When I've talked to her on the phone, she seems pretty cold.

Liz explores Susana's feelings of rejection by Judy and comments on Susana's experience of either being neglected or maintaining connection by focusing on the needs of the other. Toward the end of the session, Susana expresses a very slight dissatisfaction with the fact that she is paying for the dates with Carlos, and Liz simply reflects her statement without any further comment.

Review of Session 26

Susana's caretaking of Liz is evident at the beginning of this session, and she is more deferential and less collaborative than in sessions before Liz's vacation. Liz is consistent in her focus on Susana's feelings, and she maintains the warmth of her feelings toward Susana rather than pulling back in reaction to Susana's distance. She encourages Susana to talk about her feelings from the previous week when Susana correctly perceived Liz's surprise about Carlos.

When Susana describes Jan as upset and Judy as mad, Liz is aware that Susana may have experienced Liz's anger even if she isn't consciously aware of it. Liz continues to express interest in and understanding of Susana, and she doesn't take a position on Susana's relationship with Carlos. While Liz doesn't believe resuming the relationship is a wise decision for Susana, she chooses to emphasize Susana's strength and autonomy in order to remain steady in focusing on Susana's feelings and experience. This leads Susana to express some of her own dissatisfaction rather than being reactive to feeling judged or misunderstood.

Update of Assessment and Treatment Plan

After session 26, Liz reviews the assessment and treatment plan that she had completed 6 months earlier. In the next session, she asks Susana to complete the BDI-II and AUDIT again to compare the results with her original scores. Susana does not want to complete the AUDIT because she says it was upsetting, but she does complete the BDI-II with a score of 10. They have the following discussion about Susana's treatment goals.

Liz:	I'd like to talk about your treatment goals because it's been about 6 months since we originally talked about them. Is that ok with you?
Susana:	Yes, that's ok. I know I probably haven't done as well as I should on some of them.
Liz:	I can tell you're still worried about me evaluating you. As I said before, your treatment here isn't dependent on a certain amount of change. I'm interested in helping you make the changes you want to make that will improve your life. If you haven't been able to make the changes you wanted to make, we'll need to talk about what's gotten in the way and how we can work together to make those differences.
Susana:	It's hard for me to think about what I want in my life because so many things just happen to me and I need to pay so much attention to the kids.
Liz:	That's why I think it's so important that you've made time for your therapy when I know it's not easy for you. Here is the treatment plan we talked about 6 months ago. The first goal was to reduce your depression, which has happened. Your score this time was 10 compared to last time when it was 18. That's really good to see. I know you've been feeling a lot better in the last couple months especially.
Susana:	Yes, I don't really think I'm depressed any more.
Liz:	The second goal was that you wanted to have only one or two drinks on Friday and Saturday only. How has that been going? I know there are times when it's hard to not drink on other days and times when you have had more than two drinks.
Susana:	The last 3 weeks I've only had one or two drinks when I go out with Carlos on the weekend, usually both Friday and Saturday.
Liz:	The third goal was something we decided on as part of our discussion about family therapy. You weren't sure you wanted to do that, but you did want to talk about your relationship with your kids. The goal was that you would identify one thing that was working well in your family

and one thing you wanted to change. When you were making the decision to do family therapy with your kids, we talked about several things that are working well, like the fact that they all have friends and are getting good grades in school and the fact that you started having one family dinner together every week. As I remember, your decision to see Jan was because you wanted help in talking about difficult things when your feelings are different from your kids' feelings.

Susana: That's still hard. It seems like she takes the kids' side whenever we feel different about something, like about Carlos.

Liz: I know it's been hard to feel like she understands you and that you often think there's a winner and loser when people have different feelings or needs. Is there something related to the family therapy that we could work on here?

Susana: The thing we've talked about there in the last few sessions has been Carlos. I know the kids don't like me seeing him, and Jan seems to think I shouldn't see him if it upsets them. I've started to notice some problems, but I'm afraid of being depressed and lonely again if we break up. Maybe I talk about that with you so you can help me figure out what to do.

Liz: In the language we use for goals here, I'd say "Client will identify at least three feelings and needs in an intimate relationship," and I'll help you by asking questions and making comments about different possibilities for you to consider.

Susana: I think that's a good idea. What about the other goals? I'm not depressed anymore and I'm staying with my goal about drinking.

Liz: Is there anything related to depression you want to focus on? You just mentioned a fear that you'd get depressed if you and Carlos broke up.

Susana: It's happened every time before, and it seems like it would probably happen again.

Liz: It sounds like it would be helpful for us to look more at how you came to feel guilty and responsible for making your partners happy, which we've talked about some but there's probably more to look at. Maybe we'd say, "Client will feel less guilt and responsibility for the happiness of her partner and will develop at least one alternative explanation for his feelings." I can help by pointing out how you blame yourself and supporting you to challenge those thoughts.

Susana: If I can do that, do you think I won't get depressed if Carlos breaks up with me?

Liz: I can't say for sure but I think your depression has had a lot to do with blaming yourself.

Susana: What about the goal about drinking? I'm doing what I said I would do.

Liz: Yes, and how has that felt to you?

Susana: I haven't really thought about it. I just tell myself that's all I can drink, and then I do it. It's easier now that I'm not depressed.

Liz: I can understand that. Is there anything related to drinking that you'd like to look at and talk about here? One thing I wonder about is whether it would be helpful to talk about your dad's drinking and how that affected you. We've touched on it a few times, but there may be more to understand about that.

Susana: Maybe that would be a good idea. I know I didn't like it, and I feel bad that my kids saw me drinking more than I probably should have.

Liz: I could put that as a goal of "Client will maintain her current level of one to two drinks on Friday and Saturday only, and client will identify three ways she was affected by her father's drinking." I can support you in exploring the impact of your father's drinking and in continuing to ask about your use. How does that sound?

Susana: That's fine.

They continue the session with a discussion of the last family therapy session and Susana's irritation about her children telling her in that session that they want her to stop seeing Carlos. Liz empathized with Susana's feelings, explored her ambivalence about Carlos, and provided some psychoeducation about how each of Susana's children might be experiencing her return to that relationship. At the end of the session, Liz asked Susana to sign an updated treatment plan based on their earlier discussion.

After session 27, Liz writes the following assessment review and updated treatment plan based on the format used at the Community Support Center.

Six-Month Assessment Review

Client Name: Susana Rodriguez
Date of Birth: XX/XX/19XX
Date Case Opened: XX/XX/20XX
Clinician Name: Liz Matthews
Funding/Payment: $40 per session, paid by client
Presenting Problems: Client is a 36-year-old Latina, specifically a Salvadoran immigrant, who requested services following an argument with her boyfriend, which resulted in client's 15-year-old daughter calling 9–1–1. Client reported symptoms of depression in the first session as well as conflict with her daughter. She reported ambivalent feelings about the fact that her boyfriend had moved out following the 9–1–1 incident.
Diagnosis
F33.41 Major Depressive Disorder, Recurrent Episode, In Partial Remission
Z62.820 Parent-Child Relational Problem
Z63.8 Disruption of Family by Separation or Divorce
Z65.4 Exposure to Disaster, War or Other Hostilities
Recurring migraine headaches

Current Symptoms

Client reports a reduction in symptoms of depression. Her score on the BDI-II decreased from 18 to 10, reflecting a minimal level of depression. The diagnosis has been updated to reflect partial remission of depressive symptoms.

Update of Mental Status Exam, Risk Factors, and Substance Use

Client's mood has improved. Other aspects of her mental status are within normal limits. No new risk factors are present, although client has resumed contact with her former partner with whom she had significant conflict. She has not reported any verbal or physical conflict during the last month since they have been together. Client did not complete the AUDIT, stating she found the questions upsetting. Her use of alcohol has varied during the last 6 months, and she reports current use of one to two drinks twice a week. Client does not meet criteria for an alcohol use disorder.

Additional Information and Changes Since Last Assessment

Client began family therapy with her three children approximately three months ago. Her older daughter completed 12 sessions of individual therapy, which is the maximum provided by the school, and the daughter's therapist referred them to a family therapy program at the school. Family therapy will end in approximately three weeks, at the end of the school year.

Six-Month Update of Treatment Plan

Treatment Goal 1:   Client will identify at least three feelings and needs in an intimate relationship.

Interventions: Clinician will explore client's feelings and needs and will assist client in generating possibilities to consider.

Treatment Goal 2:   Client will feel less guilt and responsibility for the happiness of her partner and will develop at least one alternative explanation for his feelings.

Interventions: Clinician will identify examples of self-blame and support client to challenge those thoughts.

Treatment Goal 3:   Client will maintain her current level of one to two drinks on Friday and Saturday only, and client will identify three ways she was affected by her father's drinking.

Interventions: Clinician will support client to maintain her current level of alcohol use. Clinician will explore the impact of her father's drinking on client.

The Next Step

Chapter 12 will discuss case management and coordination of care, which involves assisting clients with accessing other resources and contacting other professionals who are working with the client to ensure that the client's care is consistent. The case example illustrates both of these aspects of treatment.

References

Denning, P., Little, J., & Glickman, A. (2004). *Over the influence: The harm reduction guide for managing drugs and alcohol.* New York, NY: The Guilford Press.

Elliott, R., Bohart, A. C., Watson, J. C., & Greenberg, L. S. (2011). Empathy. *Psychotherapy, 48,* 43–49.

Gelso, C. J. & Bhatia, A. (2012). Crossing theoretical lines: The role and effect of transference in nonanalytic psychotherapies. *Psychotherapy, 49,* 384–390.

Linehan, M. M. (1993a). *Cognitive-behavioral treatment of borderline personality disorder.* New York, NY: The Guilford Press.

Linehan, M. M. (1993b). *Skills training manual for treating borderline personality disorder.* New York, NY: The Guilford Press.

McWilliams, N. (2011). *Psychoanalytic diagnosis: Understanding personality structure in the clinical process* (2nd ed.). New York, NY: The Guilford Press.

Miller, W. R. & Rollnick, S. (2002). *Motivational interviewing: Preparing people for change* (2nd ed.). New York, NY: The Guilford Press.

Norcross, J. C. (2010). The therapeutic relationship. In Duncan, B. L., Miller, S. D., Wampold, B. E., & Hubble, M. A. (Eds.). *The heart and soul of change: What works in therapy* (2nd ed.). Washington, DC: American Psychological Association.

Shedler, J. (2010). The efficacy of psychodynamic psychotherapy. *American Psychologist, 65,* 98–109.

Teyber, E. & McClure, F. H. (2011). *Interpersonal process in therapy: An integrative model* (6th ed.). Belmont, CA: Brooks/Cole.

Weiss, J. (1993). *How psychotherapy works: Process and technique.* New York, NY: Guilford Press.

12
CASE MANAGEMENT AND COORDINATION OF CARE

(Note: This chapter will use the female pronoun for supervisor, clinician, and client.)

This chapter discusses aspects of behavioral health treatment that involve communicating with other individuals or organizations in order to locate resources needed by your client, obtain information that will increase the effectiveness of treatment, and coordinate treatment with other health and social services. The chapter begins with a review of general guidelines and legal and ethical issues. I then examine specific issues that arise in integrated care settings, in coordinating with health care and other helping professionals, in obtaining records from others, and in working with family members.

General Guidelines

Contacting other professionals to locate resources for your client, such as financial assistance or social services, is usually called *case management* or *client advocacy*. These terms may also be used to refer to communication with others who are working with your client. In some settings, the terms *care coordination* and *care management* are used to describe this type of communication.

Case management and care coordination may be familiar to you if you have studied in a social work program or worked in a clinical environment before entering graduate school. When you begin clinical training, you will find that many clients need and benefit from multiple services, and case management is often an important part of your role. In some settings and with some populations, it is the primary way you provide service to the client. Some clinicians enjoy helping clients access and coordinate with other services, and others prefer working directly with clients. Regardless of your preference, you need to be familiar and comfortable with coordinating care and locating resources as part of your clinical work.

A situation that often occurs related to case management and care coordination is that a client complains to you about another professional. She may describe the other professional as incompetent or may report interactions that seem unreasonable to you. It can be tempting to intervene on your client's behalf by serving as a mediator or advocate. Check with your supervisor before taking an active role with another professional, so you can review your client's report to you and the different factors that may influence her interaction with the other provider as well as with you. Clients who work with multiple providers often have different expectations and reactions to the different providers, and these interactions are emotionally complex. While there are situations in which it is appropriate to intervene directly with another provider, the first step is usually to get more information about the situation.

When you contact another provider, *begin with a neutral, open statement or question.* This is especially important when the client has reported a negative interaction but is always a useful way to begin a conversation. Examples of neutral openings follow.

- I'm interested in hearing about your work with _____ so I can be more effective in helping her in therapy.
- Could you give me a summary of your work with _____?
- _____ mentioned a conversation with you about her housing request. Could you tell me the status of that?

If the client has brought a complaint to you, usually the other provider's report of the situation will be more reasonable and understandable than the client has interpreted and reported to you.

When you coordinate the client's care with other services, your *goal is to facilitate a positive outcome for the client.* Sometimes you can provide information that will influence the provider's decision. For example, a client may report that her psychiatrist has not increased her antidepressant medication despite severe symptoms of depression, and your description of the symptoms you have observed in session may lead the psychiatrist to consider a medication change. At other times, you may get information from the other provider that helps you assist the client. For example, a client may report that her application for housing assistance was rejected, and you learn that the office requires financial information from a paycheck stub or tax return before processing an application. With this information, you can then assist her in providing the documents that will move her application forward.

Legal and Ethical Issues Related to Sharing Information

The Health Insurance Portability and Accountability Act (HIPAA) includes a number of regulations related to disclosure of protected health information including records of mental health treatment (U.S. Department of Health and Human Services, 2003). In addition, the ethical codes of the profession require protecting the confidentiality of information disclosed by clients, with certain exceptions (AAMFT, 2001; APA, 2002; NASW 2008).

Principles for Sharing Information

Chapter 10 includes more detailed discussion about some of the principles to follow when sharing information about your client, summarized below.

• Ask for the client's written authorization before sharing information.
• Request authorization even when you are permitted to disclose without authorization, unless doing so would compromise the safety of the client or another person.
• Disclose the minimum information necessary for coordinating care or accessing services.
• Release information only to the individuals authorized to receive it and limit the information released to others in the organization or agency.
• Protect the privacy of information you disclose by leaving messages only on a private voice mail, sending a fax only to a location that is private and secure, addressing mail to a specific individual, and encrypting emails containing protected health information or removing information from the email that identifies the client.

Sharing Information within Your Organization

HIPAA and the professional codes of ethics apply to information that is shared within your organization as well as between you and someone outside your organization. Clients must be notified what health information about them will be shared within the agency and for what purposes. The HIPAA guideline for *disclosure of the minimum necessary information* applies to information shared within the agency. For example, a billing clerk needs to know the client's diagnosis in order to complete a billing claim but does not need access to the assessment or progress notes. A client's family therapist needs to know her diagnosis and aspects of her history that are relevant to the family therapy with her children, but the details of early trauma shouldn't be shared by you unless the client wants the family therapist to have that information. In group supervision or case conferences for purposes of your own training and consultation, eliminate the client's name and other identifying information from your presentation and discussion.

Maintaining Professionalism

Be mindful that you are in a professional role when discussing clients with agency colleagues and supervisors. These conversations should be scheduled, rather than taking place casually, and held in a private, confidential space. If you talk with your supervisor by telephone in an emergency situation, protect the confidentiality of your conversation and make sure you can't be overheard.

When you communicate with a *professional in another organization* by telephone or email, remember not to reveal more than the minimum information necessary and do not share impressions or conjectures that you haven't confirmed. It will be easier to stay alert to these parameters if you consult with your supervisor before having any communication about your client, and get her suggestions on how to prepare for the conversation. If you are planning to talk by telephone, write down your questions and summarize the information you want to share. If you send information by email, make sure it is written in professional language and that you take time to review your response with your supervisor before sending it.

Requests from Other Professionals

Sometimes another professional may want you to answer questions to help her make a decision that will affect the client's life. Talk with your supervisor before any conversation so you can remain clear about your role as a clinician and the limits of your role and your knowledge of the client. You can ask the other party to send questions to you in writing so that you can review them with your supervisor and prepare a response. You can also write down the questions yourself and let the other party know you will send a response after reviewing your records and consulting with your supervisor.

When your client is involved in a legal case, there is often great pressure and urgency on the part of the attorneys, case workers, and advocates involved in the case. This makes it difficult to remain clear about your role as a clinician separate from the legal matter. However, you will be most useful to your client when you maintain a distinction between the purpose and goals of your clinical treatment and the needs and motives of others who are involved with the client in different ways.

Informing Clients About Outside Conversations

Clients feel more engaged and involved in their treatment when you inform them about your conversations with others. When you ask the client to sign an authorization to share information, explain the reasons you are requesting her permission. I tell clients when I plan to contact another professional or when I have received a call from someone, and I give them a brief summary of the conversation. Doing this helps to alleviate clients' concerns about violations of their privacy or of being excluded from conversations about them. It also strengthens the spirit of collaboration in the treatment relationship.

Integrated Care in a Multidisciplinary Team

Integrated care has been shown to be especially effective in treating individuals with co-occurring mental health and substance use disorders (Mueser, Noordsy, Drake & Fox, 2003). Integrated care is provided by a multidisciplinary team that may include a psychotherapist, case manager, psychiatrist or nurse practitioner, addiction specialist, family advocate, and social worker. Such a team can provide coordinated behavioral health treatment for clients with mental health and substance use disorders and their family members. Services generally include individual, family, and group psychotherapy; psychoeducation for clients and family members; medication management; and support and assistance with housing, daily activities, education, and employment. Members of the team may be employed by the same organization or by different organizations.

When care is provided by a multidisciplinary team, clients are asked to authorize exchange of information among members of the team as part of their consent for treatment. This allows members of the team to share information as a group or individually to coordinate the client's care. A separate authorization is required for sharing information with professionals outside the team or with family members.

Multidisciplinary team meetings may be more or less formal than your staff meetings and group supervision. Making the transition from a clinical training setting to a multidisciplinary team can be confusing, so check with your supervisor about the appropriate level of detail to share with team members. When possible, prepare a summary of your questions for the team and an update of your work with the client in advance of team meetings or conversations with team members. This will help you discuss the case professionally and stay on task regarding the client's care.

Psychiatric and Medical Care

It is best clinical practice to exchange information with a psychiatrist, primary care physician, or other medical care provider when your client

- Is taking psychotropic medication,
- Has a serious or chronic medical condition,
- Is pregnant or recently gave birth,
- Has been given a mental health or substance use diagnosis by a medical provider, or
- Has a mental health disorder that affects her ability to maintain physical health.

Because of the interactions between physical and emotional well-being, you should recommend an annual medical evaluation by a primary care physician for all of your clients. Clients who maintain their physical health will make greater progress in behavioral health treatment, and conversely, appropriate treatment of medical conditions often improves clients' psychological symptoms.

Before you contact a medical provider, take time to think through the goals for the conversation so it will be productive for both of you. You may have specific goals such as learning more about the client's physical health condition or what medication she is taking. In addition, it is always a goal to establish a positive collaboration with the medical provider. Plan the structure and content of your conversation so that you convey a collaborative tone. If the client has expressed negative feelings about her doctor or has reported her psychiatrist giving her advice that is inconsistent with your point of view, talk with your supervisor before contacting the medical provider. Remember that you are hearing about the medical provider through your client's emotionally based perspective and that the picture is probably less extreme than she is describing.

You often contact a medical provider for information that will enhance your treatment with the client. For example, if a psychiatrist has prescribed antidepressant medication and the client presents primarily with anxiety in sessions with you, you can ask what the psychiatrist observed and heard from the client that led to the prescribing decision. If your client has an eating disorder, you need to know what aspects of her health have been impacted. For clients with auto-immune disorders, diabetes, thyroid or cardiac conditions, chronic pain, or a recent surgery, the medical provider can tell you about the impact of the condition and treatment on your client's mental health.

Make a list of your questions before you contact the provider to ensure you get the information you need. It is wise to start with a general question like, "What would be useful for me to know about _____ as we work on her depression?" You can follow with other specific questions like, "What is _____'s current weight and at what weight will her health be endangered?" or, "What benefit has _____ shown from antidepressant medication and do you think there will be continued improvement?"

Often you may have information you want to convey to the medical provider such as your impressions of the client and additional support or resources you feel she needs. *Begin by asking questions, and then share your opinions.* Medical providers operate in a hierarchical structure, and behavioral health clinicians are often viewed as having lower status than physicians. Asking for information first conveys your respect for the physician's opinion and is more likely to lead to a collaborative conversation. When you then share your impressions as they relate to the information offered by the medical provider, the medical provider is more likely to view you as an ally in the client's overall treatment.

Keep in mind that your client will be best served when you have a cooperative working relationship with her medical providers. Prepare for the conversation by writing down the information you want to convey and make sure it is objective and emotionally neutral. For example, "I have observed _____ showing a lot of tension and worry, and she has reported symptoms that fit the criteria for a panic attack. Have you seen anxiety symptoms as well as depression?" is a more collaborative approach than, "I think _____ has an anxiety disorder instead of depression." Medical providers usually rely on observations and the client's report more than subjective judgment, so you should be prepared to back up your clinical and intuitive conclusions with data.

It is often difficult to reach medical providers directly by telephone, due to the full schedules of you and the other providers. If you are unable to schedule a direct phone conversation, you can write your questions and a brief summary of your impressions in a letter to the medical provider. Check with your supervisor to see if sending a letter would be appropriate, and be sure to send it in compliance with HIPAA privacy regulations.

Other Mental Health and Addiction Treatment

Many clients receive services concurrently from multiple providers, and this is likely to be true for some of the clients on your case load. You may be doing family therapy while one of the parents is in treatment for alcohol abuse; you may see a parent in individual therapy while her 10-year-old daughter is seeing another therapist; you may lead a therapy group in which some members have individual therapists outside your agency. Collaborating with these providers is often essential to ensure the quality of care for the individual or family.

An important issue regarding treatment of substance use disorders is that these records, and all information about treatment of substance use disorders, are covered by a federal law, 42CFR, Part 2 (Substance Abuse and Mental Health Services Administration, 2011). In order for a provider of substance abuse treatment to share information, the client must sign an authorization that explicitly gives permission for sharing of information about substance abuse treatment. If you work in an agency that has programs for substance abuse and general mental health treatment, you will need to follow the more stringent requirements of this federal law when sharing information between those programs.

As when you share information with medical providers, prepare for your communication with another clinician by writing down your questions and summarizing what you want to say. Be aware that you are obligated to share only the minimum necessary information even when collaborating with another behavioral health provider. Aspects of your treatment with the client or aspects of her history that are not specifically relevant to the other clinician should not be shared. It is sometimes difficult to monitor the relevance of information in a phone conversation, which may evolve into mutual sharing of impressions. As you prepare for the conversation, think through the specific issues that fall outside the minimum necessary rule and review these issues with your supervisor. If the client has explicitly asked that you keep certain information private, you should honor this request. If you feel that the information is relevant to the client's treatment with the other clinician, discuss the issue in supervision to develop a plan for handling your dilemma.

When you talk with other behavioral health providers, you need a common language and framework for understanding the client. Since there are many different theoretical perspectives in the field, there are likely to be some differences between your formulation of the client's issues and that of the other clinician. It is generally not productive to get into discussions of theoretical differences or to introduce terminology that requires extensive explanation.

You are most likely to have a productive conversation with another provider when you use commonly accepted diagnostic terms, describe your observations and the client's report of symptoms, and share your treatment approach and goals. For example, most clinicians will understand a description like

> _____ has a diagnosis of generalized anxiety disorder, primarily showing symptoms of worry, restlessness, and tension. She has a hard time concentrating and falling asleep. I'm using a CBT approach to help her reduce the worry from an 8 to a 5 on a 10-point scale.

You might also communicate a different treatment approach with statements like, "I'm using an insight-oriented and supportive approach to help her see the connection between her current worry and her mother's recent diagnosis of cancer" or, "I'm introducing mindfulness as a technique for her to use when her worry and tension increase to an uncomfortable level."

At times when the other clinician is having difficulty with your mutual client or family, she may shift from a collaborative conversation to asking for your support or advice. Be aware that you are a fellow clinician collaborating on a case, rather than a supervisor or consultant and that you cannot take responsibility for the other clinician's treatment decisions. The best response if the other clinician is asking for your advice is to empathize with her difficulty and suggest she get support elsewhere. You might say, "As your colleague I can't really answer your question but I can hear how frustrated you are. Who can you go to for help with this?" Your supervisor can help you understand the best approach to take so that you remain clear about your role.

Education and Social Services

Teachers and school counselors are essential resources for treatment with children and families. Contacting school personnel early in treatment will give you helpful information for your assessment of the child and her family, and ongoing communication will help you identify the impact of treatment on the child's academic performance and her behavior in school. Many clients are also involved with the child welfare or probation system or are receiving assistance with housing, employment, and basic needs from social service agencies. These agencies typically assign a specific case manager, social worker, or probation officer to meet with the client on a regular basis and track the client's compliance with the agency requirements.

When communicating with professionals outside the health care field, be aware that _the requirements you must meet for protecting information are more stringent than those of the professionals in other settings._ Teachers, case managers, and social workers are likely to offer and request information that goes beyond what is necessary for your collaborative work. You are not prohibited from receiving information from another party, but you are prohibited from giving more than the minimum necessary information. Your supervisor can help you plan your questions and decide what information to share. If you feel pressured or are unsure how to respond to a question, it is best to defer answering. You can say, "I'm not sure how to answer that. I'd like to give it some thought, talk with my supervisor, and get back to you."

When an educator or social service worker asks for your advice or opinion, evaluate whether her request falls within your *scope of practice and competence*. Examples of situations in which it is appropriate to offer an opinion are (a) when a teacher asks if an evaluation for special education services would be useful or (b) when a social worker asks if your client meets the mental health diagnosis criteria for supported housing. Remember not to go beyond your role as a clinician in answering other requests such as (a) whether your client is able to be an adequate parent to her children, or (b) whether a child needs special education services. Questions like these require an evaluation that is outside your role as a treating clinician. Check with your supervisor if you are asked for an opinion on an issue that requires you to draw a conclusion rather than to report your observations.

Another reason for contacting social service organizations is to assist your client in accessing help with housing, employment, and basic needs. If you believe she is eligible for financial or case management support, you can ask about available services and application processes and pass on the information. You will need to provide more direct assistance and advocacy for clients who are in immediate danger or who are impaired in taking action on their own behalf. A good guideline is to support the client in doing as much as she is capable of doing on her own, and to step in directly only when the client is unable to do so.

Records of Prior Treatment and Evaluation

Clients often have multiple contacts with behavioral health providers over time, and these records can be useful in your assessment and treatment planning. Some clinicians prefer to meet and assess the client without prior records, fearing their judgment may be biased by reading the opinions of others. While it is true that you should form your own impressions and case formulation of the client, you may be able to reach a clear diagnostic picture more quickly if you have access to prior records. This is especially true for clients who have a complex clinical presentation or a long history of treatment. In these cases, it is best to request records of prior treatment and evaluation at the beginning of treatment while you are completing your initial assessment. In some cases, the client may not tell you about prior treatment until later, and you can request the records at that time.

Records of prior treatment and evaluation are especially useful when working with children and adolescents, young adults who are struggling with the transition to independence, adults with symptoms of cognitive deficits or developmental delays, and adults with a history of recent hospitalization and/or diagnosis of serious mental illness. You will need a written authorization for exchange of information in order to request records or talk directly with the clinician who created the records. Ideally, you will have access to a written evaluation report, assessment, or treatment summary as well as direct contact with the treating or evaluating clinician.

It is sometimes difficult to get enough information from the client or parent to obtain records of prior treatment. When working with children and adolescents, you can often get copies of educational evaluations from the school, which may include psychological testing that is relevant to your treatment planning. Obtaining this information will probably require a specific written request to the school, and you may have to persist in following up on your request. Adult clients are often unclear about the details of their treatment and any evaluations that were performed, making it difficult to get contact information for other treating and evaluating clinicians. Check with your supervisor for guidance on what information is essential and for suggestions on obtaining the records you need.

Family Members

Communicating with family members is a vital part of individual treatment with children, adolescents, and some adults. Except in emergency situations, when your client is 18 or older you must have her authorization to share information before talking with family members. You may also need her authorization if your client is under 18 but has legally consented to her own treatment, based on the laws in your state. If you are providing family treatment or if you have sessions with family members, all members of the family should individually consent to treatment, and you will need to clarify your unit of treatment as well as your practice regarding sharing of information among family members. The remainder of this section applies to individual treatment when the primary contact with family members is by telephone or email rather than in-person sessions.

Emotional Complexity of Communication with Family Members

Asking your client to authorize communication with family members may bring up complex emotions for her. The family relationships may be conflictual, and your client may be avoidant, angry, or both. It is easy to identify with your client's perspective, and view the parents and other family members as misguided at best and toxic at worst. What is more difficult but critically important is *to remember the importance of the family members as attachment figures* for the client and to recognize the value of resolution and reconciliation in the client's developmental progress.

In considering the client's family relationships, *work to set aside blame and criticism* about who is responsible for the client's difficulties. When there is a strong pattern of blame and criticism in the family, you need to disengage from that pattern in order to be helpful. One strategy is to put yourself in the position of each family member, and imagine the situation from that person's perspective. Doing this will help you develop empathy for each individual in the family including your client, as it involves holding different and sometimes conflicting perspectives on your client's symptoms and behaviors. Your supervisor can help you sort out any confusing or conflicting emotions that may arise for you in this process.

Some clients are preoccupied with anger and blame toward family members whom they see as responsible for their current difficulties. While it is important to understand and empathize with your client, she will be better served if you help her focus on her goals rather than on justifying her position. An example of a helpful response to a client who blames her difficulties on a family member is

> All symptoms and family conflicts are caused by multiple factors so I don't think it's as helpful to focus on why this situation developed as to talk about what we can do to make the improvements you want to make.

If your client's focus is on her desires for the parent, spouse, or other family member to change, you may need to bring attention back to the treatment relationship with a statement like

> I understand why you'd want X to change, but since you and I can't do anything to change her behavior, I'd like us to think about what you could do differently in relation to her that might work better for you.

Discussing Client's Authorization for Communication

The initial period of treatment and assessment is the best time to introduce the idea of contact with family members, since you will be asking about the client's current and past family relationships during that time. Keep in mind that the definition of family for a particular client may include extended family members (e.g., grandparents, aunts, uncles, older siblings) living together or separately, as well as members of the same household not related by blood or marriage (e.g., domestic partner, step-parent).

Consider the question of communicating with family members during the initial assessment period, and talk with your supervisor about the best approach before you make a recommendation to the client. The importance of involving family members varies with the severity of the client's symptoms, degree of current family conflict, and reliability of the client's self-report. In some cases, you may require the client to authorize communication with family members as a condition of treatment. When working with adolescents and with adults who have diagnoses of serious mental illness, communication with parents is usually the best clinical practice. The client's well-being, safety, and developmental progress are often enhanced by having parents involved in treatment.

In discussing with the client the issue of contact with family members, let her know what information would be helpful for you to have from them and what you might share. With the exception of issues of safety, the client can limit her authorization to topics and areas of her life that she feels comfortable for you to share with the family, and she will feel more empowered if she is able to decide what you share.

Receiving Communications from Family Members

Family members may contact you by telephone or email, even if your client has not authorized you to share information. This occurrence raises complex clinical questions that you should talk about in supervision before you decide whether and how to respond. Options include not responding, suggesting that the client talk with the family member, acknowledging the family member's communication without sharing any information yourself, and asking the client to authorize limited communication. Unless you believe it would escalate the level of danger in the family, you should tell your client about the family member's contact. In some cases, you can discuss with your client several possible responses you can make, and ask her what response she would prefer.

While your primary responsibility is to your individual client, *keep in mind that the client's condition impacts family members.* You may be able to offer empathy and support to a stressed family member without compromising your client's confidentiality. For example, you can say something that doesn't reveal anything about your client but does acknowledge the parent's distress, like, "I got your message about your son having an angry manic outburst. I've worked with many families who are affected by bipolar disorder, and I know it can be very difficult."

Exchanging Information with Family Members

When you have authorization from an adult or adolescent client or when your client is a child who has not given independent consent, your contact with family members usually involves both requesting information from them and providing information to them. At the beginning of treatment, you request historical and contextual background regarding the client's symptoms, past functioning, and current daily activities. As treatment progresses, family members can give you their perspective on the client's progress toward treatment goals and on the current status of the client's symptoms. The amount and type of information you provide is based on your client's age and developmental capacity, the quality of the family relationships, and your client's preferences.

Preparing for conversations with family members is as important as preparing for conversations with other professionals. Write down the questions you want to ask and a summary of what you are prepared to share about treatment. Feel free to say, "I need some time to think about that question and how to answer it," if you are asked for information you aren't prepared to share. Then be sure you contact the family member within a few days after you've talked with your supervisor and possibly with your client.

If your client has signed an authorization that limits what you can share, let the family member know about those limits at the beginning of your communication. For example, you might say, "Your daughter has agreed for me to share information about her diagnosis and our treatment goals with you. I'm also interested in your perspective on how things have been going at home."

Be prepared for the family member to ask questions that exceed the limits of your authorization. If this happens, be empathic with her desire to know and firm about the limits of what you can share.

Issues of confidentiality can become complex when you are talking with family members of individual clients. Family members often assume you are obligated to protect their confidentiality even though they are not the client. Talk with your supervisor about the best way to clarify the limits of confidentiality before you talk with a family member. If there is high conflict and tension within the family, you may need to state at the beginning of the conversation that you will not keep information secret from your client. Clarifying your position in this way establishes the boundaries of confidentiality, clarifies your role as therapist to your client, and prevents a clinically untenable situation. See Chapter 3 for more discussion of a policy of "no secrets."

Scheduling a Family Session in Individual Treatment

Clients sometimes ask for a family session with a parent, spouse, or partner. On occasion, they may bring a family member to a session unannounced. When this happens, let the client know you want to talk with her first before deciding whether to include the family member in the session. Do not hold a family session without prior discussion and preparation unless there is an issue of your client's imminent safety or you are in the initial assessment phase and have not established the appropriate unit of treatment.

When deciding whether to hold a family session while doing individual treatment, some of the relevant factors are

- How the idea arose (i.e., is this the client's idea or the family member's idea),
- What the client hopes to accomplish in a family session,
- What role she expects you to have in the session, and
- How she will feel if the session isn't successful in accomplishing her goals.

In exploring these questions, you may discover that the client has a wish for you to help the family member understand her or for you to influence the family member's behavior in a way the client has been unable to do. She may believe you are more capable than she is in dealing with her family, and she may want you to extend your role beyond the boundary of individual treatment.

While clients often have unrealistic goals when raising the idea of having a family session, you may arrive at appropriate therapeutic goals through examining their wishes and beliefs. An appropriate goal for a family session in individual treatment is to support the client in talking with the family member about an emotionally charged issue or an area of disagreement. The client may be able to communicate more clearly when she feels your support than she can on her own, and when you are present as a facilitator the family member may be more open to listening and reaching agreement.

If your discussions with the client result in a decision to hold a family session, the following steps will help you prepare.

- Develop a realistic goal for the session, based on the client's capacity and need as well as the family situation.
- Clarify your role as supporting the client toward her goal.
- Ask your client to talk with the family member about her goal for the family session.
- At the beginning of the family session, ask the client and family member to agree that any of you may end the session if it is not leading to the intended purpose.

Thorough preparation increases the likelihood that your family session will have a positive outcome. If the session results in an expressed desire for more family sessions, check with your supervisor before agreeing to change your unit of treatment. It is often preferable to continue individual treatment and refer the client and family member to another clinician for family therapy.

Summary

This chapter discussed different aspects of case management and coordination of care beginning with general guidelines and a review of legal and ethical issues. I provided suggestions for (a) working in integrated care settings; (b) communicating with providers of psychiatric and medical care, mental health and addiction treatment, and educational and social services; and (c) accessing records of prior treatment and evaluation. The chapter ended with a review of issues related to the involvement of family members in individual treatment. Specific areas of professional growth related to case management and care coordination are listed below.

1. Using yourself as an instrument of hope, change, and healing:
    a. Be aware of the potential to be emotionally pulled away from your therapeutic role when communicating with other providers.
    b. Notice tendencies to adopt blame and criticism when hearing about clients' family relationships, and work to develop empathy for each family member.

2. Becoming confident in your authority and professionalism:

   a. Become familiar with requirements of HIPAA and 42CFR, Part 2, regarding sharing information with other care and service providers.
   b. Prepare for communications with other providers and family members by writing questions and a summary of information to be shared.

3. Developing interpersonal skills that strengthen the therapeutic relationship:

   a. Communicate with other providers in an open, emotionally neutral way to facilitate collaboration.
   b. Maintain clarity in your role with family members of clients in individual treatment.

Case Example: Case Management in Susana's Treatment

Liz contacted three other professionals during the first 26 sessions of Susana's treatment: Susana's internist, her daughter Maria's individual therapist, and the family therapist. Liz also considered whether any records of prior treatment or evaluation were available and whether Susana and her family could benefit from any additional social service resources. Each of these areas of case management and coordination of care is discussed below.

Coordination with Medical Care

Liz contacted Susana's internist, Dr. Carl Harris, after Susana signed an authorization for Liz and Dr. Harris to exchange information. Liz prepared for their conversation by writing down her questions about Susana's migraine headaches and her general health. She planned to let the doctor know that Susana had requested treatment due to symptoms of depression, but not to disclose the circumstances of her breakup with Carlos unless the physician indicated he was aware of that.

Liz scheduled a telephone consultation with Dr. Harris through his assistant and they spoke during the fourth week of Susana's treatment. Dr. Harris confirmed that he was treating Susana for migraine headaches and that she had come in for a visit a couple months earlier reporting an increase in frequency of headaches. He said he didn't change her migraine medication at that point but did prescribe antidepressant medication due to her report of a relationship breakup and his assessment of mild depressive symptoms. Dr. Harris said he was glad to hear Susana was seeing a therapist, which he had recommended to her. Liz asked about Susana's general health and Dr. Harris reported she was in good health. They ended with an agreement to talk again as needed based on Susana's progress and symptoms. Liz didn't disclose the circumstances of Susana's breakup with Carlos or the fact that Susana did not report taking the antidepressant medication.

Coordination with Daughter's Therapy

Liz also contacted Anna Jones, the school counselor for Susana's 15-year-old daughter Maria, after receiving authorization from Susana. Anna asked Liz to fax the authorization to her, which Liz did, and they consulted by telephone in the third week of Susana's treatment. Liz was primarily interested in hearing Anna's assessment of Maria and the family, based on Maria's report and perspective.

In their telephone consultation, Anna expressed a great deal of concern about Maria's well-being and a very negative view of Susana's parenting. She described Maria as being terrified on the night of the 9-1-1 call and continuing to experience high levels of anxiety about the safety of her mother and siblings if Carlos were to return. Anna told Liz she thought Susana was narcissistic and preoccupied with her own needs to the detriment of her children. Liz was surprised by the vehemence of Anna's account and simply told her it was helpful for her to have the information Anna gave her. Liz also talked about the history of addiction in the family, knowing that experimentation with substances is common for adolescents. Anna said that Maria had reported some use of alcohol and marijuana at parties but that her primary focus was Maria's anxiety and her needs for safety. Anna reported that she would strongly recommend family therapy after the 12 sessions of individual therapy, due to the family's level of dysfunction and risk.

After talking with Anna, Liz questioned the accuracy of her assessment of Susana, especially since Anna was a licensed clinician and Liz was still in training. Liz shared the conversation with Anna in her next supervision session with Dalia and was reassured when Dalia told her that discrepancies are common between the perspectives of therapists who see family members in different contexts. Dalia observed that Anna seemed to have developed a strong bond with Maria that included protectiveness and possibly over-identification with Maria's negative feelings toward her mother.

Dalia reminded Liz that from the beginning of treatment, Liz had been aware of limitations in Susana's parenting skills, and had expressed in supervision her own concerns about Susana's ability to attend to her children's needs. Dalia and Liz agreed that the referral for family therapy was warranted, and they discussed how Liz could facilitate Susana's willingness to participate in family therapy by supporting Susana's desire for better communication with her children.

Coordination with Family Therapy

Susana signed an authorization in session 17 for Liz to speak with Jan Davis, the family therapist at Northside Family Services. Maria's therapy had ended about two months into Susana's treatment but Susana had postponed calling for family therapy. About a month before session 17, Susana reported beginning the family therapy at Maria's insistence. Liz didn't ask for an authorization immediately due to Susana's ambivalence about the family therapy. She knew that Susana was worried about being judged as an inadequate parent, and she wanted to form a stronger alliance with her so Susana would perceive Liz's communication with Jan as supportive rather than critical.

Liz and Jan had a telephone consultation after session 19, and Jan reported that Susana and her children were attending therapy regularly. She described Susana as having difficulty hearing her children's feelings and needs but said that at times she saw genuine affection in the family. Jan expressed confidence that family therapy could be beneficial. She reported seeing some signs of progress in Susana's ability to listen to her children without defensiveness.

Liz was relieved to hear Jan's view of Susana and her prognosis for the family. Liz told Jan she was working to help Susana identify her desire to provide a different environment for her children from what Susana experienced in her family of origin and that she would continue to support Susana's participation in family therapy. They agreed to consult every 2 to 3 months, unless something occurred that was pressing and warranted more frequent communication.

In supervision the following week, Liz talked about her consultation with Jan Davis. Liz asked Dalia about the views of Susana's parenting expressed by Anna and Jan, since they were quite discrepant. Dalia said it is easy for individual therapists to form views of family members that are colored by the individual client's emotions and interpersonal conflicts. She conjectured that Anna's more negative view of Susana's parenting was influenced by Anna's concern for Maria's safety in the immediate aftermath of the relationship breakup and Maria's direct and indirect expressions of anger toward her mother. Dalia encouraged Liz to continue supporting Susana's participation in family therapy and to consult with Jan as needed.

Records of Prior Treatment and Evaluation

Liz considered whether any records of Susana's prior treatment or evaluation might be available and helpful. Since Susana's only prior treatment was a hospitalization 18 years earlier, Liz did not request any records.

Social Service Resources

Liz also considered whether Susana and her family could benefit from any social service resources, a question she considered with all of her clients. Susana's income level and stability in housing and employment did not indicate any need or eligibility for other resources.

The Next Step

Chapter 13 will cover the topic of treatment termination. I will discuss planned and unplanned endings, initiated by the client or by the clinician, and will provide a case example illustration of each scenario.

References

American Association for Marriage and Family Therapy. (2001). *Code of ethics.* Alexandria, VA: Author.

American Psychological Association. (2002). Ethical principles of psychologists and code of conduct. *American Psychologist, 57,* 1060–1073.

Mueser, K. T., Noordsy, D. L., Drake, R. E., & Fox, L. (2003). *Integrated treatment for dual disorders: A guide to effective practice.* New York, NY: The Guilford Press.

National Association of Social Workers. (2008). *Code of ethics.* Washington, DC: Author. Retrieved May 4, 2012, from http://www.naswdc.org/pubs/code/code.asp.

Substance Abuse and Mental Health Services Administration. (2011). *SAMHSA's confidentiality law and regulations (42 CFR) FAQ.* Retrieved January 18, 2016, from http://www.integration.samhsa.gov/financing/SAMHSA_42CFRPART2FAQII_-1-,_pdf.pdf.

U. S. Department of Health & Human Services. (2003). *Summary of the HIPAA privacy rule.* Retrieved April 3, 2013, from http://www.hhs.gov/ocr/hipaa.

13
TERMINATION—PLANNED AND UNPLANNED

(Note: This chapter will use the male pronoun for supervisor, clinician, and client.)

This chapter discusses the ending of treatment with clients, which can happen in a variety of ways. I begin with some general guidelines, followed by a discussion of countertransference reactions to termination, and the goal and tasks involved in termination. I will then discuss four different ways in which treatment may end, initiated by the client or by the clinician, in a planned or unplanned way. The chapter closes with a discussion of sequential treatment provided by different clinicians over a period of time.

General Guidelines for Ending Treatment

Sometimes treatment will end when you and the client agree that the goals of treatment have been achieved, and you engage in a planned process of termination. However, treatment termination is often unplanned and occurs before some or all of the treatment goals have been reached. Two common situations are that clients end treatment by not coming to appointments and not responding to your efforts to contact them and that you end treatment when you leave a training placement after a year or two. Both of these situations are more common in training settings than are situations in which you and the client work toward treatment goals and agree on a planned ending date. I will describe four different ways treatment may end, but I will first discuss some common issues that occur at the end of treatment.

The professional psychotherapy literature uses the word *termination* for the end of treatment (Bender & Messner, 2003; Teyber & McClure, 2011), and this is probably the word you will use with your colleagues and supervisors. However, in general usage this word has negative—even violent—connotations, and for this reason I recommend that you use different language with your clients. Examples of alternate terms are *ending treatment, saying goodbye, discharge, graduation,* or *closing your case.* If the preferred terminology in your organization isn't apparent to you, check with your supervisor and with more advanced colleagues. With children, you can choose a phrase that fits the child's developmental level and the language you have used to discuss the treatment. Other examples of what you might say are *finishing our job here* or *ending our time of work together.*

Professional ethics require that services be ended when the client is not benefitting or no longer needs treatment (AAMFT, 2001; APA, 2002; NASW 2008). Treatment can also be terminated when the client fails to meet financial or other requirements if the client has been notified in advance of these requirements. However, under the professional codes of ethics, you cannot terminate services when a client is in a life-threatening crisis or emergency. You need to continue services until the client is out of danger, and then make a referral for continued treatment to another provider or resource.

Countertransference Reactions

All clinicians have *personal experiences with both expected and unexpected loss,* and we bring those feelings and reactions to experiences of loss in our professional lives. Ending treatment with clients is a loss, even if the ending is planned and is the result of successful engagement and progress. You may find yourself feeling angry, sad, guilty, and anxious and you may manage these feelings by avoiding and/or denying them, by becoming overwhelmed, or by focusing on the concrete details of closing and discharge.

Your feelings and reactions will be more or less intense with different clients, depending on the length and nature of your therapeutic alliance and attachment. You may also notice differences in the nature of your feelings with different clients, although most clinicians come to recognize a typical pattern to their termination reactions. In treatment with children and families, it is often easier to feel protective and sad toward the child, and to have more mixed feelings toward the parents, including anger and judgment. It is also common to have different feelings toward each member of a couple.

As with all countertransference reactions, *your feelings about ending treatment are important sources of information about yourself and the client.* Reflecting on your feelings and responses can lead to insights that influence the termination process in a beneficial way. There is always a potential for therapeutic progress as treatment ends, and understanding your countertransference will help you maximize this potential. Consultation with your supervisor and with colleagues can highlight blind spots and challenge assumptions that are outside of your awareness.

It is easier to examine your countertransference when the termination is planned due to the client reaching the end of a specified course of treatment or meeting his goals or due to your placement coming to an end. In these situations, your feelings are often fairly clear and you have a period of time to understand and use them in the service of a therapeutic ending. It is more difficult when the treatment ends in an ambiguous or abrupt way without planning. You may find that these situations trigger personal experiences of loss, with more intense emotion than occurs with planned endings. When the ending is unplanned, you may be tempted to close the case quickly and focus on your remaining clients, minimizing the value of taking time to think about a client who is no longer in treatment. These *abrupt, unplanned endings are a valuable part of your training,* and talking about these situations in supervision will give you an opportunity for self-examination and insight into the client's relationship patterns. If the parents of a child client end treatment abruptly, you are likely to feel angry with them and to look for ways to continue your relationship with the child. This situation is important to discuss in supervision so you maintain as much of an alliance with the parents as possible.

Goal and Tasks of Termination

Saying goodbye should be handled with the same care and thoughtfulness that you use in all aspects of treatment. It is ideal if the end of treatment is planned, with sufficient time for preparation and discussion over a period of several sessions. In most training settings, a planned ending occurs in a minority of cases. When the ending is not planned, however, you still have an opportunity and responsibility to find the most therapeutic way to close the relationship. In child, couple, and family treatment, the ending may be more complex than with individual clients, especially if your attachment and therapeutic alliance with different family members has varied. Your supervisor can help you determine the most therapeutic experience for each member of the couple or family who has participated in treatment.

The goal of termination is to create an ending that is less traumatic than the client's prior experiences of separation and loss and that honors the client's way of managing loss. This goal is most likely to be served when you have acknowledged and talked in supervision about your countertransference feelings and reactions. Talking with your supervisor in this way will help ensure that your ideas about how to say goodbye are primarily serving your client's needs rather than your own. As you become clearer about your countertransference, you can focus more effectively on the client's history, current circumstances, and needs.

When planning a therapeutic ending, review what you know about the *client's past experiences of separation and loss* and how he manages feelings of grief and sadness in the present. Identify the key elements in the treatment termination that may be different from the client's prior losses, and consider how the client is likely to respond. Saying goodbye to an important attachment figure is emotionally challenging, so your client is likely to rely on past coping strategies, even if he has learned and begun to use more adaptive strategies during treatment.

There are a number of tasks to be accomplished during the ending of treatment and different ways of organizing the termination process (Teyber & McClure, 2011). I will present an *organization of the ending process in three parts,* which can be accomplished in one session, over several sessions, by telephone, or in written communication from the clinician. If you are able to plan for the ending of treatment, you can talk with the client in advance about these three areas in order to provide structure and to give him an opportunity to reflect on the ending before the final session. Clients often question the necessity of having a final session or spending several sessions to end, so be prepared to explain why you think it is important and what you plan to do to end.

Final sessions in *child, couple, and family treatment* should follow the same structure as the rest of the treatment. If you have generally seen the child alone and the parents in separate collateral sessions, it is usual to spend time alone with the child in the final session, and meet with the parents alone or with the child at the end of the child's final session. If you have done couple or family treatment, your final session will usually be with both members of the couple and all members of the family who have participated.

Three tasks of ending are

- To review the treatment,
- To discuss the future and indications of a need for further treatment in the future, and
- To say goodbye and to talk about the feelings associated with the treatment relationship and its ending.

Review of the Treatment

The first task of the ending process is to review the treatment. If you are having a final session in person, you and the client can share your views of the work, what changes you have seen, and what things have remained the same. I prefer to ask the client to share his thoughts first, and then ask if he is interested in hearing mine. Although I have never had a client say no, I want to be explicit in asking his permission to share my observations.

Sharing your view of the treatment is an opportunity to highlight and support the gains the client has made. It is especially powerful to offer comparisons of his presentation at the beginning of treatment with what you have observed more recently. For example, you might say, "I remember how much anxiety you had when we first began talking about your past, and the last several times we've had those discussions you seem more calm."

If there are areas that haven't changed, acknowledge those as well, using neutral rather than judgmental language. The client is likely to be more trusting of your supportive comments if you acknowledge the full range of issues in his life. You can address areas that haven't changed with a statement like

> I know we haven't made much progress in the area of romantic relationships, which is something you wanted to work on. However, I think we've started to identify some of the things that get in the way, and I hope you'll

continue to develop your thoughts about this area of your life or get support in other ways after we end.

As part of the review of treatment, talk about ways the client can sustain his progress and continue to make further improvement. Encourage him to use the new skills and capacities he has developed, to ask for support from family members and friends with whom he has positive relationships, and to engage with community organizations and other health care providers. If you believe the client is ending prematurely, you can offer him information about other providers or resources that you believe would be helpful.

Discussion of the Future

A second task of ending treatment is to discuss the future and indications of a need for further treatment. Your client may have a risk of increased symptoms when certain life events or developmental markers occur. You can alert him to the circumstances that could present a risk for him, based on his specific history and current life. Examples of life events are (a) entering an intimate relationship, (b) parental divorce or separation, (c) anniversaries of traumatic events, or (d) achieving sobriety anniversaries. Examples of developmental markers are (a) becoming a parent, (b) having a child reach the age at which the client experienced a significant trauma, (c) reaching the age at which a parent died, (d) entering a new school, or (e) leaving home for college.

In talking about the conditions that could lead to a need for future treatment, remind the client of his symptoms at the beginning of treatment and what you have learned together about the early stage of those symptoms. Clients often delay entering treatment, and you can provide psychoeducation to help the client identify early signs and seek treatment before symptoms have escalated. Having this discussion helps to normalize the fact that many people benefit from multiple episodes of treatment and helps to support the client's self-awareness of internal cues and symptoms.

Include all family members who have been involved in the treatment in the discussion about the possible need for future treatment. You can encourage them to share their individual perspectives on the symptoms or issues that led to treatment and you should stress the importance of ongoing communication about their areas of concern. In child treatment you can model this communication by having a portion of the final session with the child and parent together. In the session you can discuss how each family member can identify and address the possible return of symptoms or concerns.

Saying Goodbye

A third task in ending treatment is to say goodbye and to talk about the feelings associated with the treatment relationship and its ending. Many clients are reluctant to do this explicitly, and some clients may be unable to do it. As you prepare to say goodbye, think about your client's capacity to express his feelings and his response to hearing others' expressions of feelings. The depth of emotional sharing between you and your client can vary greatly, depending on the depth of sharing you have experienced in your work together and on the client's comfort and skill in handling strong emotions. The degree of emotional sharing you can expect with your client lies along a continuum, with a mutual sharing of complex feelings at one end, and at the other, your decision to make a simple statement like, "I want you to know our work together has been important to me," without asking the client to respond.

Your expression of feelings related to the goodbye process should be genuine, reflective of the quality of the emotional interaction you have had with your client, and focused on the client and your relationship. Your self-disclosure and personal sharing are often very meaningful to the client, as long as you stay within professional boundaries and keep your focus on the client's well-being. For a client who has maintained a close, positive therapeutic alliance, you might say, "I've enjoyed working with you and I feel sad as our work comes to a close, even though I'm glad to see the tremendous changes you've made in this last year." With a client who has presented some relational challenges and who has triggered difficult emotions in you, it might be authentic to say, "We've been through a lot together, and I've gained more understanding of the treatment process by working with you." Other statements you could include, if they reflect your genuine feeling, are, "I'll miss seeing you," or, "I'll think about our work together in the future."

As you think about saying goodbye to your client, consider his history, his experience with other endings, and how he may interpret your statements and requests. For example, if he is accustomed to feeling used and exploited in relationships, express your feelings with some reserve and do not make an explicit request for him to disclose his feelings. He will then feel freer to express himself and be less likely to praise or compliment you out of a sense of obligation.

With couples and families, your comments should reflect your general feelings about the family unit and should not include distinctions between individual family members. If you have seen a child individually and the parent in separate sessions, check your countertransference feelings with your supervisor to ensure that your remarks are balanced and do not convey preference or judgment.

You may choose to mark the ending of your treatment relationship with a ritual. Doing this is only possible when the ending is planned and is more appropriate when the treatment has extended over a number of months. Discuss this option with your supervisor in advance to ensure your client's needs are the primary focus. Children often like to have a little party that includes food and an activity such as a creative art project that you exchange with each other. A party can be a nice way to end family therapy as well, depending on the age of the children and the circumstances of the ending. With couples and adults, the tasks of termination themselves often serve as a ritual, and clients sometimes suggest ways to mark the final session. If you feel a ritual will be helpful to the client, examine your countertransference feelings and discuss the issue in supervision before you raise it with the client. Be mindful that many clients will feel obligated to comply with your requests.

In some cases, it is appropriate to give the client a small gift as part of the ending process. However, be cautious about doing this, especially if you have strong feelings about a client for whom you want to buy a gift. If you and your supervisor agree that a gift is an appropriate way to mark the ending, it should be a small, inexpensive symbol of the treatment relationship. Examples are a small token with an inspirational image or word, a card with a personal note expressing your thoughts and feelings about your work with the client, or an object from nature (shell, rock, dried flower) that symbolizes something about the treatment relationship. Gifts that are moderately costly or involve a great deal of your time to acquire or create can unintentionally imply a hierarchical relationship involving superiority or privilege, leaving the client feeling inadequate and shamed. In child treatment, refrain from giving a toy to the child, since the gift of a toy blurs the uniqueness of your role as clinician and can stir feelings of resentment or shame in the parents. All aspects of the ending should reflect the professional nature of your relationship, and this means saying goodbye differently from the way you say goodbye in your personal life.

Different Circumstances of Termination

In this section, I discuss the types of endings and the issues that are relevant in different circumstances leading to the ending of treatment. Each type of ending will be illustrated with a conclusion of the case example of Liz and Susana. The following update of the case example sets the stage for the four endings.

Case Example: Introduction to Termination Process

Liz and Susana have worked together for 11 months and 40 sessions. Since session 27 reported in Chapter 10, Susana has remained free of the depressive symptoms that were present when she began treatment. About a month after that session, she began discussing her dissatisfaction with Carlos, and a few weeks later she made a decision to end that relationship. The family therapy ended at the end of the school year, during the time Susana was making her relationship decision. Since then, she has talked with Liz about her loneliness and guilt, and she has gained insight into the impact of her early trauma and family relationships on her adult life. About a month ago, Susana made a decision to stop drinking alcohol, which she shared with Liz in session 36. Susana had been maintaining her pattern of reduced drinking after ending her relationship with Carlos, but she told Liz she wanted to stop relying on alcohol to numb her feelings of loneliness because she felt more confident in being able to handle those feelings in other ways.

Initiated By Client, Unplanned

Clients end treatment in many ways, and unplanned endings are common. Often the client's life includes relationships that ended unpredictably, suddenly, and without direct acknowledgment or discussion; thus, it is not surprising when clients end treatment in a way that is consistent with their life experience. An unplanned ending may happen after a few sessions or after many months. The client may be explicit in stating, by message or in person, that he doesn't want to continue the work, or he may simply stop attending scheduled sessions and not respond to your efforts to make contact. The ending may be abrupt with a sudden shift in engagement, or it may develop over time with lapses in attendance or recurrent expressions of dissatisfaction. If you have a final call or session, the client may be critical of you and the results of treatment, or he may attribute his decision to external factors such as lack of time or money.

An unplanned ending to treatment *generally elicits feelings of helplessness, confusion, and, sometimes, inadequacy* in the clinician. When this happens, you are likely to question the value of the treatment and your understanding of the client and the treatment relationship. You may feel angry and dismissive of the client, or you may feel insecure and look for mistakes you may have made that precipitated the client's decision to leave prematurely. It is a valuable learning experience to review the treatment process and recent sessions in supervision. Doing this allows you to reflect on any interactions that may have contributed to the unplanned ending; however, unplanned endings are usually ambiguous and can be explained in several different ways. Consider alternative explanations, and learn to tolerate uncertainty as part of the clinical process. Sometimes clients return to treatment after ending abruptly, and their explanation of why they left treatment generally differs from what you assumed at the time.

In an unplanned ending, you are likely to feel pulled into either pursuing the client in an effort to persuade him to continue or distancing from him while denying your feelings of attachment and connection. As you experience unplanned endings with multiple clients, *notice your personal tendency to pursue or distance*. It is best to move toward a neutral position, although it is sometimes appropriate to express your view that the client could benefit from continued treatment, taking care not to be overly zealous in your pursuit of him. Noticing your emotional pull toward pursuing or distancing will give you important material for supervision, where you can develop greater self-awareness and have an opportunity to process endings more fully.

Communicate your perspective that the client is making or has made a decision to end the treatment, even when he hasn't made this explicit. Guilt, shame, and a desire to avoid the loss and sadness of a goodbye are a few reasons he may avoid talking directly to you about ending. You may perceive a disconnection between the client's statements and his behavior; for example, he may say he wants to stay in treatment but frequently miss appointments. Stating *your observation that the client is making a decision* communicates your belief that he has agency and takes initiative in his life. This sends a powerful message to clients who often experience themselves as helpless in the face of circumstances or the actions of others. An example of a straightforward, nonjudgmental statement is, "Since you haven't been able to come in for the last three weeks and I haven't been able to reach you, it seems you've made a decision to end our work together."

If the client expresses dissatisfaction with you and the treatment in the ending process, it will feel difficult to say goodbye without either becoming defensive or agreeing with the client's criticisms. It is helpful in these situations to acknowledge the client's perspective while holding your own, even if you don't share your differences directly. You might say something like, "It sounds like you've decided to end our work together because it hasn't helped as much as you hoped. Given your disappointment, I can understand the decision you're making."

As a practical matter, the circumstances of the client's ending will affect how you accomplish the goal and tasks outlined above. If you are unable to have a final session in person or if the circumstances of your final session make it difficult to address these tasks, you can communicate in writing as a way to create a more complete and optimal goodbye to your relationship. As you compose a final letter to the client, you will become aware of countertransference feelings which you can reflect on and process in supervision. This awareness will enable you to express your thoughts to the client in a professional manner.

Case Example: Susana Ends Treatment without a Final Session

Session 40 begins with Susana arriving 10 minutes late. After apologizing, she opens the session by saying:

Susana: I have some big news. I decided to move to southern California to live close to my family.

Liz: Wow, that is big news. How did you make that decision?

Susana: I've been talking more often to my mom lately as you know, and she's been telling me it would be better for me and the kids if we were closer to family. My kids don't really know their cousins, and I think it would be good for them to know each other better before they get older. I didn't know what I would do for a job, but my sister talked to a friend of hers and found out about a job at the friend's company. I sent in my application a couple weeks ago and found out today I've been accepted.

Liz: It sounds like you've worked out a way to make this happen. When do you plan to move?

Susana: They wanted me to start the job next week but I told them I needed at least 2 weeks to give notice here and move, maybe 3 weeks. I don't know if they'll wait 3 weeks or not though, so I may have to start working in 2 weeks. I've already started packing, and I gave notice at my job. Amelia is excited about living close to her cousins, and Jorge and Maria are okay with it although they say they'll miss their friends. I'm sure it will be great once we're there.

Liz feels quite shocked at Susana's news and the fact that she didn't bring up the move or job application until she had made the decision. Liz is concerned about the effect of a sudden move on Susana's children and doesn't think Susana has thought through her decision carefully. However, she is also aware that questioning or challenging Susana is likely to create a rift between them. She expresses interest in Susana's decision and encourages her to talk about her thoughts and plans. Although the move seems impulsive, Susana expresses greater feelings of closeness with her mother and siblings, and Liz supports her in this. She knows Susana's feelings of estrangement from her family have been painful and are not normative in her culture. Liz reflects Susana's reasons for moving, and she supports Susana taking action on something that she believes will be good for herself and her family. She asks Susana about her children's reactions and how she plans to help them in the transition.

With about 10 minutes left in the session, Liz raises the question of ending treatment since Susana hasn't done so.

Liz: It sounds like you've thought about the steps you need to take for this move. Have you given thought to ending our work together?

Susana: I thought it was better for me to come in and tell you goodbye than just call and tell you about the move. So that's why I came in today.

Liz: I agree it's good to have a chance to say goodbye in person so I'm glad you came in today. I wonder if you'd be willing to come in one more time for a final session. I find it's helpful to do that.

Susana: I don't know if I can. I'm so busy with packing and everything else with the move. Why do we need to meet again? I can just tell you goodbye today.

Liz: I realize it may seem like all we need to do is say goodbye which won't take long. But if you're willing to fit in one more session, it would give us a chance to talk together in a more complete way about the work we've done. I usually like to review what has changed and what we're still working on and talk about what things might come up in the future that could be helpful to talk about with a counselor. It would also be good to talk about what it's like for you to end this time we've had.

Susana: I didn't think about doing all that. I thought we'd just say goodbye. When we ended the family therapy we talked about those things, but we knew ahead of time the school year was over and that was why we stopped. This seems different.

Liz:	This is different in a lot of ways from your family therapy. Do you think it would be possible to come in once more? I know there's a lot going on.
Susana:	I'll try.
Liz:	It may feel harder to say goodbye here than in your family therapy because our time together has been focused just on you and because we've worked together for almost a year now. That's a long time.
Susana:	I didn't realize it had been that long. I'll do my best to make it in next week.
Liz:	OK. I'll plan to see you then.

After the session, Liz feels sad and worried about Susana's move. She wonders why Susana didn't talk about her plans, and she reviews the issues they discussed in the last few weeks. Liz questions her confidence in the strength of the therapeutic alliance and goes to supervision with feelings of self-doubt and loss.

In supervision, Dalia reminds Liz of Susana's history of difficult separations, beginning with her family's move from El Salvador during the war. She helps Liz develop understanding and empathy for Susana's need to make an abrupt separation. They discuss Susana's lack of experience in managing feelings of loss and her vulnerability to caretaking, both of which would make it hard for her to use Liz's support in planning her move. Dalia also reminds Liz of the significant progress Susana has made in treatment and suggests that the move toward her family is a culturally congruent coping strategy for her loneliness, which has been a primary focus of recent sessions. Liz is able to use this supervisory input to put the session in perspective and see it as part of the treatment rather than a change of course. She talks with Dalia about her plan for the final session.

Susana doesn't come to the final session, and she doesn't respond to Liz's calls over the next few days. Liz becomes increasingly anxious about not having a chance to say goodbye and asks Dalia for consultation before their next supervision hour. Dalia offers Liz an additional half-hour of supervision, and Liz begins by asking what she should do to try to reach Susana before she leaves the area. Dalia invites Liz to talk about the nature of her anxiety. Liz is aware of her personal pattern of pursuit when faced with a separation that is outside of her control, and Dalia helps her shift back to a focus on Susana's experience and needs. They agree that Susana may experience Liz's calls as a pull toward caretaking, and Liz decides to write a letter to Susana, hoping that it will either arrive before she leaves or be forwarded to her new address.

Liz gives the letter to Dalia for review and makes some changes in the content before sending it. As she is writing the letter, she becomes aware that her surprise at Susana's decision to move interfered with paying attention to Susana's desire to have that session be the final one. She realizes it would have been preferable to say goodbye in that session, even though it would have been abbreviated and somewhat incomplete. She sends the following letter:

Dear Susana,

I'm sorry we didn't have a chance to say a final goodbye in person before your move and I want to share some of my thoughts about our work together. I know you have a lot to do to get ready for your move, and I realize you may have felt pressured by my suggestion to have a final session.

You have made some important changes during the time we have worked together. I am impressed with your strength and determination to face difficult feelings and circumstances in order to have a better life for yourself and your children. You have learned new strategies for managing feelings of loss and loneliness and have used them in the last several months after you chose to end your relationship. You also have developed a better understanding of how some of your earlier experiences have affected you in your adult life.

I hope the benefit you have experienced in treatment will lead you to seek help in the future if you find some of your familiar patterns coming back. You have learned different ways of coping, but sometimes it is useful to go back to a counselor when facing stressful events. Specifically, you may experience an increase in symptoms when your children leave home or when you enter another romantic relationship.

I have enjoyed working with you, Susana, and I wish you well in your new home and job. I am pleased that you have made a decision that benefits you and your children, in being closer to your family.

Sincerely,
Liz Matthews

Liz continues to think about Susana and the ending of treatment over the next several weeks. She feels regretful that she didn't use their last session together as an opportunity to review their work and say goodbye. Liz talks with Dalia about her feelings and the insight she has gained into her response to separation. After a few weeks, Liz shares with Dalia that she feels more prepared for a sudden ending when that circumstance arises in the future.

Initiated By Client, Planned

Clients also end treatment in a way that allows for discussion of the reasons for ending and for planning the number and frequency of sessions leading up to a final one. Planned endings occur when:

- The client puts a time limit on the number of sessions due to financial constraints,
- A new job requires a schedule change or a planned move to a different city, or
- The client has seen improvement in symptoms and has met all or most of his goals for treatment.

In these circumstances, the client usually raises the issue of ending treatment without having a plan for a termination process. He may be consciously or unconsciously conflicted about making the decision, and his inner conflict may affect the tone of the conversation and your countertransference feelings. Be aware that you need to support his expression of autonomy and self-determination, while encouraging an ending that is different from his past experiences.

Your initial response to a client who is initiating the end of treatment should include *acknowledgment of the progress he has made* and the self-efficacy evident in his decision. When the ending is due to an external circumstance, you can say

> I can understand you've thought through this decision and are doing what you feel is best. You've made progress on some of the issues you wanted to change, and I hope we can talk about how you can continue that process.

A response to a client who is ending due to improvement could be, "I have noticed the changes you have made in managing your stress, and I understand you're feeling confident about continuing without treatment."

You can then continue with a suggestion about the timing and structure of an ending process. Once they have made the decision to end, clients are unlikely to agree to meet more than four more times and often are reluctant to meet more than one additional session. Taking this into account, you can say, "I find it's often helpful for people to meet three or four times after making a decision to end, in order to review what we've done together and say goodbye. How does that sound to you?" If the client feels one or two sessions is sufficient, support his initiative in making the decision rather than insisting on more time for the termination process. This is especially likely when the treatment has lasted six months or less.

A different approach is more appropriate when the client raises the issue of ending *without a specific external precipitant and without having met the treatment goals.* In these cases, ask the client about his thoughts related to ending and listen carefully for the meaning he is expressing. He may be concerned about your view of his pace of progress, he may be repeating a pattern of self-sabotage, or he may be acting out of fear of closeness or a feeling that he is undeserving of help.

Planned endings are likely to be less emotionally intense for you than unplanned endings. In these cases, there is a greater sense of collaboration and accomplishment, and it is easier to acknowledge the meaning and value of the treatment relationship. As you reflect on your countertransference feelings, think about the client's previous experience in ending relationships, especially when leaving parental attachment figures.

Keep in mind the overall goal of the termination process: providing an experience of non-traumatic separation and honoring the client's way of managing the loss. His past experience creates expectations related to the ending with you, and your goal is to make the ending different enough from his past experience to facilitate further growth. You may have some concern about how the client will manage on his own, especially if you are seeing a child or family and you feel the parents' decision is not in the child's best interest. However, once the decision is made, you need to shift your attention to providing a positive experience of separation. Talk about any strong countertransference feelings in supervision to ensure that you do not inadvertently undermine the client's growth.

Accomplishing the goal and tasks of the termination is relatively straightforward in a planned ending. You usually have sufficient time to review the treatment, anticipate the need for future treatment, and share the feelings associated with saying goodbye. When you express your feelings about the ending, you model the capacity for self-awareness and the ability to express a range of feelings. Your feelings will probably include sadness as well as pleasure and pride. Clients have often avoided painful feelings related to separation, and they may fear that feeling sad implies doubt about their decision. You may talk about this issue explicitly or simply express your own feelings with a statement like, "I'm really pleased to have shared in your growth over these months and I also will miss our sessions together since I've enjoyed working with you."

Some clients are reluctant to discuss a planned ending but express a desire to *take a break from treatment*. They may have a time frame in mind or they may be more open-ended about when they will return. It is usually preferable to have a final session with the option for the client to return when he wishes to do so, since the client's desire to take a break from treatment may represent ambivalence and avoidance related to separation. It is possible he will not return as planned, and you will have missed the opportunity to have a final session. The tasks of termination can be adapted somewhat if there is an agreement that the client will return after a break, but it is possible and preferable to acknowledge and discuss the treatment progress and relationship even when the possibility of returning to treatment is open. You will need to talk with your supervisor about the agency policy regarding holding cases open and reserving time in your schedule for a client to return.

It may be appropriate to consider meeting on a less frequent basis as part of the ending process, if it is acceptable practice at your agency. For example, if you are meeting weekly, you could meet every 2 weeks for two sessions, then every month for two sessions. This gives the client an opportunity to experience longer separations and to come back to discuss how he felt during the 2-week or month-long separations. Clients who have felt abandoned or neglected by parental caregivers or who have been unsuccessful in separating from attachment figures can often benefit from gradually extending the length of time between sessions. The longer separations build the client's confidence in his ability to negotiate life circumstances.

Case Example: Susana Ends Treatment after Discussion and Planning

Session 40 begins in the following way:

Liz: What is on your mind today?
Susana: I wanted to tell you about something that I feel really good about. I was at the mall last weekend and saw Carlos' brother. He stopped and

said hello, and we talked for a little bit. He didn't mention Carlos, and I decided not to ask about him. I thought about it, but I knew I would start thinking about him all the time again and it would probably make me upset. So I didn't ask, and I was really glad. I did think about him some more later that day, but it wasn't bad. If this had happened a month ago, I don't think I would have stopped myself from asking.

Liz: I see why you feel good about how you handled this. It's a change from focusing on Carlos to focusing on you and what's good for you. You've been working hard on that.

Susana: It seems like it's not so hard now, and I could really see the change.

Liz: It's really rewarding to work hard at something and see that it makes a difference in how you feel.

Susana: Yeah. So I wanted to ask you about when you think I'll be ready to stop coming here since I'm doing so much better.

Liz: It's not really my decision; it's yours, although we can talk about how things are going and what you'd like to do from here.

Susana: I don't know how to decide. I feel like things are going well with the kids. I'm not depressed, and I'm not drinking like I was before. I actually feel pretty good most of the time even though I don't have a man in my life. That hasn't been true before.

Liz: I'm really glad to hear that. You're experiencing your life in a different way than you were when we started working together. When I think about the goals we've been working on, it seems like you've made progress on all of them.

Liz reminds Susana of the goals on the most recent treatment plan and they review her progress. Susana says again that she doesn't know how to decide whether to end. Liz feels confused at Susana's indecisiveness and passivity. She tries to help Susana clarify her thoughts in order to make a decision but there is no resolution.

Liz: It seems like we're going around in a circle about this question of whether you're ready to end. I feel tempted to tell you yes or no, but then it would be my decision and not yours.

Susana: I'd like you to tell me because it would be easier.

Liz: How would it be easier?

Susana: I wouldn't have the responsibility in case it didn't work out.

Liz: Can you tell me more about that? Are there other decisions you're thinking about?

Susana: I'm thinking about pretty much all the decisions I've made or that other people have made. Except for this last time with Carlos, every other man has left me even though I knew it wasn't working out. I never wanted to be the one to end it, so I would wait until he decided to leave. Even when I went to college I went back and forth all summer about whether to go or not until finally my dad blew up and told me to leave because he was tired of hearing me talk about it.

Liz: Oh, that's really interesting. What was going on that made it hard for you to decide about going to college?

Susana: I didn't know then, but after talking with you about my parents, I guess I was worried about my dad's drinking and my mom's depression. I probably thought they might get worse if I wasn't there. I was fixing dinner most of the time and checking on my sister's homework to make sure she was doing okay in school.

Liz: So with that separation you worried about your parents and your sister being able to manage their lives without you. Is it possible you're worried about whether I'll be okay if you leave?

Susana: That seems crazy. You're not my mom, or dad, or my sister. You have other clients to see and probably have friends and a partner or husband. I know you don't need me to feel okay in your life.

Liz: We can have different thoughts and feelings at the same time. You may know in one way that I'll be okay and you may worry in another way that I won't be okay, like you worried about your parents and sister when you went to college.

Liz and Susana continue to talk about her college experience and the suicide attempt that led her to drop out. The session ends with Liz suggesting they continue to talk about this period of Susana's life. Susana agrees it seems important.

Liz talks about this session with Dalia in her next supervision hour, ending her description by saying, "So it looks like she won't be leaving after all." Dalia comments that Liz seems to feel relieved that Susana decided to continue. She asks Liz about her feelings, and Liz becomes teary as she describes her feelings about Susana's treatment and the possibility of treatment ending. Liz acknowledges the intensity of her countertransference and tells Dalia that she will bring this up with her therapist. In therapy, Liz explores some of the feelings she had about parting from her family and friends when she left for college, and she feels more able to separate that experience from her feelings about Susana's treatment over the next several weeks.

During the next four sessions, Liz and Susana talk about Susana's pattern of caretaking, guilt, and responsibility, and they identify how those feelings are stimulated by Susana considering the end of her work with Liz. In session 45, Susana tells Liz she understands much more about her problems with separation and why she has been depressed each time a relationship has ended. She reports feeling less burdened by worry and less lonely. She asks Liz how they can end in a different way than she has ended other relationships.

Liz: How would you like this ending to be different than others?

Susana: Maybe not stopping our sessions all at once, but I don't know if that's possible. There are probably other clients that you need to see.

Liz: It sounds like you're saying you'd like to have our ending be gradual, maybe stretching out the time between sessions for awhile instead of meeting every week and then not at all. Is that right?

Susana: Yes, but I don't know if that's okay. I don't want you to get in trouble with the clinic.

Liz: I have enough flexibility in my schedule to be able to plan our ending in that way. I've done that with other clients, too. People often find it helpful to plan out a schedule of meeting less frequently as we approach the end date.

Susana: That sounds good if you're sure it's okay.

Liz: Yes, I'm sure. What period of time would you like to use for our ending?

Susana: A couple of months? Maybe I'll see you next week and then skip a week.

Liz: That sounds fine. We can meet next week, then every 2 weeks for two times, then wait 3 weeks for our last session. That would give us 2 months. What do you think about that?

Susana: Yeah, let's try that.

When Liz meets with Dalia for supervision, she reports on the schedule of termination she has planned with Susana. She has used a similar schedule with other clients, so she knows the agency procedures allow for clients to extend the time between sessions as they approach the end of treatment. Dalia asks Liz about her current feelings about ending with Susana, and Liz is able to express her strong attachment to Susana, her appreciation for Susana's commitment to therapy, and her sadness at saying goodbye.

In the next three sessions, Susana talks about feelings of anxiety related to the treatment ending. She tells Liz she has reconsidered her decision numerous times, and she asks Liz what to do. Liz reminds Susana that the ending is her decision, and she reviews what they have learned about Susana's earlier family experiences. At the end of each session, Susana returns to her decision to end. Liz prepares Susana for the final session by telling her she would like to review their work together, talk about future circumstances that might indicate a need for further treatment, and share their feelings about saying goodbye.

Liz talks with Dalia about each session and the different feelings that emerge for her. She reports that she sometimes feels impatient with Susana's ambivalence and sometimes feels worried about whether Susana will be able to sustain the gains she made in treatment. Dalia comments on the parallel between Liz's feelings and the feelings of a parent toward an adolescent child preparing to leave home. Liz appreciates this perspective, and they discuss how Liz's countertransference feelings indicate that Susana is reworking her developmental transition from adolescence to adulthood. Liz also talks about her desire to give Susana something as a reminder of their work together, and Dalia suggests some options.

Liz and Susana spend the final session sharing their thoughts about their work together, and Liz is able to support Susana's view of the progress she has made. Liz talks with Susana about indications that treatment might be useful in the future, reminding her of depression and increased alcohol use as signs that she needs additional support. Liz also says Susana may find counseling useful in the future when her children leave home, since that was a difficult developmental stage for Susana. She also recommends that Susana consider counseling when she begins another romantic relationship, in order to receive support for continuing to care for herself.

Liz and Susana then share their feelings of sadness about saying goodbye. Susana gives Liz a bouquet of flowers and expresses her gratitude for Liz's patience and care. Liz gives Susana a small stone painted with the word *strength* and shares her desire that the stone serve as a reminder to Susana of her internal strength. After Susana leaves the office, Liz feels teary and takes a few minutes to acknowledge the importance of this relationship before she meets with her next client. She continues to talk with her therapist and Dalia about the ending with Susana until she feels she has fully acknowledged the impact of her work with Susana in her own personal and professional development.

Initiated By Clinician, Unplanned

Clinicians generally avoid unplanned endings with clients, but circumstances can arise that require ending prematurely with a client. Examples are medical conditions, a family emergency, and job assignment changes with short notice. The effects of making a decision to end treatment with little or no notice should not be taken lightly, but if this kind of ending is necessary, it can be handled in a way that minimizes the negative impact on the client. An advantage of working in an agency setting is that your supervisor and other colleagues are available to support and assist you and to provide continuity of care to your clients.

If it is necessary for you to leave your work or training setting in an unplanned way, you will probably have difficult feelings related to your personal circumstances in addition to your feelings about leaving clients. Be sure to get support from your supervisor and other colleagues so that you can provide an ending focused on your clients' experience and needs. If it is hard for you to think through the practical aspects of the ending, follow your supervisor's advice. With each client, you may feel a different mixture of guilt, worry, and relief about ending. If you are moving to a new job assignment, you may feel excited about the new opportunity. If you are leaving due to a change in your personal or family life, you may feel worried and preoccupied about those circumstances and have difficulty focusing on your work.

When you need to initiate an unplanned ending to treatment, keep the overall goal of termination in mind: ending the relationship in a way that is less traumatic than the client's previous experience and that honors his way of managing loss. If your circumstance is such that you cannot have a final session in person, communicate something directly to the client by phone or letter. If you can have only one final session, inform the client by phone of your plan to leave the agency and tell him that the next session will be your final one. If you can have more than one session, you can inform the client that you are leaving in one session and decide with the client on the timing of your final session.

You may be inclined to minimize the negative impact of an unplanned ending, in order to avoid feeling guilty or worried or because you are preoccupied with the circumstances that necessitate your leaving. Give as much attention as you can to the ending process, both for the clients' benefit and for yours. It is difficult to hold the necessity of your decision along with awareness of the clients' loss, but doing so will provide the best ending for both of you.

You can expect different responses to an unplanned ending, based on clients' past and present experiences of sudden separation. Some will fail to attend the final session, due to feelings of rejection, sadness, and anger that they may not recognize or feel able to talk about with you directly. Others will be reassuring and caretaking of you, and it is important for you to acknowledge your clients' concern for you while shifting attention back to their experience of the ending.

If you end treatment due to your own circumstances, talk with clients about continuing treatment with another clinician. Most clients experience a sudden ending as a rejection and confirmation of historical messages or internalized beliefs that they don't deserve to get support and help. Agency resources may make it difficult to offer continued treatment to all of your clients, so review possible options with your supervisor as well as specific procedures for transferring the client's treatment. Clients may be put on a waiting list, seen on a less frequent basis, or given a referral to another local agency. If possible, consult with the new clinician in person about the client's current issues. Whether the client plans to continue with another clinician, update the client record to include a recent summary and an overview of the treatment. In some agencies, a specific document will include this summary, and at other agencies your summary can be included in the note for your last session or client contact.

Case Example: Liz Ends Treatment Due to Unexpected Circumstances

Liz cancels session 40 with Susana due to an injury she sustains while hiking. She lets Susana know she expects to be out for 2 weeks and confirms a date for their next session. During that time, Liz learns that she needs to have surgery which usually requires a 6-week recovery period and a reduced schedule for several months following the surgery. Since Liz is in a graduate program as well as working in a clinical placement, she decides to take a leave of absence from school which requires a leave from her placement.

Liz talks with Dalia by phone about her decision. They discuss the stress and worry Liz feels about her physical condition and the interruption of her career goals. Dalia identifies other clinicians who can take on Liz's cases, and she helps

Liz think through the practical aspects of this unplanned ending. They agree that Liz will call each client to inform each of them of Liz's need to end and the date of the final session, which Liz will hold before her surgery. Liz has the following conversation by phone.

Liz: Hello, Susana. I want to give you an update on my hiking injury and our next session.

Susana: How are you feeling? I've been doing pretty well so I don't need to come in next week if you need some more time.

Liz: I can see you next week as we planned, but I need to let you know that I have learned I need surgery. Because I may need several months recovery time after surgery, I have decided to leave my placement at the Community Support Clinic. That means next week will be our last session.

Susana: Oh. I'm sorry to hear that. I really am doing fine, so it's all right to not meet if it's hard for you to come in.

Liz: No, it's all right for me to come in. I'd like to see you in person to say goodbye and tell you about your options for continuing at the clinic.

Susana: I don't know if I want to see anyone else, but I guess I can come in to see you again if your doctor says it's okay for you.

Liz: Yes, it's fine. I'll plan to see you next week.

Liz talks with Dalia by phone again after scheduling final sessions with her clients. They discuss Susana's response to Liz's news and Liz's concern that Susana will not be receptive to continuing with another clinician. Dalia helps Liz identify options she can present to Susana that foster a sense of choice and autonomy. They discuss Susana's feelings of abandonment and rejection—probably unacknowledged— and her pattern of caretaking, which they recognize as the likely response to Liz leaving. They also discuss Liz's grief and her sense of losing control due to her injury, upcoming surgery, and time needed for recovery. Liz recognizes her desire to plan for her clients' continued care as a way of feeling more in control in her powerless situation.

Susana arrives 15 minutes late to their final session, which begins in this way:

Susana: Sorry I'm late. My boss needed me to stay late, and then traffic was really bad.

Liz: I'm glad to see you. I wanted to have a chance to say goodbye to you in person.

Susana: I'm really sorry about your surgery and I hope it fixes the problem.

Liz: Yes, so do I. My doctor is optimistic about it being successful, but there will be a long recovery time which means I need to take a leave of absence from school and my work here. I'd like to use our time today to talk about our work together and what you may want to do next. Is that okay?

Susana: Sure. You've been great in helping me. Things are going so much better for me now. I know you mentioned seeing someone else here at the clinic, but I don't think I need that.

Liz: Before we get to that specifically, I think it's important for us to acknowledge the changes you've made and how you are handling things differently now.

Liz refers to the goals of their treatment plan and the progress Susana has made in those areas. Susana continues to compliment Liz and attributes the change to Liz's skill.

Liz: I'm glad I've been helpful to you, and I appreciate your thanking me. I also am aware that you've worked really hard here. I know that some of the changes you've made, in your drinking and in ending your relationship with Carlos, were new for you. You had to face feelings that you have avoided in the past, and you used things we talked about here to deal with those feelings of loneliness and loss. I want you to know I've been impressed with how determined you have been in doing this work.

Susana: Thanks. It seemed like it happened slowly, but I guess it is a pretty big change.

Liz reviews some of the specific strategies Susana has used and what helps her remember to respond to difficult situations in new ways. She then decides to bring up the issue of continued treatment again.

Liz: I know you said earlier you didn't want to see anyone else at the clinic now, but I thought it might be useful for you to know about the alternatives.

Susana: I guess that's a good idea.

Liz: There is another clinician who would be available to see you if you wanted to continue. She could see you alone or with your children, depending on your preference. You could also wait and contact the clinic later if you want to pursue counseling at another time. If you want to consider seeing someone outside our agency, I can recommend other agencies in this area or you could check on providers covered by your health insurance.

Susana: I really have been doing pretty well, and I don't want to start over again with someone else right now. It took awhile for me to get to know you, and I'm not sure I want to do that again.

Liz: I understand, and I'm sorry I have to leave before our work came to a natural ending. You're the only one who can know what will work best for you now.

Susana: How long do you think it would take for someone else to get to know me?

Liz: It's hard to say. I think the progress you've made in this last year of work means that it might not feel as hard this time. If you want to continue with someone here or somewhere else, the clinician could have access to the record of your treatment here which would provide him or her with some information about your history and what we've worked on together.

Susana: I just don't know. It's kind of sudden. I had been thinking about asking you if it was time to end anyway, before you called to tell me about your injury.

Liz: I know this has been very sudden. Because of that, my supervisor has offered to call my clients in a couple of weeks to check in and see what they'd like to do next. Would you like her to check in with you?

Susana: Yes, that would be okay. I'd have a chance to see how I feel then. I've done pretty well during the last 2 weeks when I didn't see you.

Liz: Okay. She'll call you in about 2 weeks and talk with you about how things are going. If you want to see someone here or somewhere else at that time, she could help you with that.

Liz and Susana then say goodbye. Liz expresses her regret about ending in this way and shares her admiration of Susana's strength and courage. Susana thanks Liz for helping her make the changes she has made and gain an understanding of the impact of her past. Liz gives Susana a business card with her supervisor's name and contact information and wishes her well.

Initiated By Clinician, Planned

You will probably end treatment with clients in a planned way several times during your clinical training. You may choose to change clinical placements, or your graduate program may require you to take different placements in order to get different types of experience. You may also leave placements for paid employment or change employment during your training.

If you are in a placement or an employment contract for a specified period of time, part of the informed consent process is to tell the client how long you expect to be at the agency. Clients don't always hold this information in mind, especially if the treatment continues for a number of months, but you need to provide that information at the beginning of treatment. See Chapter 3 for more information about informed consent.

You are likely to feel both sadness and anticipation when you end treatment due to a change in your placement or employment. You will experience a termination process with your agency as well as with your clients, which brings up feelings and reactions to separation as you say goodbye to your supervisors, colleagues, and mentors. Terminating with the agency and ending with your clients are related and simultaneous events, but there are differences between the two processes. When you *begin with attention to your feelings about leaving the agency,* your feelings about ending with clients will be more apparent and distinct. If you are leaving for a new job, you may have limited time for reflection but try to be aware of the full range of feelings that accompany your transition. Think about what you will miss and what you have learned in the agency you are leaving, as well as what excites you about the new position.

When you leave a treatment setting, you will find that your *countertransference reactions* are different with each client, and these reactions will parallel the feelings you have had with the clients during treatment. You may feel relieved to end with clients who have presented clinical challenges, sad and protective with clients who have engaged deeply in treatment, and indifferent toward clients who have been ambivalent or inconsistent in attending sessions. As is true in other phases of treatment, these countertransference feelings are a source of information about yourself and the client. Identify your reactions, and talk about them in supervision before you plan for the practical aspects of ending treatment. Doing this enables you to plan the best ending while minimizing the effects of your countertransference reactions.

There are usually several options related to continued treatment for your clients after you leave. Some of your clients may have an opportunity to continue working with another clinician. If you are in a clinical training placement, there may be a waiting period before the next group of clinicians is trained and begins to take cases. Other clients will have made sufficient progress on their goals to end treatment when you leave, and some may have reached the limits of the funding allowed by a third party. It is often appropriate to recommend other treatment agencies, community organizations, or support groups to clients who are not continuing with another clinician. Occasionally, it may be possible for a client to follow you to your new work or placement, but due to geographic considerations, funding restrictions, and differences among agencies in mission and population served, this rarely happens. Check with your supervisor about the agency policy before talking with clients about transferring with you to a new setting.

After you have identified and discussed with your supervisor your feelings about leaving and the options available to your clients, you are ready to have conversations with your clients. It is optimal to *give clients at least 1 month's notice* when you are leaving, although this may not be possible if you are leaving to take a new job. If you are leaving a training placement, you usually know many months in advance, so it is possible to talk with clients four to eight weeks in advance, depending on the length of treatment and their history of attachment disruptions.

When you let the client know you are leaving the agency, *be specific about scheduling the date of your final session* because clients may misinterpret or misremember a more general statement about the number of weeks remaining. Begin to address some of the termination tasks before the final session, since some clients will miss the final scheduled session. When this happens, you may be tempted to reschedule or extend your availability beyond the date you have set. However, doing this breaks the therapeutic frame you have established and probably serves more to meet your needs than the client's needs. If you have consistently reminded the client of the date of the final session and he doesn't attend, he is probably unable to face the painful feelings associated with the separation and loss. When the client fails to attend the final session, you will need to manage your feelings with the support of your supervisor and colleagues. Writing a final letter to the client can be appropriate in these instances, following the guidelines outlined above in the section "Unplanned Endings Initiated by the Client."

Case Example: Liz Ends Treatment Due to Planned Circumstances

Liz and Susana continue meeting beyond session 40. As Susana's self-understanding grows and she becomes more accustomed to managing her feelings of loneliness without using alcohol, the focus of treatment shifts to her relationships with her three children. Susana begins to talk about specific interactions with her children, and Liz helps her identify her own thoughts and feelings as well as what her children's experience may be. Susana's empathy and understanding for her children grows. Shortly after session 46, Liz got a job at another agency, effective after her graduation. Liz told Dalia about the job and said she would be leaving in three months. She expressed excitement about moving on to another placement after graduation and sadness about leaving the agency and her colleagues and supervisors there. Liz then began to share her thoughts about her clients and talked with Dalia about who she thought needed to continue in treatment and who might be ready to end. Dalia stopped her and suggested they explore Liz's feelings about leaving before planning for her clients.

In the next 2 supervision hours, Liz and Dalia talked more about Liz's upcoming departure, and Liz also brought it up in her own therapy. She discovered some unresolved issues related to her separation from her family and friends when she left her hometown for college. As Liz explored these feelings with the support of her supervisor and therapist, she was able to differentiate feelings about past separations from feelings about her current departure from the agency and clients. She and Dalia then began to plan for the ending of treatment with Liz's clients. Liz's new job was in a program serving individuals with serious mental illness, so she was unable to transfer any of her clients into that setting.

Liz and Dalia discussed the termination process for each client in light of the length of treatment, modality, presenting issues, and diagnosis. Dalia suggested that Liz tell Susana about her intention to leave the agency 8 weeks before her departure, since Susana's treatment was long-term. Liz expressed her sadness about saying goodbye to Susana as well as some guilt about leaving, as she knew that rejection and abandonment were part of Susana's past. Dalia helped Liz think about ways their termination could allow Susana to experience a separation differently than in the past. She also stressed the importance of talking with Susana about her choices regarding the end of treatment, in order to foster a sense of control and autonomy in the face of an ending initiated by Liz.

Liz began session 52 in the following way:

Liz: I need to bring up something with you today. I have taken a job at another agency and plan to leave in 8 weeks. I'd like us to take some time to talk about that today.

Susana: Oh, I was wondering when that would happen. I remember you telling me you were in school, and I thought you'd probably leave when your school finished.

Liz: As you've been wondering about this, have you had thoughts about what you'd like to do?

Susana: I think I'll be ready to end. I've been doing really well as you know, and I feel ready to try it out on my own. What do you think?

Liz: I think it will be good for us to continue talking about it during the next eight weeks so you'll have a chance to consider what it will be like for you to stop now or to continue with someone else. Would you like to do that today or are there other things on your mind today?

Susana: I really wanted to talk with you about how to handle a situation with Maria. She wants to apply for an internship for next summer, but I wanted her to get a job and she can't do both. I thought it would be good to talk it over with you before I have a conversation with her to make sure I handle it well.

Liz: That sounds important. I'll bring up the issue of my leaving again and we can talk more about it. As we get closer to ending, I'll suggest we spend more time on it. What are your thoughts about Maria's choices for the summer?

Liz and Susana talk about the decision facing Maria and Susana's conflicting feelings about Maria's two choices. Susana looks to Liz to give her advice, and Liz is aware of her own bias toward Maria's internship, since Liz benefitted greatly from her volunteer work in high school and college. However, she stays with her clinical stance of exploring Susana's feelings and expressing confidence in her judgment. The session ends with Susana deciding she will talk to Maria more about the advantages and disadvantages of each choice so that Maria can participate in the decision making. When Liz discusses this session in supervision, Dalia comments on the parallel between Liz's collaborative approach with Susana and Susana's decision to talk about the decision with her daughter. They view this parallel as an indication of Susana's gradual internalization of the therapeutic relationship.

Liz brings up the issue of ending treatment each week, and they spend time discussing Susana's thoughts about continuing with another clinician or ending when Liz leaves the clinic. This discussion includes exploration of Susana's experience with separations and focuses especially on her ambivalence about going to college and her return home after her suicide attempt. Susana continues to talk about her relationship and communication with her children, and she seems to have a greater ability to empathize with and attune to their needs.

When they have four sessions remaining, Susana cancels, stating she has a meeting with Amelia's teacher that evening. In the next session, Susana says she has made a decision to end treatment when Liz leaves, knowing that she can contact the clinic and see another clinician in the future. Liz notes that this decision follows the cancelled session, and remembers Dalia's statement about Liz's clients needing to experience control and autonomy in light of Liz initiating the end of treatment. She supports Susana's decision as reflecting the sustained progress she has made in therapy. She gives Susana the date of their final session and reminds her that they have three sessions remaining.

During the next two sessions Liz continues to bring up the issue of saying goodbye, and they spend time discussing Susana's thoughts and feelings about the end of treatment as they relate to the events in Susana's life that she brings in to each session. Before the final session, Liz suggests they spend time reviewing their work together, talking about what might indicate a need for treatment in the future, and saying goodbye, and Susana agrees with Liz's suggestions.

In the final session, Susana gives Liz a card expressing her gratitude for the help she received from Liz and describing Liz as compassionate and insightful. She also brings a small cake she has baked for the two of them to share. Liz has purchased a round metal token with the word *peace* engraved on it, and she shares with Susana her view that Susana has begun to find peace within herself.

Liz and Susana review the progress Susana has made, and Susana explores the question of her ability to be in an intimate relationship differently from the past. Liz summarizes the insights that have come from the therapy and encourages Susana to continue reflecting on the issues that led her to stay in unfulfilling relationships. In terms of planning for the future, Liz reminds Susana of the symptoms she had at the beginning of treatment and encourages her to return to the clinic or seek counseling elsewhere if she finds those symptoms returning, even if at a mild level. Liz refers to Susana's children leaving home and the beginning of an intimate relationship as times of transition when Susana might benefit from counseling. Susana says she appreciates Liz thinking ahead and advising her about seeing another counselor. They come to saying goodbye in the following way:

Liz: It's time for us to say goodbye. I want you to know that our time together has been really meaningful to me. I know I'll remember you and our work together as I continue in this field. I admire the strength you've shown in facing some really tough issues, and I feel sad that we're at the end of our time together.

Susana: As I said in my card, I think you're a great counselor. You helped me a lot by being understanding and not judging me or rushing me when I wasn't changing very quickly.

Liz: Thank you. I know this process wasn't easy for you. We talked about times in the past that were painful and stressful, and I appreciated how open you were with me. You could have given up, but you kept coming in to make the changes you wanted to make. The work you've done here has benefitted your kids as well as yourself.

Susana: Yes, I know the kids are doing better now. I told Maria that tonight was my last session with you, and she said, "Tell her thanks from us, too." All three of them know that you've helped me be a better mom to them.

Liz: I'm glad I was able to be part of that process for you. You told me early on that you wanted things to be different with your kids, and they are. The way you've described your conversations with them these last few months makes that really apparent.

Susana: I hope your new job goes well. They're lucky to have you.

Liz: Thank you. I feel like it's a good fit for me, and I'll also miss being here. It's about time for us to end. Goodbye, Susana. I wish you all the best. Thanks for sharing your journey with me.

Susana: I can't thank you enough. Bye.

Liz has scheduled her final session with Susana at the end of her day. She feels more attached to Susana than to some of her other clients who she has worked with for a shorter time, and she expects to have a stronger emotional reaction to their final session. She spends some time alone with her feelings of sadness, pride, and respect. Later that week she talks with her therapist and Dalia about her feelings in ending treatment with Susana and other clients. She also spends time saying goodbye to her colleagues at the agency and has a final session with Dalia in which they share their thoughts and feelings about the supervision.

Review of Case Examples

The examples above illustrate the interplay between Liz's and Susana's prior experiences of and feelings regarding separation. Liz uses supervision and her own therapy to help her understand her countertransference reactions and to refocus her attention on Susana's needs when her own feelings become preoccupying. The exploration of the three tasks of ending treatment happens differently based on the circumstances: by letter and in one session when the ending is unplanned, and over four to eight sessions when the ending is planned. Liz fosters Susana's feelings of choice and autonomy in response to Susana's pattern of caretaking, which arises especially strongly when the ending is initiated by Liz. She acknowledges Susana's progress and the importance their relationship has had for her. In all four examples, Susana has an experience of a separation that is less traumatic than her experience in childhood and in her earlier adult relationships. Liz does her best to create an ending that honors their time together and supports Susana returning to treatment when her symptoms or life circumstances change.

Sequential Treatment by Different Clinicians

It is common for clients to be seen sequentially by different clinicians in clinical training settings. This may occur in a planned way, when a clinician formally transfers the case to a new clinician, or it may occur when clients begin and end treatment over a number of years as their symptoms improve and recur. Funding limitations and difficult experiences with trust and vulnerability in relationships can also lead clients to seek treatment for relatively brief periods over a number of years.

Sequential treatment often occurs within the same organization but may also happen across different agencies if the client is able to choose among different health providers. For this reason, *treatment with some of your clients may be one part of a longer treatment process* involving several clinicians at the same agency or at different organizations. Many of the clients you will see in clinical training have multiple diagnoses, presenting problems, and psychosocial stressors, and you will be able to assist the client in only some of the difficulties he is facing. You can feel reassured when you are assigned a client who has already formed an attachment to your organization, which helps him weather the transition between clinicians who come and go each year or two. For clients who are in treatment for the first time, a positive outcome of your work can be an increased receptiveness to seeking help after your time with them has ended.

When working with a client who has a treatment history in your organization, you usually have *access to information about the client before meeting with him*. This includes the formal documentation in assessments, treatment plans, and progress notes, as well as informal descriptions or impressions of the client from clinicians who have worked with or have knowledge of the client. As mentioned in Chapter 12 regarding obtaining records of prior treatment, some clinicians prefer to meet each client without the benefit of any prior information; however, doing this can be unwise when working with a client who has a complex diagnosis and treatment history or who has a history of volatility or violence. In these cases, it is preferable to read or hear the information that is available while being open to forming your own impressions based on your experience with the client. Each therapeutic relationship is a unique combination of the client's and clinician's manner of relating to others and is also being influenced by aspects of the client's clinical presentation that are consistent over time. Reading other clinicians' documentation and hearing their impressions can often help you avoid mistakes as long as you don't allow yourself to become biased or fixed in your expectations.

As in all aspects of treatment, you will have *countertransference feelings* regarding clients who have worked with other clinicians. You may dread beginning treatment with someone described as volatile and narcissistic; you may be excited about working with someone described as engaged and committed; or you may feel burdened at the thought of working with someone described as dependent and victimized. If you have direct contact with the previous clinician, you may have competitive feelings with him or you may feel inadequate to meet the client's and clinician's expectations.

When you are ending treatment due to leaving your placement or job, you will also have *countertransference feelings about transferring your clients' care to other clinicians.* You may focus on the transfer of care as a way to avoid feeling guilty or responsible for your clients' reaction to the separation or to avoid your own feelings about the separation. If you notice strong feelings about transferring care of your clients, it may mean you are masking your own feelings about leaving the agency and your clients. Your feelings about the separation and ending are important to discuss in supervision. Your decisions about transfer of care should be motivated by the client's needs and well-being, which may be overshadowed if you have not acknowledged your own reactions.

Although it is common for clients to engage in sequential treatment, there are *obstacles to clients engaging successfully with a new clinician* when the transfer is due to the clinician's schedule or decision rather than the client's need to end and resume treatment. The client may avoid expressing anger or disappointment toward the clinician who is leaving and may then experience those feelings toward the new clinician, making it difficult to form a new treatment relationship. The clinician who is leaving may unintentionally foster in the client an idealization of the relationship that is ending, which makes it likely that the client will devalue the new relationship. An ending that is initiated by the clinician is likely to trigger feelings of abandonment and loss in the client, and he may need to experience control over the abandonment by leaving the new clinician and returning to the same or a different organization after some time has passed.

Given the complex issues involved in transferring care, the best preparation for the client when you leave a placement or job is to:

- Acknowledge the ending of the current relationship,
- Provide the client with an opportunity to discuss this as much as he can,
- Present him with the options available for continued treatment, and
- Support him making the decision he feels is best.

If the client decides to end treatment and you have concerns about his safety, you can let him know you plan to have someone check in with him after you leave. He is more likely to be able to form an attachment to a new person if he doesn't feel coerced to do so because of your decision to leave.

Summary

This chapter focused on issues related to the termination or ending of treatment. I presented general guidelines including the goal and the three tasks of termination, followed by discussion and case examples of four different types of endings. Finally, I offered suggestions related to sequential treatment provided by different clinicians. Specific areas of professional growth related to treatment termination are listed below.

1. Using yourself as an instrument of hope, change, and healing:

    a. Reflect on your personal experiences of separation and loss and the feelings you currently associate with the ending of relationships.

    b. Be aware of your countertransference responses throughout the termination process and use them to inform your approach to ending treatment.

    c. Balance prior treatment information with openness to new possibilities when working with a client whose prior treatment records are available to you.

2. Becoming confident in your authority and professionalism:

    a. Develop a structure for the ending process of treatment incorporating the tasks of reviewing progress, anticipating the future, and saying goodbye.

    b. Make recommendations and referrals for continued care and support as appropriate.

3. Developing interpersonal skills that strengthen the therapeutic relationship:

    a. Learn to provide an ending process that is less traumatic than the client's past experience and honors his ways of managing loss.

    b. Practice therapeutic skills in a final session, phone call, or letter.

References

American Association for Marriage and Family Therapy. (2001). *Code of ethics*. Alexandria, VA: Author.

American Psychological Association. (2002). Ethical principles of psychologists and code of conduct. *American Psychologist, 57,* 1060–1073.

Bender, S., & Messner, E. (2003). *Becoming a therapist: What do I say, and why?* New York, NY: The Guilford Press.

National Association of Social Workers. (2008). *Code of ethics*. Washington, DC: Author. Retrieved May 4, 2012, from http://www.naswdc.org/pubs/code/code.asp.

Teyber, E., & McClure, F. H. (2011). *Interpersonal process in therapy: An integrative model* (6th ed.). Belmont, CA: Brooks/Cole.

14
DEVELOPMENT OF PROFESSIONAL IDENTITY

(Note: This chapter will use the female pronoun for supervisor, clinician, and client.)

Whether you are reading this book before you begin clinical work, while you are in training, or after you have been in practice for several years, you are engaged in a process of developing a professional identity. This identity will evolve throughout your career as you gain in skill, knowledge, and wisdom. Your relationships with clients will impact you in ways that are sometimes welcome and sometimes uncomfortable. I have found it helpful in my own professional development and in mentoring others to hold an acceptance of the ever-changing nature of our identity as professionals. If we are bringing ourselves fully into clinical work, we are always engaged in a dynamic process of identity formation.

In this chapter, I will summarize the issues and tasks that emerge in the development of professional identity, using the three areas of clinical practice that have served as an anchor throughout the book:

1. Using yourself as an instrument of hope, change, and healing.
2. Becoming confident in your authority and professionalism.
3. Developing interpersonal skills that strengthen the therapeutic relationship.

Using Yourself as an Instrument of Hope, Change, and Healing

The theme in all of the suggested areas for professional growth related to this task is the development of mindful self-awareness, noticing our experience without reacting to or judging it (Siegel, 2015). Mindful self-awareness is related to the ability to integrate all aspects of our experience—physical, intellectual, and emotional. This integration has been described as flexible, adaptive, coherent, energized, and stable (Siegel, 2011). We aren't able to achieve this optimal state consistently in every moment, but it is helpful to practice paying attention to what we are thinking, feeling, and doing. This practice leads to greater awareness of our experience with our clients, which informs us about them as well as about ourselves, and lowers our levels of reactivity, judgment, and blame. Mindful self-awareness includes:

- Holding different perspectives on a single situation,
- Managing intense emotions,
- Exploring your countertransference responses, and
- Developing healthy strategies for self-care and coping.

Holding Different Perspectives on a Single Situation

When we develop the skill of mindful self-awareness, we are able to recognize the diversity of perspectives that can be held by two or more people who have experienced the same outward situation. Clinical work provides multiple opportunities to observe the interpersonal conflicts that arise when each person insists that his or her version of the situation is the only correct version. In working with individuals, couples, or families, you are likely to experience and remember interactions differently from how the client experiences and remembers them, and members of a couple or family are likely to experience interactions different from each other and from you.

The capacity to view your own perspective as one of several possible views is essential to being a professional clinician. Developing this capacity assists you in understanding and empathizing with a client who may report feeling hurt or rejected by you. If you are able to hold in mind different perspectives, you can explore the client's experience without feeling a need to explain yourself or correct the client's view of your intervention.

Your capacity to hold multiple perspectives when working with couples or families can help shift the focus from a quest to identify who is right to an appreciation for each individual's unique emotions, needs, and motivations. For example, a couple may begin a session with the wife reporting an argument in which the husband yelled at her, and the husband reporting that he didn't raise his voice but only asked his wife to move her car into the garage. You can help both clients feel heard and understood by pointing out that the wife felt criticized and bullied, even though her husband may not have intended to criticize her, and the husband felt ignored when his wife objected to his request.

Divergent viewpoints about the same situation may also be present when you collaborate with colleagues who are working with your client in a different capacity and when you experience supervisory disagreements. The ability to hold your perspective while being interested in another is invaluable in these situations.

Managing Intense Emotions

Being skilled at maintaining attention and a calm presence in the face of fear, anxiety, confusion, hostility, grief, sadness, disgust, and grandiosity is critical to competent clinical practice. By now, you are probably aware of some of your familiar strategies for handling emotions when they arise in you and in others. You can increase your awareness by asking some of the following questions, in relation to your clinical work.

- When do you shut down and withdraw?
- When do you become escalated or triggered?
- Do you feel comfortable with sadness but withdraw from anger or vice versa?
- Do you understand fear but overlook confusion?
- How do you respond to guilt?
- Do you become intellectual when grief or other emotions enter the room?

Work to become more comfortable with emotions that you may have previously avoided or struggled to manage. As you make progress in this area, you will develop a broader range of coping strategies and skill in maintaining equilibrium when emotions are heightened in the therapeutic relationship.

Exploring Your Countertransference Responses

Training settings and programs vary in the extent to which they focus on using your countertransference reactions as a source of information about the client and about yourself. Whether countertransference is discussed in your supervision and training, you will find it useful to develop a greater understanding of the thoughts and feelings that emerge in you when you engage in clinical work. We can gain important insights by looking closely at the specific client interactions in which we felt a strong emotional pull, either positive or negative. Personal psychotherapy is one of the most powerful ways to do this, and it gives you an opportunity to get feedback from a more seasoned clinician. Personal psychotherapy for therapists often combines elements of learning, mentoring, emotional exploration, and intellectual discovery.

Other ways to support your self-reflective capacity are

- Discussing countertransference in supervision,
- Using audio and video recordings of sessions to review your clinical work,
- Using meditation and other mindfulness practices, and
- Reading case studies written by experienced practitioners in which you compare your responses to those of the writer.

These methods of learning about yourself as a clinician will enhance your ability to pause before responding or reacting to a difficult situation in a session and to incorporate your observation of your thoughts and feelings into your therapeutic interventions.

Developing Healthy Strategies for Self-Care and Coping

Throughout the training process and into independent practice, many clinicians struggle to develop and maintain strategies for taking care of their own needs and for managing the emotional impact of their work on them and their relationships. As you change practice settings and client population or take on new roles in your personal life, you will find a need for new routines and methods of self-care. Ask your supervisors and colleagues for their suggestions and practices so you can expand your self-care repertoire. You may also find it useful to return to personal psychotherapy at times of change such as when you take a new job, open a private practice, become a parent, enter or leave an intimate relationship, or take on a new caregiver or volunteer responsibility.

Becoming Confident in Your Authority and Professionalism

There is a paradox inherent in developing confidence in your authority and professionalism. In order to become confident, you first need to acknowledge what you don't know and open yourself to feedback from your supervisor, peers, and consultants in order to acquire the skill and knowledge you need. The ability to know what one knows and what one doesn't know has been called metacompetence (Falender & Shafranske, 2007). It takes some time to achieve metacompetence because in the early stages of training you are more aware of how much you have learned and less aware of how much you have yet to master. Metacompetence requires introspection and self-assessment as well as access to supervisors and others who can provide guidance, and it includes:

- Being open to balanced evaluative feedback,
- Differentiating personal and professional roles, and
- Holding a developmental perspective.

Being Open to Balanced Evaluative Feedback

It is difficult to seek out and take in evaluative feedback from your supervisor especially when the feedback contains suggestions about the need for change and improvement in certain areas. It is natural to begin supervision as though it were an academic class in which the goal is to get an A. It is also natural to feel anxious when your supervisor points out the skills that you haven't yet mastered. On the other hand, becoming a clinician wouldn't require extensive training under supervision if it weren't a complex process requiring repeated practice and corrective feedback.

If you hold an internal standard of perfection for yourself, it is challenging to be a novice with much to learn. However, if you can loosen your expectations and accept the fact that you still have much to learn, your skill and knowledge will increase much more quickly. If your supervisor's feedback doesn't include suggestions for improvement, ask for them. Supervisors are trained as therapists before becoming supervisors and often emphasize support over constructive criticism.

If you believe your supervisor is being too critical of you, ask about what you are doing well but also remember that metacompetence is difficult to achieve early in training. You will probably become more aware of what you don't know after you have reached a higher level of mastery and are able to appreciate the full scope of clinical work with a particular client population.

Differentiating Personal and Professional Roles

Like many clinicians, you probably came to clinical work being a good listener, showing kindness and empathy, and having the ability to make helpful suggestions. These characteristics are tools we bring into our professional role, and they can be the building blocks for professional growth. As we develop more tools and skills professionally, we often find ourselves taking those clinical skills into our personal relationships. This transfer of skills may be welcomed by our friends and family, who may begin to comment on their desire for free therapy, or it may feel stigmatizing to loved ones who want us to stop treating them like clients.

An important step in developing a professional identity is to begin to differentiate our role in personal relationships from our professional role. Sometimes this means making a change in some of our interpersonal patterns as they manifest in our personal relationships, especially if we have taken on a caretaking role in those relationships. Satisfying personal relationships involve mutuality and reciprocity, whereas in our therapeutic clinical relationships, our focus is on the well-being, needs, and goals of our clients. When I talk with a friend, I expect both of us to share the events of our lives and to support each other in our joys and our challenges. If I begin to feel that I am being asked to play the role of therapist, I need to clarify the nature of the relationship in a more or less direct way. A direct way is to say something like, "As your friend I can't really delve into why these things are an issue for you, but I certainly support you seeing a therapist. I can give you some recommendations if that would be helpful." A less direct statement would be, "I'm sorry you're having a hard time and I hope you get the support you need to regain your equilibrium."

As you experiment with differentiating your personal and professional roles, you will become clear about how much your caretaking role is expected in your personal relationships, and you will be able to identify the internal and external pressures you feel to continue to function in that way. Personal psychotherapy can be invaluable in helping you sort through your familiar interpersonal patterns and make the changes you want and need to make as you progress in your professional work with clients.

Holding a Developmental Perspective

Most clinicians in training that I have supervised and trained have expressed some level of discomfort or guilt that they are too inexperienced to provide the quality of clinical care that their clients need. One of their concerns arises from the fact that the behavioral health system in the United States is structured so that people who live in poverty are especially likely to receive treatment from clinicians in training. However, an offsetting factor in this situation is the amount of time, attention, and emotional investment you devote to your clients. This investment is very high when you are in training, probably higher than it will be at any other time in your career. It is generally true that clients seen by clinicians in training feel disenfranchised and devalued by the larger society, and I believe that clients experience the dedication of clinicians in training and that this contributes to the healing that can take place. The client may not be directly aware of how many hours the clinician has spent in training, supervision, personal research, and reading as well as in musing about and analyzing each session. However, the value the clinician holds for the client and the treatment, which is reflected in these hours and emotional energy, is nonetheless transmitted to clients.

Developing Interpersonal Skills That Strengthen the Therapeutic Relationship

All of the suggestions I have offered throughout the book require that you expand your capacity for interacting with your clients in a therapeutic way. You will face situations and tasks that are unpleasant, that bring up discomfort or distress in you and/or your client, and that require new skills. Even if you have faced similar situations in prior personal or professional contexts, it will be challenging in your work as a clinician to maintain a clinical role and to remember that your therapeutic goals are primary. While developing new interpersonal skills can be demanding, doing so will enhance your effectiveness as an instrument of healing and will increase your professional confidence. Some of the skills to develop are

- Learning to address difficult and uncomfortable situations,
- Cultivating a calm, non-reactive presence in clinical work, and
- Increasing the variety and flexibility of interpersonal relating.

Learning To Address Difficult and Uncomfortable Situations

All clinicians enter the behavioral health field with a history of emotionally challenging experiences interacting with family members, intimate partners, and friends. We have become accustomed to dealing with these emotional challenges in ways that may be more avoidant or reactive than is therapeutically useful. The developmental process for clinicians, therefore, involves working toward an ability to talk directly and calmly about difficult topics, interactions, and situations. Some common examples of emotionally challenging situations that are often part of clinical training are (a) dissatisfactions with supervisors, (b) disagreements with peers and colleagues about management of a client, and (c) the need to enforce agency policies with clients whose behavior is disruptive in some way.

Many clinicians are reluctant to address challenging situations with supervisors or colleagues, choosing instead to view these situations as temporary annoyances that they hope to leave behind when the training year is completed or when they move on to another job. I encourage you to get support for identifying and addressing these difficulties during your clinical training in order to expand your comfort zone and prepare for the inevitable interpersonal challenges that will continue to be part of your clinical practice. Having a license to practice independently does not eliminate the need to work collaboratively with colleagues, some of whom may hold perspectives different from yours. It does not eliminate the reality of having to report to a clinical or administrative supervisor in an agency or organizational setting. Nor does it eliminate the need to set expectations and requirements for clients who you see in a private practice or organizational setting. If you take the risk to develop more skill in facing these challenges directly while in training, you will benefit from the experience and will continue to grow throughout your career.

Cultivating a Calm, Non-Reactive Presence in Clinical Work

There are moments in every therapeutic relationship in which your ability to be a calm, non-reactive presence is vital to the client's progress. Learning to identify these moments and to value this aspect of your professional role takes time. Therapeutic progress will not be complete without these moments, although active intervention is also part of the therapeutic process.

During training, you may end a session feeling as though you didn't do anything or that you didn't do enough. This often happens when a client is overcome with grief or the suffering that accompanies memories of trauma. It can also happen with clients who insist that you should do something immediately to help them feel better or get rid of their symptoms. It is important to learn techniques that are helpful in these clinical situations, but your work also needs to include times when you simply witness and share the client's grief and suffering, or when you empathize with the desperation and helplessness of the client who wants something that is out of reach.

One way to understand the importance of your calm presence is to think about the fact that most clients you will see during your training, and many you will see throughout your career, have had no experience with someone who is able and willing to sit with them in their pain. Doing nothing more than staying emotionally present and attuning to your client's feelings may be uncomfortable for both you and the client, but it can provide a vital experience that has been missing in the client's other relationships. When you move away from the client's feelings too quickly, you may convey a message that emotions are overwhelming, shameful, or wrong. The client may then experience a repetition of the earlier painful experiences. Your presence conveys a desire to share and understand the emotion that the client has learned to avoid or judge. Far from not doing enough, you are doing something uniquely important that cannot be accomplished by therapeutic technique alone.

Becoming More Expansive and Flexible in Your Style of Interpersonal Relating

As you work with a variety of clients and in several settings, you will find the interpersonal style that is most comfortable for you, and you will have the greatest success and satisfaction with clients who respond to that style. However, remember that your professional growth involves expanding your capacities so that you can be helpful to a broader range of clients and in different stages of clients' growth.

Some of the interpersonal styles that tend to fall on a continuum are

- Being supportive or confrontive,
- Taking initiative or following the client's lead, and
- Stressing the importance of change or acceptance.

You may feel competent and comfortable on only one end of the continuum, or you may have received supervisory feedback suggesting that you focus on a skill that you underutilize. If you have received such feedback, make a conscious effort to identify clinical situations in which your underdeveloped capacity is needed and to expand your interpersonal repertoire. Also notice the thoughts and feelings that arise when you employ an interpersonal style that is unfamiliar to you. Talking about these reactions in supervision as well as in personal psychotherapy will increase your awareness of the reasons you may have inhibited yourself from developing certain capacities.

Concluding Remarks

In closing, I want to offer encouragement to you wherever you are in the process of professional development. One of the realities of this profession is that there is always more to learn, both about oneself and about the therapeutic process. These opportunities for growth are part of what keeps me fulfilled and stimulated in my work as a clinician, and I feel grateful to have found a career that continually calls me to deepen and grow. However, you may feel somewhat daunted when you are at the beginning of your career and have learned enough to recognize how much more there is to know.

In my own professional development as well as in supervising others, I have found it useful to remember that as clinicians, we are engaged in a process of inner growth. There are milestones along the path—graduation, completing licensure hours, passing the licensure exams, becoming certified or approved in various therapeutic methods—but our inner growth is a process without a fixed endpoint or clearly marked signs of accomplishment. Finding satisfaction in the process rather than the outcome can help us to counter our harsh expectations or unrealistic standards, as does a practice of cultivating acceptance over judgment.

At the beginning of training, an alternative to focusing on expectations and standards is to view our progress on a continuum that allows us to track where we began, where we are, and where we are headed. Your supervisor's feedback is one source of information that will help you place your growth on this continuum. Feedback from colleagues and your own self-reflection are also helpful. Viewing your progress along a developmental continuum allows you to note and celebrate your growing skill and confidence while acknowledging that there is more growth ahead. In tracking most aspects of your clinical development along this continuum, you will observe and experience three general stages of growth. First there is a stage of confusion and overwhelm in which you rely heavily on your supervisor's advice and suggestions; then comes a middle stage of growing confidence in familiar techniques and strategies in which you rely on your supervisor's validation and corrective feedback. Finally, you move to a stage of engagement in your therapeutic work in which the therapeutic relationship itself is the primary source of feedback, and in which you turn to supervisory consultation only when you need assistance in problematic or difficult situations.

You may recognize that my description of these stages of professional growth could apply equally well to your personal life. This connection brings me to a final principle that I have found to be true: personal growth and professional growth intersect and overlap such that each contributes to and enriches the other. The insights you gain from personal psychotherapy and life experience will impact your clinical work, and conversely, the insights and relational experiences you have as a clinician will change who you are in the world outside of your work. As clinicians, we are blessed to experience this positive synergy between our lives and our work, and I congratulate you on choosing a career path that promises such rich rewards, both personally and professionally.

References

Falender, C. A., & Shafranske, E. P. (2007). Competence in competency-based supervision practice: Construct and application. *Professional Psychology: Research and Practice, 38,* 232–240.

Siegel, D. J. (2011). *Mindsight: The new science of personal transformation.* New York, NY: Bantam Books.

Siegel, D. J. (2015). *The developing mind: How relationships and the brain interact to shape who we are.* New York, NY: The Guilford Press.

INDEX